Statehood and Union

MIDWESTERN HISTORY AND CULTURE

General Editors
James H. Madison and Thomas J. Schlereth

STATEHOOD

AND

U ☆ N ☆ I ☆ O ☆ N

A HISTORY OF THE NORTHWEST ORDINANCE

Peter S. Onuf

INDIANA UNIVERSITY PRESS

Bloomington & Indianapolis

Library of Congress Cataloging-in-Publication Data

Onuf, Peter S.
Statehood and union.

(Midwestern history and culture)
Bibliography: p.
Includes index.
1. Ordinance of 1787.   2. Northwest, Old—
History—1775–1865.   I. Title.   II. Series.
E309.058   1987   977'.02   86-43046
ISBN 0–253–35482–X

1 2 3 4 5 91 90 89 88 87

Dedicated to

Kristin Kirkman Onuf

C ☆ O ☆ N ☆ T ☆ E ☆ N ☆ T ☆ S

M ☆ A ☆ P ☆ S

ACKNOWLEDGMENTS

Much of the research for this book was done at the American Antiquarian Society in Worcester, Massachusetts, where I was a National Endowment for the Humanities Fellow in 1984–85. With its unparalleled collections and excellent staff, the AAS is a wonderful place to work. I am grateful to Director Marcus McCorison and staff members Keith Arbour, Nancy Burkett, John Hench, Dennis Laurie, and Joyce Tracy for making my stay at the society so pleasant and productive. Other scholars in residence, most notably Michael Bellesiles, James Henretta, Linck Johnson, and Steve Nissenbaum, provided good criticism and stimulating fellowship.

Earlier versions of several chapters were presented at scholarly conferences. The hospitality and support of the Claremont Institute, the Center for the Study of Federalism, the Liberty Fund, Ohio Historical Center, and Johns Hopkins University are gratefully acknowledged. Terry Barnhart made me feel particularly welcome in Columbus, as did my mentor Jack P. Greene in Baltimore. Portions of the book have been previously published: substantial sections of chapters 1 and 2 appeared in the *William and Mary Quarterly*, 43 (April 1986); scattered sections of chapters 4, 6, and 7 are taken from *Ohio History*, 94 (Winter-Spring 1985).

I am indebted to numerous friends and colleagues for criticism and support. Over the years George Billias has regularly provided good advice and a sympathetic ear. Joyce Appleby, Terry Barnhart, Robert Berkhofer, Jr., Drew Cayton, Paul Finkelman, Jack Greene, Drew McCoy, and Dick Ryerson read portions of the manuscript, offering useful criticism and encouragement. Timo Gilmore pushed me to be more assertive in developing my argument. Several chapters have been markedly improved by Robert R. Dykstra's superb editing and many insightful suggestions. Ruth Smith's helpful reading of the entire manuscript spurred me through revisions. As has been so often the case, many of my ideas were developed through conversation and collaboration with Cathy Matson. Herb Sloan, in typically generous fashion, gave the completed manuscript a close, critical, and extremely useful reading.

My biggest intellectual debt is to Nicholas Onuf, a brilliant man and a loving brother. My daughters Rachel and Alexandra are a constant joy to me. Kristin, to whom this book is dedicated, is my source of strength.

INTRODUCTION

On July 13, 1787, the Continental Congress, then meeting in New York, enacted "An Ordinance for the Government of the territory of the United States North West of the river Ohio." The Northwest Ordinance is one of the most important documents of the American founding period. Through the Ordinance Congress established a "colonial" government on the Ohio frontier to protect its property interests, at the same time promising settlers they would recover all the rights of self-governing citizens when new states were created and admitted to the union. But the Ordinance is more than a blueprint for continental expansion. Drafted at a time of sectional division and constitutional crisis, it also embodies a vision of a more harmonious, powerful, prosperous, and expanding union.*

To plan for the addition of new western states when the existing union appeared to be on its last legs was an act of faith. The West that policy makers imagined—peopled by orderly, industrious settlers, connected to the old states by common interests and loyalties, and busily contributing to the national wealth and welfare—was nothing like the West that already existed. Speculators, squatters, and other adventurers infested the new settlements, promoting their private interests, defying state and national authority, and entertaining overtures from foreign powers; north of the Ohio, hostile Indians remained a formidable presence. The frontier would have to be transformed before the West could play its part in a revitalized union, a transformation that required the exercise of authority—to maintain order, protect legitimate land titles, and foster economic development—by a strong national government.

This book is a history of the federal government's promises to the pioneer settlers of the Old Northwest. It is also a history of the promise western development represented for the preservation and expansion of the union and the perpetuation of republican government. Properly developed, the incredibly rich western lands offered unprecedented opportunities for enterprising settlers; they also would enable the new nation to trade on favorable terms with the rest of the world—or to turn away from it and become "a world within ourselves."[1] This promise was not soon or easily fulfilled: for the founding generation, a flourishing, republican West remained a "dream," a

* The text of the Ordinance is printed in chapter 3.

visionary world that only existed "within ourselves." But their belief that the enlightened pursuit of private interest would ultimately serve the public good in a harmonious, expanding union helped define the future of American liberal culture. This faith in the ultimate harmony of interests—and in the possibility of transcending sectional differences—was crucial to the creation of a stronger central government under the Constitution.[2]

The enterprising settlers who developed the Northwest were among the chief legatees of the founders' vision. The early growth of the Northwest was slow and fitful, even after the federal Constitution was ratified and the central government was better able to exercise effective authority on the frontier. The vision of western development survived, however, both because of Americans' faith in their national destiny and because of their boundless optimism as enterprising individuals. At last, in the early decades of the nineteenth century, settlement began to spread rapidly across the Northwest. Then northwesterners made the founders' vision their own, identifying the Ordinance as the source of their free institutions and the ultimate cause of their unprecedented prosperity. Ironically, however, a vision that had once promised to cement the bonds of union among enterprising Americans was now increasingly allied with a regionally distinctive political economy and culture. In resisting efforts to legalize slavery in their own new states, many northwesterners were already convinced that slavery and freedom were fundamentally incompatible. Further economic development—and a more perfect "union" among free men—depended on excluding the "curse" of slavery. And, almost despite their love of the American union, proponents of free institutions and enterprise in the Northwest began to define "union" in ways that excluded their slaveholding neighbors.

Northwesterners came to celebrate the Northwest Ordinance because of the freedom and prosperity they thought it had secured to them. But if the promise of development was fulfilled, to their own obvious benefit, the Ordinance's constitutional legacy—the history of its specific promises to settlers in the Northwest—was much more ambiguous. Together, the Ordinance and the Constitution supposedly settled the constitutional future of the new national domain. Article IV, section III of the Constitution *permitted* Congress to admit new states to the union; in the "compact" articles of the Ordinance, Congress *promised* to do so "whenever any of the said States shall have sixty thousand free inhabitants therein." But this and other "compacts" proved controversial, in the Northwest and in the nation at large. Thus, even while the Ordinance gained authority and prestige as the founding document of rapidly developing new states, disputes over specific provisions undercut its constitutional force.

I. Interpreting the Text

This book examines the drafting and interpretation of the text of the Northwest Ordinance. In the early chapters I deal with what I take to be the intentions of congressional policy makers, focusing specifically on their plans for the economic and political development of the national frontier and their hopes for preserving and strengthening the American union. Westward expansion was a controversial project in 1787; many easterners feared that it would lead to the depopulation and impoverishment of their states and to the weakening of the union. The Northwest Ordinance and the companion Land Ordinance of 1785 were designed to meet these objections: they would control new settlement in a way that would enrich both East and West while guaranteeing strong bonds of common interest.

I do not offer a detailed account either of the legislative history of the Ordinance or of political developments under its provisions. Nor do I provide a comprehensive explication of the Ordinance's text. Instead, my goal is to discover what the text meant to its authors by reconstructing the complex of assumptions that they brought to their work. The first three chapters thus constitute my own reading of the intentions of congressional policy makers. To this end, I discuss contemporary prescriptions for preserving and extending the union of East and West (chapter 1) as well as Congress's efforts to implement them in the Land Ordinance of 1785 (chapter 2). Plans for territorial government culminating in the Northwest Ordinance can only be understood in relation to land policy: the price of lands, their location, and the process of acquiring them determined who would settle the national domain and the kind of communities they would form. Policy makers had to adapt territorial government to the needs of those prospective settlements. In chapter 3 I trace the evolution of government plans from 1784 to 1787, emphasizing the redefinition of western "statehood" in the wake of land policy development.

My next task is to see how the Ordinance was interpreted as its provisions were implemented in the era of northwestern state making. I am less interested in assessing the actual impact of the Ordinance on political development than in uncovering what the text—particularly the supposedly permanent "compact articles"—meant to the people of the region. Chapters 4, 5, and 6 reconstruct distinct, though related episodes in the Ordinance's history as a "constitutional" document. The discussion is organized thematically around specific Ordinance provisions: chapter 4 focuses on portions of compact Article V concerning state formation; provisions in the same article governing new state boundaries are considered in chapter 5; and chapter 6 traces the sustained controversy over Article VI, which excluded slavery from the Northwest. These treatments are by no means exhaustive, and other parts of the Ordinance certainly merit further study. But the controversies I consider present a rich array of materials for recovering the meaning of the Ordinance to the people of the Old Northwest.

Northwesterners first asked what the authors of the Ordinance had intended to accomplish. Despite controversy over specific applications, most agreed that related goals of rapid economic and political development were paramount. Assuming that the Ordinance was intended to guarantee the region's population and prosperity and its accession to political privileges and power, northwesterners disagreed about how these goals could best be implemented: would the Ordinance's authors have insisted on the exclusion of slavery, had they known it would retard immigration? Would they have insisted on their boundary provisions, had they known they would lead to the creation of unequal states?

Debating "intentions" naturally led to questions about how the various parts of the Ordinance were to be read in relation to each other: in what way, if at all, did the compact articles control the exercise of territorial government authorized in the first part of the Ordinance? Could one compact article control another? The meaning of specific words and phrases was also controversial: when, for instance, Congress said that two additional states could be formed north of a line running through the "southerly extreme" of Lake Michigan, did this mean that that line would be their southern boundary or that the states could be formed *anywhere* north of it? As commentators looked closely at the text of the Ordinance, they also questioned the authority of its authors. Northwesterners who wanted to evade the effect of specific provisions inevitably challenged the constitutional force of the entire document. Denying the authority of the Confederation Congress to control the present generation, they invoked instead Congress's continuing, unlimited power over the territories or the right of the sovereign people to draft their own constitutions.

Large issues were at stake in the debates over the constitutional authority of the Ordinance. Most important for the future of the American union was the constitutional status of the territories: was statehood a right, or merely a privilege extended at Congress's discretion? To what extent were Congress and the people of the Northwest bound to adhere to the new state boundaries set forth in compact Article V, or to exclusion of slavery required in Article VI? The answers are clear enough now: under the Constitution, Congress's authority over the territories was unlimited and it could do whatever it pleased; on the other hand, once admitted to the union, the new states (probably) could do whatever they pleased (except challenge federal ownership of the public lands). But this was by no means clear to all northwesterners—or even to many congressmen—a half century after the Ordinance was passed. Congress finally settled these issues in 1835–1836 by blocking Michigan's entry to the union until it receded from boundary claims based on Article V. The constitutional authority of the Ordinance was effectively demolished. And, by asserting its unlimited authority over new state creation, Congress guaranteed that the further expansion of the federal union would be held hostage to the increasingly intractable differences between slave and free states.

Yet the declining constitutional authority of the Ordinance is only part of the story. Chapter 7 shows how northwesterners came to think about the Ordinance as they reviewed their own history and groped toward a sense of regional distinctiveness. The declining authority of the Ordinance as a constitutional text parallels its apotheosis by northwestern writers as a charter for freedom and development. The two developments are, of course, closely related: only when the Ordinance's specific provisions ceased to be controversial in the Northwest—and the last efforts to legalize slavery were finally rebuffed—could the Ordinance begin to function as a regional icon. Only then could its text be seen to articulate the fundamental principles of freedom that defined the region. This celebration of the Ordinance—like its "failure" as a constitutionally authoritative text—contributed to the larger sectional crisis that it expressed.

Statehood and Union tells the story of the drafting of an important state paper and of how its meaning was contested and redefined by subsequent generations. Northwesterners' efforts to interpret the Ordinance—to ascertain its authors' intentions and to determine the extent of its continuing authority—provide a narrative thread through a series of connected essays on various controversies over Ordinance provisions. While such an approach offers only glimpses into the political life of these territories and new states, it enables us to explore broader, recurrent themes in regional and national history. The two parts of the book stand as commentaries on each other: in the early chapters I reconstruct the founders' vision of the future; then, beginning with the Ohio statehood movement, I show how the people of the Northwest interpreted both the letter and spirit of the founders' legacy. This continuing dialogue between past and future was characteristic of constitutional politics in the new republic.

II. A Constitution for New States?

At the heart of all the controversy surrounding the Northwest Ordinance was a simple question: was it an authoritative constitutional text? Yet, as with so many constitutional questions, the answer would remain elusive because the authors of the Ordinance never felt compelled to confront it directly. Undoubtedly, the Ordinance was intended to have constitutional effect, even though it was enacted as simple legislation by an enfeebled Congress looking forward to its own early demise. But the Ordinance pledged Congress to perform acts—in admitting new members to the Confederation—that, according to the best informed contemporary opinion, were probably beyond its constitutional authority.[3] Despite these formal flaws, the Ordinance was treated as a constitutional document. The "new state clause" of the federal Constitution laid to rest misgivings about Congress's right to admit new states; and once the first new Congress had reenacted the Ordinance in 1789 to make its provisions compatible with the new constitutional regime, the constitutional future of the West seemed secure.[4]

How could Congress have drafted a constitution for the territories when its own constitutional standing was so tenuous? The answer to this question hinges on the contemporary cluster of meanings surrounding the word "constitution."[5] The modern idea that constitutions must be drafted and ratified by the sovereign "people," according to standard forms and procedures, is a legacy of the era of the American Revolution. According to such standards, the Northwest Ordinance is certainly defective and therefore "unconstitutional." But American Revolutionaries also used the word "constitution" to describe the organic acts—charters, covenants, or compacts—that originally gave political life to their communities. And because they were concerned with relations among their distinct, sovereign communities, they used "constitution" interchangeably with "compact" or "treaty" to describe interstate agreements. These later meanings were most relevant to the problem of organizing the West. The expansion of the union through the creation of new states depended on organic acts—calling them into existence—and compacts or "treaties"—securing their place in the American union. Modern constitutional standards did not apply because the Ordinance did not prescribe "constitutions" in the modern sense for the new states. To do so would have been to substitute the will of Congress for that of the sovereign people.

The Ordinance was occasionally described as a "treaty." Territorial delegate Paul Fearing told Congress in 1802 that the Ordinance "compact is the supreme law of the land, and is in the nature of a treaty."[6] The comparison implicitly recognized the potential bargaining power of the new states. The challenge to the founders of the territorial system was to preserve the union while encouraging settlement. Rufus King and other pessimistic antiexpansionists warned that no "paper engagements" could "insure a desirable connection between the Atlantic States, and those which will be erected to the Northwestward."[7] King's more optimistic contemporaries agreed that the problem of "connection" was central. Thomas Jefferson believed that the union would be extended only if generous terms were offered. If the westerners' interests were not properly secured, they would "end by separating from our confederacy and becoming it's enemies."[8] As the independent republic of Vermont demonstrated, frontiersmen were capable of forming their own new states.[9] Therefore Congress had to bind itself by anticipatory "compacts" or "treaties" with the new western states that would guarantee their equal place in the union.

The sale of the national domain under terms laid down in the Land Ordinance of 1785 was supposed to be a panacea for the new nation's financial woes. Congress had a tangible interest in offering acceptable terms to prospective settlers. In order to make its property valuable to potential purchasers, Congress's own title had to be established, as it apparently was by international agreement (the peace of Paris in 1783) and by the cession of state claims (notably Virginia's in 1784)—and by ignoring Native American property rights. Purchasers' titles then had to be protected and their political rights secured. No self-respecting American citizen would venture into the national domain without the assurance that these rights eventually would be restored: this could only take place under a state government.[10] The sale of public lands thus became inextricably linked with promises about the political future of the West.

As titleholder to the western lands Congress had the authority to prescribe terms of purchase and forms of government. Some sort of government clearly was necessary. Revisions of the territorial government ordinance between 1784 and 1787 reflected a growing awareness of the connection between land sales and the maintenance of law and order. In 1786 a congressional committee reported that promoting settlement and securing "rights of property and of personal safety" made it imperative for "Congress to adopt and publish, previous to the sale of any part of the said territory, the plan of temporary government for said State or States."[11] The elaboration of guarantees for purchasers in the national domain led to the institution of a more "tonic" or "colonial" form of temporary government for the territories.[12] The promise of effective government by federal officials while population remained sparse was harmonious with the promise of eventual statehood. It was, indeed, a crucial inducement to potential investors in national property.

The idea that a program for settlement could have constitutional force was a natural one for early Americans. Colonial charters which defined boundaries and provided for the future distribution and government of unsettled lands were obvious precedents. On the eve of the Revolution, many colonists argued that these charters functioned as fundamental limitations on British authority in America.[13] The "constitutionalizing" of charters was a crucial stage in the development of claims to colonial "statehood" that justified the rejection of British authority. The colonists argued that the British violated the "compacts" under which their colonies had been founded.

The Revolutionaries' penchant for charters coexisted with natural rights ideology. The combination is particularly striking in early new state movements. Vermont separatists advanced the spurious claim that the British government had granted a charter for their "colony" before the Revolution; in the early 1780s they sought a new colonial charter. In the meantime they invoked their "charter of liberty from Heaven."[14] Not surprisingly, the Northwest Ordinance, blueprint for American colonization of the West, was considered a "charter." In this context "charter" and "constitution" could be used interchangeably, as when Governor Arthur St. Clair told the territorial council in 1795 that the Ordinance "is unquestionably the constitution or charter of this colony."[15] In 1834 the Michigan Legislative Council still regarded the Ordinance compacts "as their charter."[16] This usage permitted the identification of new states with old: the American colonies in the West would recapitulate the colonial experience of the original states and then be recognized as their equals. The original states had been colonies—and as colonies had been "states"—whose constitutional claims had justified the Revolution.[17] Similarly, statehood was immanent in the American concept of territory. But because of the Ordinance, the territories would not have to resort to revolution to vindicate their constitutional rights.

Settlers could look forward to full incorporation in the union precisely because the national domain was first organized into "colonies" or "territories." In creating new communities, Congress was simply following British precedent. The British sovereign had prescribed boundaries for the old colonies and brought them to political life. As titleholder and "sovereign" in the West, Congress constituted new states by enacting a new charter, the Northwest Ordinance.

Though the Ordinance's provisions for temporary, territorial government were rapidly altered—and eventually discarded—the promise of membership in the union for the "states" marked out in Article V, when they attained populations of sixty thousand, was considered "sacred" and "inviolable" before the 1830s. The Ordinance's compacts were supposed to be equally binding on Congress and on the new communities emerging in the West.[18] In the 1820s, commentators like William Rawle still assumed that the United States was "bound" to recognize the "right" of a territory to "form a constitution" and gain admission to the union when conditions stipulated in the Ordinance were met.[19] The constitutional limitations set forth in the compact articles cut both ways. According to an 1832 Ohio Supreme Court decision, the compacts were "as much obligatory on the state of Ohio as our own constitution." Indeed, the court continued, the Ordinance was even "more" binding than the constitution: "The constitution may be altered by the people of the state," whereas changes in the Ordinance required the concurrence of the United States as parties to the original compact.[20]

The Ordinance's limitations on Congress and on future new states filled a constitutional void. Though, according to the first clause of Article IV, section III, Congress was permitted to admit new states, it was not required to do so. The subsequent clause empowered Congress to "make all needful rules and regulations" for national territory, an apparently plenary grant of authority. The Ordinance extended crucial guarantees to western settlers—who might not otherwise have ventured into the national domain—that they would not be kept in a state of perpetual dependency under Congress's sovereign authority. For a time the result was, as Arthur Bestor notes, "a stable constitutional system" for the West, "a set of promises about the future, secured by institutional arrangements that command general assent and respect."[21]

Yet, as the Missouri crisis of 1819–1821 made clear, the American system for making new states proved to be anything but stable. Territorial constitutional claims were demolished by the sectional crisis. By 1850, Chief Justice Roger B. Taney could declare the Northwest Ordinance itself a constitutional nullity: the compact articles, though "said to be perpetual . . . are not made part of the new Constitution. They certainly are not superior and paramount to the Constitution."[22] Taney was registering a change that had already occurred in the constitutional climate. While the future of slavery in the territories and new states—and slave-state solicitude for states' rights—was undoubtedly the leading cause of this change, the process of state making in the Northwest had already exposed immanent contradictions in territorial constitutionalism. The Northwest Ordinance lost its constitutional aura because of controversies over specific compact article provisions as well as because of the increasingly tenuous position of the territories in American law and politics.

The history of the Northwest Ordinance raises fundamental questions about American political and constitutional development. Why was the Ordinance so readily accepted as a constitutional document when it was first adopted? How did it become so rapidly "deconstitutionalized" in the decades before the Civil War that it ceased to control state making in the Northwest or elsewhere in the national domain? This book will attempt to provide answers to these questions. Establishing the limits of the Ordinance's constitutional regime will help to show how the American state system expanded, and ceased to expand—at least in a predictable, "constitutional" way—as the sectional crisis deepened.

Statehood and Union

1.

Liberty, Development, and Union

☆

VISIONS OF THE WEST IN THE 1780s

After the Revolution, American policy makers looked west with mingled expectation and anxiety. They entertained high hopes for the growth of national wealth and power through expansion of settlement and addition of states. At the same time, in darker moments, they feared that the opening of the West would release energies that might subvert social order and destroy the union. Images of anarchy and disorder in postwar America were drawn from, and projected onto, the frontier. Semisavage "banditti," squatters, and land speculators were seen spreading over the western lands. European imperial powers—British to the north, Spanish to the south and west— supposedly stood ready to exploit frontier disorder and Indian discontent to reverse the outcome of the Revolution.[1] The success of the American experiment in republican government thus seemed to depend on establishing law and order on the frontier.

As republican ideologues, Americans found the idea of territorial expansion profoundly unsettling. History demonstrated that republics were vulnerable to decline and decay as citizens turned toward private pursuits. Would vast new opportunities for individual improvement—or for escape from the restraints of the "civilized" East—subvert republican virtue?[2] Would Americans be able to preserve the wide distribution of property, the "happy mediocrity" that students of James Harrington considered essential to the broad distribution of power?[3] Expansion also raised the familiar issue of size. Montesquieu and other writers warned Americans that republicanism was best suited to small states and that a republic's effective authority progressively diminished as it expanded.

During the mid-1780s the West presented a challenge both to policy makers and ideologists. Once the states began to relinquish their western claims to the United States, Congress had to organize, distribute, and defend the new national domain. Given the new nation's straitened circumstances, congressmen were determined to finance the costs of western government through land sales; they also anticipated that land sales eventually would help discharge the burdensome national debt. But the realization of these goals hinged on the market for western lands. Were these lands valuable enough, now or in the forseeable future, to attract sober and industrious purchasers and settlers? The answer depended on Congress's ability to protect new settlements and on the region's prospects for economic development. Would farmers be able to get their crops to market? Would merchants and manufacturers be attracted west, thus creating local markets as well as links to the outside world?

This chapter will explore the ideological implications of policy imperatives faced by congressmen as they drafted ordinances organizing western land sales and government. Regardless of their prior political preferences, policy makers were compelled to embrace a vision of an economically developing, commercial frontier. But the endorsement of private enterprise implicit in this program for western development was apparently at odds with long-cherished republican premises. American republicans needed to invent a new vision of their future prospects that would transcend and invalidate the grim predictions of republican theory. Advocates of territorial expansion had to portray the private pursuit of profit—the impulse that would draw purchasers into the western land market—as the source of national wealth and welfare.

Prescriptions for commercial development of the frontier challenged the conventional opposition of self-interest and public interest. Opponents of expansion argued that the centrifugal force of private enterprise pushing outward the frontiers of settlement threatened to weaken the states and subvert republican liberty. In response, promoters of western development boldly asserted that private interest, properly channelled, was the true foundation for liberty and prosperity in an expanding "republican empire." This assertion suggested a broad reconception of the relation between public and private realms. In effect, promoters of expanding economic opportunity in agriculture, commerce, and manufacturing in the West—and by extension throughout the union—redefined liberty. For them, "a Love of liberty" and "a spirit of enterprize" were complementary, perhaps even identical, impulses in the forming of American character.[4]

In May 1784 a student orator at the College of Philadelphia captured the sense of opportunity and adventure that helped transform republican premises: "A new country, partly uninhabited, and unexplored, presents the fairest opportunity to the industrious and enterprising, of making most useful and curious discoveries—of serving mankind, and enriching themselves." How, exactly, the "noble, patriotic desire of serving mankind and ourselves" would advance the cause of republicanism was not yet altogether clear.⁵ But the formulation of a coherent western policy in the years after the Peace of Paris suggested the shape of things to come.

I. Visions of the West

The far-receding hinterland provoked grandiose visions of future greatness. It also presented a set of problems that demanded immediate attention. Congressmen had to formulate effective policies for novel conditions, understanding that a few false steps could transform the dream of western development into a nightmare of lawlessness, frontier warfare, and disunion. The challenge was to regulate the westward thrust of settlement in ways that would strengthen the union, preserve peace with the Indians and neighboring imperial powers, and pay off the public debt while permitting enterprising settlers to pursue their own goals. Congress's solution, embodied in the western land and government ordinances of 1784–1787, was to attempt to create a legal and political framework conducive to both regional and national economic development. Promoters of western expansion believed that the commercial development of the frontier would increase the population and wealth of the entire union; most important, it would produce a harmony of interlocking interests without which union itself was inconceivable.

Enthusiastic reports about the fertility of America's inland empire made economic development on an unprecedented scale seem possible, even "natural"; the dangers of disorderly expansion made developmental planning seem imperative. The western lands problem thus forced Americans to think in new ways about their future. They began to make crucial new connections between private enterprise, economic growth, and the national destiny. Such thinking undoubtedly came easily to "commercial republicans" dedicated to the pursuit of profit and imbued with a spirit of free trade.⁶ But the necessity of wartime sacrifice and public spiritedness inhibited the open advocacy of enterprise. After the war, conflicts among farmers, merchants, and manufacturers over the direction of economic policy reinforced traditional misgivings about the place of private interests in public life. Ironically, it was in opening the way west—precisely where European philosophers saw *homo Americanus* escaping the baneful reach of commerce and preserving his republican virtue in rustic simplicity—that American expansionists saw an unprecedented opportunity for a higher synthesis of agriculture, commerce, and manufactures.[7] For them, the development of the frontier would be a movement forward in the history of civilization, not a refuge from it. In the West, interests so often in conflict in long-settled parts of the country would be harmonious and interdependent: farmers needed merchants to find markets; by processing local products and supplying farmers' basic needs, manufacturers would help the new settlements avoid unequal terms of trade with the outside world. Even Jefferson, with his well-known partiality for agrarian localism, promoted the development of commercial agriculture on the frontier.[8] Only by rapidly developing the frontier economy and integrating it into the national economy could the West be preserved for the union, and the union itself be preserved.

In many ways, the debate over how to begin disposing of the national domain, culminating in the land ordinance of May 20, 1785, anticipated the reconception of the American union later embodied in the federal Constitution.[9] American policy makers faced a "critical period" in the West: frontier lawlessness threatened Congress's tenuous hold over the domain recently created by state land cessions. The federal lands were potentially an "amazing resource" for paying off Revolutionary War debts: on the day the land ordinance passed, Richard Henry Lee exulted, "these republics may soon be discharged from that state of oppression and distress" caused by indebtedness.[10] But if settlers refused to pay Congress for their lands and looked beyond the United States for markets for their produce, disunion would inevitably follow. Westerners would then "become a distinct people from us," George Washington predicted. "Instead of adding strength to the Union," they would become "a formidable and dangerous neighbour," especially if they turned to Britain or Spain for protection.[11] In effect, by fracturing the continent, the loss of the West would recreate European conditions in America. The weakness of the new nation in conventional military terms would then be telling. This disintegration was precisely what Americans—"the hope of the world"—had to avoid, according to Turgot, the French economist and statesman. America must never become "an image of our Europe, a mass of divided powers contending for territory and commerce."[12]

Not only did the United States stand to forfeit tremendous economic resources and a vast area for growth by failing to maintain federal authority in the West, but it would also become increasingly vulnerable to disunion and counterrevolution. Most commentators agreed that the alternative to expansion was disintegration; even the most superficial knowledge of western conditions confirmed that such fears were well grounded. This mix of hope and fear was characteristic: the West was thus a mirror for Americans in the critical years after the Revolution.

II. Economic Development

Western policy makers promoted the commercialization of the frontier in order to gain much-needed revenue from the sale of federal lands. A policy that maximized land values by controlling the available supply and clustering new locations near existing settlements and transportation routes would also make the frontier easier and less costly to defend. From both financial and strategic perspectives western development was an immediate, practical imperative. But for more enthusiastic commentators, economic development served loftier goals. For them the new nation's future prosperity and power depended on the commercial conquest of western nature. In late 1785, a New Yorker blasted the "pusillanimity and irresolution" of state and national economic policies that caused Americans to "totter about like infants." Yet "bountiful Nature" might still preserve Americans against their folly, yielding "spontaneously every natural resource we can ask of or even think of."[13] "Without doubt," "Observator" explained, it "was the original design of nature and providence" that Americans should "have recourse to the luxuriancy of our soil, and the industry of our hands."[14] "The grand object of America," the English writer "Candidus" advised, should be "to improve these immeasurable tracts of land" in the "bosom" of the continent.[15] "Observator" agreed; economic development alone "would render us truly independent."

The key issue for political economists who contemplated the productive potential of the West was whether or not Congress would implement policies that would guarantee development. As Enos Hitchcock posed the question to a convocation of the Society of the Cincinnati at Providence, Rhode Island, on July 4, 1786, would the United States

> rise superior to all her enemies, and extend her hospitable arms for the reception of the oppressed every where? How would the inexhaustible sources of agriculture be continually pouring into her lap, wealth and opulence; opening every avenue to commerce, and extending it from pole to pole? How would the rapidity of her population cover the vast tracts of uncultivated lands, now the rendezvous of wild beasts, with virtuous and useful inhabitants?[16]

For Hitchcock and other proponents of constitutional reform, one obvious answer to these questions was the institution of a stronger federal union.[17] Certainly the generally perceived weakness of Congress jeopardized its effectiveness in enforcing its land policy, as in all else. But wealth would not pour forth from the western cornucopia by simple fiat, even one issued by a powerful central government. Instead, the vast project of western development depended on the mobilization of private initiatives. The ultimate strength—and even survival—of the union would be based on the resulting growth of national population and wealth.

Congressional land policy, it appeared, would determine not only the pace of settlement but also the ultimate size of the western population. Proponents of western development suggested that overly rapid, unorganized settlement in advance of, and at the expense of, the development of markets and transportation facilities would retard long-term population growth. Just as disorganized settlement jeopardized revenues from land sales, it also endangered the region's—and the nation's—long-term prospects for economic growth: the promise of the West could easily be forfeited.

The vision of western abundance, as well as more practical policy considerations, led to a significant divergence over the character of continental expansion between Americans and sympathetic European commentators. Looking at the New World from afar, European writers hoped that Americans would sustain a pastoral balance between nature and civilization as they pushed out across the West, thus avoiding the excesses of commercial civilization. They had a "whole world to people," wrote Mirabeau: "From the sea, quite beyond the mountains, stretches out an immense territory, which must be covered with cottages, with peasants, and with implements of husbandry."[18] This would be a world without commerce, a utopia for independent farmers. English radical Richard Price also predicted that Americans would "spread over a great continent and make a world within themselves." Both writers were captivated by the image of America as an agrarian paradise peopled by an "independent and hardy yeomanry, all nearly on a level."[19] Neither made the connections between agriculture, trade, and manufactures that American policy makers believed essential to western development.

American policy makers were impressed—and frightened—by the volatility of the frontier. They were convinced that the federal government's authority and property interests depended on effectively directing the course of western political and economic development. As a result, congressmen were less interested in creating the material conditions for Price's "hardy yeomanry" than in sustaining links with—and control over—a rapidly dispersing frontier population. Under frontier conditions, the rustic simplicity and personal independence celebrated by foreign commentators posed a problem. In the new country, beyond the discipline both of established local institutions and of the marketplace, the lines between liberty and license and between private enterprise and rampant privatism inevitably blurred. Congressmen were skeptical about the possibility of republican self-government on the frontiers. They concluded that Congress would have to take an active role in regulating westward settlement and securing the union of East and West.

Students of early territorial history have generally held that this fear of anarchy prompted a reactionary insistence on social order by a new class of unelected, autocratic territorial officials.[20] Certainly, the need for a more effective "colonial" authority in the West helped spur passage of the Northwest Ordinance in 1787. But, even though American policy makers came to believe that Congress had to impose strong government on the frontiers during the settlement period, they also recognized that union could not be indefinitely sustained by force alone. Jefferson's conclusion that, if westerners "declare themselves a separate people, we are incapable of a single effort to retain them," was equally warranted by Congress's slender resources and by the potential power of western settlers united in opposition to its authority.[21] If force could not preserve the union, perhaps, Madison suggested, multiplying "ties of friendship, of marriage and consanguinity" would suffice.[22] Yet, as Jefferson argued (in the letter cited above), such ties would only serve to make recourse to force impossible: "our citizens can never be induced . . . to go there to cut the throats of their own brothers and sons."

Whatever their ideological affinities, most commentators concluded that the only effective bond between East and West was "interest." Exhortations to virtue and good citizenship were irrelevant in the absence of commercial connections. Proponents of opening the navigation of the Potomac thus celebrated the "political" as well as "commercial" advantages of their project: "it will be one of the grandest Chains for preserving the federal Union[;] the Western World will have free access to us, and we shall be one and the same people, whatever System of European Politics may be adopted."[23] The genius of republican government decreed a separation between East and West unless the wealth and welfare of both sections benefited equally. Colonial rule was seen as a temporary necessity, both for maintaining order at the outset of settlement and for allowing common interests to develop, not as an enduring foundation for union. "No proud despot" would exercise authority in this "new-found world," wrote sailor-poet Philip Freneau; nor, added soldier-poet David Humphreys, would "feudal ties the rising genius mar."[24]

Freneau's poem, "On the emigration to America," captured the prevailing sense of the importance of commercial development for westward expansion. The problem was not simply to establish trade links between settlements: the West would have to be transformed in order to become an integral part of the union. Freneau's description of western rivers epitomized his developmental, antipastoral vision:

> No longer shall they useless prove,
> Nor idly through the forest rove.

Instead, he continued, now addressing the rivers directly:

> Far other ends the fates decree,
> And commerce plans new freights for thee.[25]

The attraction of the West was not that it could provide a "rural retreat" for a virtuous yeomanry. Instead, Freneau imagined a western landscape transformed from its natural state by the new uses decreed by advancing commerce.

An unimproved, undeveloped West was unimaginable. "Its fertility of soil, and navigableness of waters" guaranteed that it would "become a source of immense wealth and strength to these states, when it shall be fully cultivated and peopled."[26] "Farmer" was convinced that the continent had "been designed for the subject of much industry, application, and improvement."[27] "Lycurgus" also held forth on the "fertile and flourishing" landscape with its extensive "inland navigation." Here was "a prospect of wealth and commerce which future ages alone can realize."[28]

Yet the land must be reduced to cultivation, land company promoter Manasseh Cutler explained, before it would "exhibit all its latent beauties, and justify those descriptions of travelers which have so often made it the garden of the world, the seat of wealth, and the center of a great empire."[29] Until touched by the white man's transforming hand, the western lands would remain "barren wilds" and "immense deserts." The promise of development was thus counterpoised to the dangers of underdevelopment, the reassertion of the wilderness's natural sway over savage man. Even while celebrating nature's bounty and asserting their natural rights to exploit it, Americans defined the "state of nature" as the lawless reign of anarchy and vice. The undeveloped, unconnected frontier provided the objective correlative to this conventional formula. In turn, conventional political ideas helped clarify and focus the alternative, radically distinct visions of the future, hopeful and despairing, that were latent in the wild, undeveloped West. By no means was it foreordained that the American "wilderness [would] be made to blossom like the rose."[30]

Political and economic concerns converged when polemicists and policy makers looked west. Union depended on commercial links that, in turn, depended on the possibilities for profitable enterprise. In this light, the very fertility of the western lands constituted a problem for the new nation.

Traditionally, republican theorists looked askance at luxury and opulence and, therefore, at commerce. Mountainous Switzerland therefore provided optimal conditions for a hard-working, virtuous, republican people. How could Americans be both virtuous and prosperous? American political economists who addressed this issue argued that an instrumental attitude toward natural abundance could resolve the apparent paradox. The challenge was to give settlers adequate incentives to exploit their property's commercial potential: "the exertions of ingenuity and labour" should be suitably rewarded. Economic development would create a context in which useful labor was possible; then Americans would "improve the bounties of a benign Providence."[31]

The vision of economic development not only suggested a solution to the problem of natural abundance but also promised to resolve chronic conflicts among interest groups. Tench Coxe, an enthusiastic supporter of manufactures, promoted internal improvements that would open the hinterland and so activate "the dormant powers of nature and the elements."[32] Farmers would provide primary materials for manufacturers while both groups depended on merchants to keep the wheel of trade turning. All market-oriented productive labor was essentially the same, whether in agriculture or manufacturing. By the same logic, "land . . . must [be] consider[ed] as a raw material."[33] It is "our great staple," wrote William Barton, and agriculture is "our principal manufacture."[34]

The political economists argued that productive labor properly rewarded would help frontiersmen avoid the temptations of easy subsistence and make them sober, industrious, and useful citizens. The economists warned that the failure to guarantee economic development would be disastrous, both for the settlers themselves and the nation as a whole. Writing "on American Manufactures" in the first issue of the new *Columbian Magazine*, "Americanus" (probably Barton) appealed to the authority of British economist James Anderson, according to whom,

> If the soil is naturally fertile, little labour will produce abundance; but, for want of exercise, even that little will be burthensome, and often neglected:—*want will be felt in the midst of abundance,* and the human mind be abased nearly to the same degree with the beasts that graze the field. If the region is more barren, the inhabitants will be obliged to become somewhat more industrious, and therefore more happy—But miserable at best must be the happiness of such a people.[35]

"Want . . . in the midst of abundance": this, in a phrase, was the nightmare of underdevelopment. Only when industry was applied to abundance—not substituted for it—was true "happiness" attainable.

Development theorists like "Americanus" emphasized that the fate of the nation was inextricably linked to the future of the West. The same reasoning suggested that the failure to promote economic growth in settled areas would roll back the frontier. "A Plain, but Real, Friend to America," explained how the encouragement of manufactures would transform "sparse scattered settlements" into prosperous villages, "full of people, and as industrious as a bee-hive." But the collapse of infant industries and the decline of trade would make America over in the image of the frontier wasteland. The countryside would "wear a horrid deserted aspect"; without work, "our own poor" would be forced "to wander in the woods and wilds of the back countries, to live like Indians."[36]

Frontier whites, besotted with an effortless subsistence, might imagine themselves "happy." But in the developers' view this was a beggarly, savage happiness at best. After all, the native Americans were a melancholy race: they had failed to exploit nature's bounty, a failure reflected in their scattered and declining numbers. Properly developed, the West could support an infinitely larger, more prosperous people. In these pre-Malthusian days, the equations between population and power and between population and prosperity still made sense. To permit settlers to be satisfied with mere subsistence was to choose a small, semisavage population over the large, industrious and civilized population that these fertile lands could so easily be made to support.[37]

Whatever America's role in the world, or as a world unto itself, the development of the West was essential. Even those who celebrated the redemptive influence of American agriculture conceded that frontier farms would have to be commercially viable. If federal lands were to have any value, purchasers had to be assured that they would find markets for their crops and a return on their investment. Congress was not about to give away its property, however desirable it might be to colonize the West with virtuous farmers. Thus, while David Howell considered "cultivators of the soil" the true "guardians" of republicanism, he was also impressed by the "amazing prospect" of a "national fund" presented by the western lands. The "gods of the mountains" who settled on the frontiers would have to purchase their lands and thus pay for the privilege of defending American liberties.[38] Colonel Humphreys hailed

> agriculture! by whose parent aid,
> The deep foundations of our states are laid.

Through agriculture the western wilds would be conquered, and so converted into an "Arcadian scene," poised between "too rude and too refin'd an age." Yet even Humphreys betrayed developmental premises: agriculture was not only the "earliest friend of man"—the means of subsistence—but also, potentially, a "Great source of wealth" for enterprising Americans. The West would have to be developed to support agriculture, and agriculture would be the means of future development.[39]

Thomas Jefferson, the preeminent agrarian theorist, had no illusions about the future commercial character of the frontier, or of his countrymen. Though, from a global perspective, Jefferson endorsed the idea that the new nation's "workshops" should remain in Europe and that a modern commercial-industrial economy constituted the leading threat to republican liberty, the opening of the West prompted him to assume a less doctrinaire posture.[40] Writing to Washington in March 1784, at a time he was playing a key role in formulating congressional western policy, Jefferson dismissed the classic question of whether agriculture or commerce was the true source of man's happiness. "We might indulge" in such speculations, he wrote, "Was it practicable to keep our new empire separated" from the rest of the world. But this could never be done. "All the world is becoming commercial," including the American people: "Our citizens have had too full a taste of the comforts furnished by the arts and manufactures to be debarred the use of them."[41]

The commercial character of the American people may have been regrettable, at least in theory, but in practice Jefferson sought to exploit the private pursuit of profit which he thought propelled the massive emigration to the West in order to advance the interests of his state and of the United States. Along with Washington and other like-minded Virginians, Jefferson was determined that Virginia command its fair share of the vast wealth to be created by western development. "Nature . . . has declared in favour of the Patowmac," he wrote, "and through that channel offers to pour into our lap the whole commerce of the Western world." Yet nature's offer was contingent on Virginia's and Maryland's willingness to undertake extensive internal improvements. Other states were all too eager to divert the western trade into unnatural courses: Pennsylvanians, traditional rivals for economic control of the Ohio Valley, were busily promoting new routes west; even New Yorkers were beginning to consider ambitious proposals for connecting their state with the Great Lakes.[42] Responding to this incipient regional rivalry, Washington agreed (on Jefferson's urging) to head a company jointly sponsored by Virginia and Maryland to extend the navigability of the Potomac. Here, according to Maryland legislator David McMechen, was a potentially "immense source of wealth" for the Chesapeake region.[43] And now was the time, Washington insisted repeatedly throughout 1784 and 1785, for "fixing . . . a large portion of the trade of the Western Country in the bosom of this State irrevocably."[44] The successful completion of the Potomac project, an Alexandria writer predicted, would raise his city "in importance, and distinction, to an equality at least, with the first commercial cities in the United States."[45]

Whether as a financial resource for governments straining under an "oppressive" burden of debt or as a source of commercial wealth for eastern entrepôts, the western lands had to be properly developed and integrated into the American and world economy. Commerce was an essential adjunct of western agricultural development: without access to markets settlers would have no incentive to improve the landscape. Similarly, political economists foresaw ample scope for the founding of new industries in the western world as well as vast new markets for eastern manufactures.[46]

Promoters of manufactures were forced by their relatively small numbers to embrace the vision of a harmony of interests and integrated economic development. Writers like Tench Coxe did not question the "pre-eminence of the agricultural interest." Indeed, the opening of the West, "the settlement of our waste lands, and subdividing our improved farms," would reinforce the dominance of agriculture. But it was a mistake to assume that the ascendancy of the agricultural interest would come at the expense of other interests. Instead, in Coxe's inflationary scheme, "agriculture appears to be the spring of our commerce, and the parent of our manufactures."[47]

Of course, for theorists like Coxe, the measure of agriculture's vitality was determined by market criteria—represented by the price of land—which depended in turn on the growth of other sectors of the economy. A "Farmer," writing in the *Maryland Journal* in early 1786, thus sought to "impress it on the minds of those who hold lands in this state, that they are as much interested in promoting its commerce, as the merchant can possibly be." "Farmer" surveyed land prices in neighboring states, demonstrating, to his own satisfaction at least, that the value of land was not determined by fertility alone. The best lands were to be found in Virginia, but they were worth considerably less than inferior lands in Pennsylvania. The explanation for this "great diversity in price" was "the great encouragement they [the Pennsylvanians] give to commerce."[48] Conspicuously missing from this account was any notion that agriculture should be a privileged activity in the new nation, that its "value" consisted in the independence it afforded yeoman farmers at least relatively immune to market forces. On the contrary, it was a crucial premise for Barton, Coxe, and the many other writers who promoted economic development in the mid-1780s that "interests" were not only equal, and thus equally entitled to protection and assistance from government, but that they were, in essential respects, identical. Agriculture was really a form of manufacturing, the application of labor and capital to America's most abundant natural resource. In their varied, but complementary pursuits, Americans were all driven by a "spirit of enterprize."[49] The result of all this busy-ness, according to Joel Barlow, would be "progress of arts, in agriculture, commerce, and manufactures"—if Americans acted prudently to secure the union and guarantee development.[50]

In one of the boldest formulations of the development idea, William Vans Murray pursued the new logic to the limits of republican theory. Murray rejected the old republican bias toward rustic, uncorrupted virtue, supported by equal distribution of landed property. He argued, instead, that only in an advanced state of civilization could a government be "created under a just conception of human rights." Such rights would not, perhaps, be "relished by a rude society." The "perfect equality of rights" and "enlightened adoption of a free form of government" was possible in America because of its social maturity, not because it remained at some semi-developed, middle stage of civilization. Material abundance, or in Murray's forthright language, "luxury," was as "natural" to civilized Americans as poverty was to savages. It was simply a "romantic . . . fiction," Murray concluded, that "luxury and true liberty are incompatible in a democratic form."[51] A contributor to the *Pennsylvania Gazette* made the same point. "To despise wealth," he wrote, "is to depreciate the first of republican virtues, and to overturn the basis of freedom and empire in our country."[52] In a debate at Yale College, master's candidate David Daggett also defended republican luxury: "as soon as you cause us to exchange our refinement for barbarity, our learning for ignorance, and our liberty for servitude, then may we see parsimony take the place of luxury, and I may add too misery and wretchedness triumphing over happiness."[53]

These proponents of luxury showed how republican values could be transformed under the exigencies of nation making. Though many contemporaries would have stopped far short of their conclusions, they articulated some of the core values in American liberal theory. Advocates of commerce and economic development saw the need for a harmonizing of interests and the creation of a true national community founded on free exchange and interaction. In this formulation, the public good—the creation of a more durable union—coincided with the pursuit of private interest. The crucial bridge between public and private realms, which classical theory sought to keep distinct, was a developing economy that rewarded private enterprise and directed it toward productive ends.

Independence Day orator John Gardiner described the American promise to a Boston crowd in 1785:

If we make a right use of our natural advantages we soon must be a truly great and happy people. When we consider the vastness of our country, the variety of her soil and climate, the immense extent of her sea-coast, and of the inland navigation by the lakes and rivers, we find a *world within ourselves,* sufficient to produce whatever can contribute to the necessities and even the superfluities of life.[54]

Gardiner's world was a dynamic one, in which land was valued for what it could produce and self-sufficiency was the goal for a continent, not merely a household. Bodies of water affording easy communication and commerce were the most conspicuous natural features, the keys to future greatness. Made accessible by these natural highways, the western lands opened astonishing prospects for individual enterprise. But individual and collective success for the American people depended on making a "right use" of nature's gift.

The importance of development to Americans like Gardiner suggests, on one hand, an enthusiastic endorsement of private initiatives from all sectors of society and, on the other, an awareness that the expansion of the union—and perhaps even its continuing existence—was problematic. If timely measures were not taken to secure cooperation among the states, "Observator" warned, "our public, political interests, and with them individual interests (for they will stand or fall together) cannot be promoted, but must be neglected, and in the end inevitably ruined."[55] Development and union were counterpoised to underdevelopment, anarchy, and counterrevolution: both outcomes were plausible. This sense of contingency magnified the agency of the American people in determining their own, and the world's future: according to Barlow, "every free citizen of the American empire ought now to consider himself as the legislator of half mankind."[56] In the developers' scheme the new world could expand or disintegrate depending on how or if settlement was regulated and on what provisions voters would make for preserving and extending the union.

In development rhetoric, the ideas of enterprise, progress, and material abundance served as solvents for differences among sections as well as economic interests that, when conceived in static, mutually exclusive terms, threatened to destroy the new nation. Economic growth would resolve conflicts that grew out of scarcity: all interests would benefit from an expanding pie. A writer in Worcester, Massachusetts, suggested that "agriculture will flourish" with the rapid settlement of the "inland part" of the country; as a result, the cost of the "necessaries of life" would drop, promoting "manufactures of all kinds, and it is to be hoped in a few years our exports will so far exceed our imports, as to make us a wealthy, and we hope a happy people."[57] Americans would come to see the interdependence of agriculture, manufacturing, and commerce that development proponents considered axiomatic and, thus enlightened, would no longer pursue shortsighted measures at each other's expense. Of course, the harmony-of-interests idea was often invoked as a rationale for promoting specific interests: manufacturers wanted protection, merchants wanted a coherent commercial policy, farmers wanted land. Differences among interests could not always be concealed by fulsome rhetoric—or by imaginary abundance. From this perspective, the dream of western development can be seen as a kind of oblique recognition of differences among Americans that often seemed intractable, a denial of political realities that proponents of development confronted and sometimes helped to create. In the case of regional competition for control of the western trade, developers like Washington and Jefferson were expressing and promoting the very forces that a stronger, more developed union—their ostensible goal— was supposed to overcome.[58] Skeptics might reasonably conclude that national land policy, for instance, would simply enrich particular groups of well-situated traders and speculators. But the dream of development, even if traceable to self-interest, was broadly appealing. It represented an authentic impulse toward national integration, while giving a new legitimacy to the boundless ambitions of countless Americans. The developers taught that in a properly regulated New World economy the pursuit of private interest would rise above interest group politics and guarantee the nation's wealth and power. Unlike the leaders of the Revolution, proponents of union through development sought to mobilize private interest and enterprise, not self-denial and sacrifice, to bring forth a new order.

III. Population Growth

The 1780s were a "critical period" for the American union. Congress's ordinances for distributing and governing the western lands in the national interest represented the first great effort to transcend sectional interests and provide for expansion of the union. To optimists like Washington, the westward movement of wealth and population would liberate Americans from insular loyalties and prejudices: "time" would "disarm localities of their power."[59] But a leap of faith was necessary before many of Washington's contemporaries could truly believe in the harmony of interests in an expanding republic. Such harmony defied the contemporary realities of American politics. Further, old-fashioned republicans questioned the wisdom of expansion, even if it were possible: large polities were supposed to be incompatible with individual and local liberties. The western problem thus raised larger questions about the durability and desirability of union itself.

Congress's program for western development was designed to cement connections between East and West. The crucial first step was to create a national market in western lands. Only then would expansionists be able to answer arguments that expansion would depopulate and impoverish the old states. By positing the rapid integration of new settlements into the national economy, they could insist that all parts of the country would benefit. Controlled expansion would spur economic development, population growth, and internal improvements throughout the union. The growth of intersectional commerce would expand the scope of common interests and counter the effects of growing distances, making republicanism possible on a continental scale.

Some observers flatly denied that a continuing union between East and West was possible.[60] Many others entertained serious doubts. Madison outlined some of these for Jefferson in August 1784. Those who "remain in the Atlantic States" would be "sufferers by the encouragement of the Western settlem[en]ts," he explained. The old states would experience "depopulation," "depreciation" of land values, and the "delay of that maritime strength which must be their only safety in case of war." Finally, Madison concluded, the Confederacy itself would be endangered by "multiplying the parts of the Machine."[61]

All of the objections recounted by Madison were based on "zero-sum" premises; they assumed expansion without economic growth or development. Population was the central concern since population density was the key determinant of both land prices and political power. This focus on population became clear during debates over closure of the Mississippi in 1786. James Monroe was convinced that by acceding to Spain's conditions northerners meant to "make it the interest of the [western] people to separate" from the union, thus precluding the addition of new states and "throw[ing] the weight of population eastward and keep[ing] it there, to appreciate the vacant lands of New York and Massachusetts."[62] For their part, northerners such as Rufus King were persuaded that "an entire separation" between East and West was inevitable. If so, he asked, "in true policy ought the U.S. to be very assiduous to encourage their Citizens to become Settlers" in the trans-Appalachian region? If westerners were free to trade through the Mississippi, King added, "I should consider every emigrant to that country from the Atlantic States, as forever lost to the Confederacy."[63]

The challenge to western policy makers was to minimize the losses to the seaboard states in population, wealth, and power that expansion apparently would cause. According to a typical complaint, "selling or settling" the West too "speedily" would open "a door for our citizens, to run off and leave us . . . depreciating all our landed property already settled, and disabling us from paying taxes, and funding the debt already contracted."[64] A program for the gradual extension of settlement, or what Washington called "progressive seating," would address these concerns. First, the "door" would not be flung wide open: the old states would retain populations sufficient to secure their welfare as well as customers for their land offices. But, at least in theory, regulated expansion would do more than this: by guaranteeing that wester- ners would become "useful" citizens, congressional land policy would in- crease the wealth of the entire union and provide an abundant subsistence for a growing population.

In practical terms, the population issue reduced itself to the question of where Congress would find suitably industrious settlers to develop the national domain. Many policy makers and commentators anticipated an influx of European emigrants, a solution that would prevent the depopula- tion of the old states.[65] But those states were also producing population surpluses that could be directed west. President Ezra Stiles of Yale College, a diligent student of demographic trends, predicted a national population of fifty million by 1876 and concluded that even "if the present ratio of increase should be rather diminished in some of the elder settlements, yet an *acceler- ated multiplication will attend our general propagation*, and overspread the whole territory westward for ages."[66] The result would not be an absolute loss of numbers for places like Connecticut: indeed, that state had continued to grow even as great numbers of its sons and daughters hived off to Vermont and Pennsylvania. "You are not desirous to send colonists to this side of the mountain," a western Carolinian wrote to an eastern friend, "but thousands may come every year without reducing your numbers."[67] Stiles and other population theorists predicted the ultimate equalization of rates of growth, not the redistribution of existing numbers or the simple extrapolation of the low densities that could be supported by subsistence agriculture.

Madison explained the connection between economic development and population growth in the same letter to Jefferson in which he reviewed conventional objections to western expansion. "Vacancies . . . in an indus- trious country" caused by emigration "are not only Speedily filled but that population is ever increased by the demand of the emigrants & their descen- dants."[68] Simultaneous increase in the demand for products of the more densely settled, "industrious" parts of the country and expansion of commer- cial agriculture over fresh western lands would promote a continuing, re- ciprocal explosion of population.

The key factor in this conception of dynamic population growth, according to Benjamin Rush, was a distinctively American "passion for migration." "This passion" might appear "strange and new," but it "is wisely calculated for the extension of population in America; and this it does, not only by promoting the increase of the human species in new settlements, but in the old settlements likewise." Local population surpluses, unless directed toward more promising regions, would retard growth, introducing a "languor in population."[69] The compelling conclusion was that the nation should encourage internal migration, even as it welcomed immigrants from abroad. Both were sources of increasing population, whether by redistributing excess population or by encouraging more rapid growth rates. In either case, the encouragement of population required freedom of movement. No one knew better than the people themselves when the material conditions for reproduction were most propitious. And no "political maxim [was] better established," William Barton wrote, than that "a high degree of population contributes greatly to the riches and strength of a state."[70]

Properly managed, the western lands would guarantee the future greatness of the new nation. "Can any physical reason be assigned," a South Carolina writer asked, "why all the lands to the westward of the Allegany mountains should not, in some distant period of time, become as populous as Swisserland, Austria, or Germany?"[71] Fulfillment of this promise depended on a variety of related, problematic conditions. The free movement of population, particularly of the more industrious and useful sort, presupposed political stability, law and order, clear property titles, and peace with the Indians. The present disordered "state of things," Tench Coxe warned in 1787, "deters all who have the means of information" from coming to America.[72] Though Washington was confident that the western "Country . . . will settle faster than any other ever did," its prospects clearly depended on preserving the peace.[73] He wrote Lafayette that he hoped to see the "sons and daughters of the world" flock to the "fertile plains of the Ohio" where they would find "agreeable amusement" in "fulfilling the first and great commandment, *Increase and Multiply*."[74] But this would be impossible in the event of the frontier warfare that unregulated settlement would necessarily provoke.

How could "freedom" be reconciled with regulation? Clearly, western policy makers did not sanction all private initiatives. Instead, they hoped to recruit from all over the world industrious immigrants eager to gain a better return on their capital and labor, as well as a more abundant subsistence. The population theorists assumed just this sort of rational, market-oriented behavior in their predictions of population growth. They expected not only that population would vary with the means of subsistence—a common-sense premise—but also that the spread of settlement would invigorate and accelerate interregional commercial transactions. Better-situated producers would be better equipped to satisfy each other's needs: through the workings of the marketplace they would become closer—more interdependent—even as they moved apart.

In elaborating the development theme, political economists stretched republican ideology to its limits. Intersectional economic development would reward and promote private enterprise and provide the foundation of a durable union. Therefore, they concluded, the pursuit of private interest did not jeopardize republican virtue: without common interests grounded in commercial exchange the survival of the extended republic was inconceivable.

Certainly all congressmen did not share the economists' boundless enthusiasm for commerce and development. But the western problem did compel them to think carefully about the need for economic as well as political connections between new settlements and old states. Congress's program for westward expansion represented a vote of confidence—an act of faith—in the face of pervasive doubts and misgivings about the future of the union. The dangers of disunion, anarchy, and underdevelopment figured prominently in discussions about the western lands, anticipating themes that would be repeated during the "critical period." Juxtaposed to the grandiose visions of the development theorists, such warnings reinforced the sense that the fulfillment of America's destiny in world history depended on union and that union depended on development. The alternatives were unthinkable.

IV. Union

In attempting to determine the pace and direction of western development, congressmen grappled with the problem of union at a time when deepening sectional conflict, notably over the navigation of the Mississippi, prompted widespread doubts about its survival. Could sectional interests merge harmoniously in western expansion? Would the union of East and West survive? The Land Ordinance of 1785 represented affirmative answers to these questions. Congressmen hoped that the rapid development of frontier lands and the spread of commercial connections across the continent would preserve and extend republican government in America.

Political economists supplied the conceptual foundation for republicanism on a continental scale. They insisted that population growth, linked with and fueling economic growth, provided an American answer to traditional warnings against overlarge states. In his "Lectures on Political Principles" Samuel Williams of Vermont argued against Montesquieu's "pernicious opinion" that "Civil Liberty can only exist in a Small Territory" and that only a despotic government could maintain order over extended territory. Williams identified political obligation with reciprocal interests and free exchange: "whatever be the size of the territory, the celerity of all motions would be greater in free constitutions." Under "judiciously constructed" republican institutions that permitted Americans to pursue their own ends freely, common interests would help overcome the growing distances entailed by expansion. But "tyranny" was unsuited to a large state because the imposition of the ruler's "caprices" guaranteed resistance by his subjects in defense of their interests. Tyrannical "motion" would be sluggish, not speedy, and the effective size of the state—and the difficulty of governing it—would increase.[75]

A liberal conception of civil society and civil liberty grounded on assumptions of rational economic behavior and on the ultimate harmony of interests in the marketplace enabled theorists like Williams to imagine an expanding empire of liberty in the New World. Long-term trends, notably in population growth rates and in the demand for American agricultural products, seemed to justify optimism about expansion. From this perspective, the future of the "union" was primarily a problem in political economy: no constitutional reforms could preserve the United States if they were not bound by common interests.[76] Therefore, congressional land policy, by determining the orientation of interests in the new settlements, was crucial to the prospects for continuing union between East and West. At the same time, the sale of federal lands spurred by western development promised virtually inexhaustible revenues to promote the common interests of all the states and strengthen the national government.

Throughout the 1780s, commentators who looked west for financial succor assumed that Congress's supply of lands soon would rapidly rise in value in response to a growing demand from a rapidly expanding population: the West would then become marketable at prices high enough to meet public revenue needs but not to discourage industrious settlers. In 1782, even before Congress had established its authority in the West, Pelatiah Webster confidently described "prospects of vast population and national wealth." These, he conceded, "may at first sight appear chimerical," but, supposing that the American population would continue to double every twenty-five years and given the renowned fertility of the western lands, "it will appear very probable that our own eyes may live to see the commencement of a great demand and rapid sale of our western territory."[77]

However promising these ultimate prospects, policy makers faced an immediate, practical dilemma in linking supply to demand. They had to create a market for a commodity, unimproved frontier land, that historically only had speculative value in anticipation of future development. Population pressure on a dwindling land supply might produce potential settlers, but Congress had to persuade them that their capital would be safely and profitably invested in federal lands. This was the challenge facing the authors of the Land Ordinance of 1785.

2.

Squatters, Speculators, and Settlers

☆ ☆

THE LAND ORDINANCE OF 1785

On May 20, 1785, Congress passed an ordinance for organizing the survey and sale of the western lands. Deliberations had begun more than a year earlier when Virginia ceded its claims to the region northwest of the Ohio to the United States. But consensus on the goals of western policy and the best means to achieve them emerged only gradually. Determined to work out an acceptable compromise, Congress named a new land policy committee in March 1785 including a delegate from each state (except Delaware, then unrepresented). After weeks of strenuous debate—and more than a dozen recorded divisions—the ordinance was finally adopted.[1]

Although the debate over how to organize the national domain revealed predictable sectional differences, there was substantial agreement on basic principles. Despite widely divergent land-granting practices in their own states, northern and southern congressmen alike endorsed prior surveys, controlled development, and compact settlement in the Northwest. They also agreed that industrious, market-oriented settlers should be encouraged to buy federal lands. A financially strapped Congress could not afford to let squatters or speculators monopolize the best lands. Furthermore, congressmen were convinced, the preservation of the union and the creation of republican governments on the frontier depended on the character of the first settlers.[2] These concerns are reflected in the text of the Land Ordinance, excerpted below.

An Ordinance for ascertaining the mode of disposing of
Lands in the Western Territory

Be it ordained by the United States in Congress assembled, that the territory
ceded by the individual States to the United States, which has been purchased
of the Indian inhabitants, shall be disposed of in the following manner:

A surveyor from each state shall be appointed by Congress, or a committee of
the States, who shall take an Oath for the faithful discharge of his duty, before
the Geographer of the United States, who is hereby empowered and directed to
administer the same; and the like oath shall be administered to each chain
carrier, by the surveyor under whom he acts. . . .

The Surveyors, as they are respectively qualified, shall proceed to divide the
said territory into townships of six miles square, by lines running due north and
south, and others crossing these at right angles, as near as may be, unless where
the boundaries of the late Indian purchases may render the same impracticable.
. . .

The first line, running north and south as aforesaid, shall begin on the river
Ohio, at a point that shall be found to be due north from the western termination
of a line, which has been run as the southern boundary of the state of Pennsylvania; and the first line, running east and west, shall begin at the same point,
and shall extend throughout the whole territory. . . . The geographer shall
designate the townships, or fractional parts of townships, by numbers progressively from south to north; always beginning each range with number one;
and the ranges shall be distinguished by their progressive numbers to the
westward. The first range, extending from the Ohio to lake Erie, being marked
number one. The Geographer shall personally attend to the running of the first
east and west line; and shall take the latitude of the extremes of the first north
and south line, and of the mouths of the principal rivers. [See Map 1.]

The lines shall be measured with a chain; shall be plainly marked by chaps on
the trees, and exactly described on a plat; whereon shall be noted by the
surveyor, at their proper distances, all mines, salt springs, salt licks and mill
seats, that shall come to his knowledge, and all water courses, mountains and
other remarkable and permanent things, over and near which such lines shall
pass, and also the quality of the lands.

The plats of the townships respectively, shall be marked by subdivisions into
lots of one mile square, or 640 acres, in the same direction as the external lines,
and numbered from 1 to 36; always beginning the succeeding range of the lots
with the number next to that with which the preceding one concluded. . . .

As soon as seven ranges of townships, and fractional parts of townships, in the
direction from south to north, shall have been surveyed, the geographer shall
transmit plats thereof to the board of treasury, who shall record the same, with
the report, in well bound books to be kept for that purpose. . . . The Secretary at
War shall have recourse thereto, and shall take by lot therefrom, a number of
townships, and fractional parts of townships . . . as will be equal to one seventh
part of the whole of such seven ranges, as nearly as may be, for the use of the late
continental army; and he shall make a similar draught, from time to time, until a
sufficient quantity is drawn to satisfy the same, to be applied in manner hereinafter directed. The board of treasury shall, from time to time, cause the
remaining numbers, as well those to be sold entire, as those to be sold in lots, to
be drawn for, in the name of the thirteen states respectively, according to the

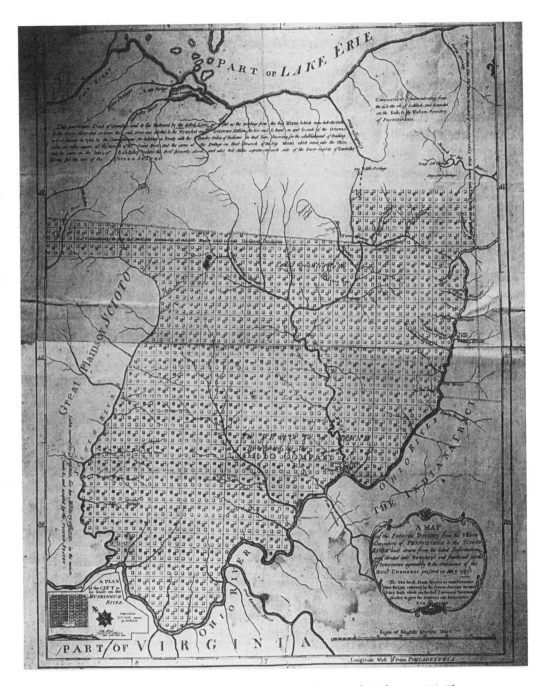

MAP 1: A Map of the Federal Territory (Salem: Dabney and Cushing, 1788). This map was distributed in conjunction with Manasseh Cutler's pamphlet, *An Explanation of the Map which Delineates . . . the Federal Lands* (Salem, 1787). (Courtesy of the American Antiquarian Society)

quotas in the last preceding requisition on all the states; provided, that in case more land than its proportion is allotted for sale, in any state, at any distribution, a deduction be made therefor at the next.

The board of treasury shall transmit a copy of the original plats, previously noting thereon, the townships, and fractional parts of townships, which shall have fallen to the several states, by the distribution aforesaid, to the Commissioners of the loan office of the several states, who, after giving notice not less than two nor more than six months, by causing advertisements to be posted up at the court houses, or other noted places in every county, and to be inserted in one newspaper, published in the states of their residence respectively, shall proceed to sell the townships, or fractional parts of townships, at public vendue, in the following manner, viz: The township, or fractional part of a township, N 1, in the first range, shall be sold entire; and N 2, in the same range, by lots; and thus in alternate order through the whole of the first range. The township, or fractional part of a township, N 1, in the second range, shall be sold by lots; and N 2, in the same range, entire; and so in alternate order through the whole of the second range . . . and thus alternately throughout all the ranges; provided, that none of the lands, within the said territory, be sold under the price of one dollar the acre, to be paid in specie, or loan office certificates, reduced to specie value, by the scale of depreciation, or certificates of liquidated debts of the United States, including interest, besides the expense of the survey and other charges thereon, which are hereby rated at thirty six dollars the township, in specie, or certificates as aforesaid, and so in the same proportion for a fractional part of a township, or of a lot, to be paid at the time of sales; on failure of which payment, the said lands shall again be offered for sale.

There shall be reserved for the United States out of every township, the four lots, being numbered 8, 11, 26, 29, and out of every fractional part of a township, so many lots of the same numbers as shall be found thereon, for future sale. There shall be reserved the lot N 16, of every township, for the maintenance of public schools, within the said township; also one third part of all gold, silver, lead and copper mines, to be sold, or otherwise disposed of as Congress shall hereafter direct. . . .

Done by the United States in Congress assembled, the 20th day of May, in the year of our Lord 1785, and of our sovereignty and independence the ninth.

CHARLES THOMSON, *Secretary*.　　　　　RICHARD H. Lee, *President*.

Congress had to decide quickly how to organize and sell its western lands. The rapid movement of unauthorized settlers and speculators across the Ohio jeopardized congressional authority in the region and threatened to embroil the frontiers in Indian warfare.[3] As congressional land policy was debated and defined in 1784–1785, attention focused on the kinds of settlers who would be encouraged to move into federal territory as well as on the proper organization of new settlements. Congressmen had to establish a context and limits for private enterprise that would secure and advance the public interest. In doing so, they groped toward a working, practical definition of republican liberty.

Serious deliberations began when a committee headed by Thomas Jefferson reported a land ordinance on April 30, 1784, a few weeks after Congress had finally come to terms with Virginia on conditions attached to that state's cession of its trans-Ohio claims.[4] The 1784 proposal, authored by Jefferson and Hugh Williamson of North Carolina, introduced the idea of dividing the western lands by a perfect grid keyed to the new state meridian lines in the companion government ordinance of April 23.[5] But the related questions of how purchasers were to locate their lands (that is, the process by which they would acquire good title) and of how much they would pay became locked in an intersectional stalemate. At first, southern and middle state congressmen favored indiscriminate locations: settlers would identify desirable lands, pay the land office, take out land warrants, and run surveys. The Jefferson-Williamson proposal rationalized this system: holdings could be located anywhere on the public lands but would have to conform to the grid pattern. New Englanders objected to the scattering of settlement and the speculation in prime locations that this plan would predictably encourage. They sought instead to sell surveyed townships to associations of purchasers actually intending to settle in the Ohio country.

The debate over the best way to sell lands and organize settlement might never have been resolved—a transcript of congressional deliberations "would fill forty volumes," Virginia Congressman William Grayson reported—if Congress's hand had not been forced.[6] Settlers would not wait. The fertility of the Ohio Valley was already common knowledge; there emigrants would find "the finest land in the world," according to geographer Jedidiah Morse.[7] John Filson's popular firsthand account of "the Present State of Kentucke," published in 1784, reported and encouraged mass migration down the Ohio.[8] The "amazing" growth of the Kentucky District, just across the river from the national lands, made westward emigration seem a powerful natural force, a veritable human "torrent."[9] The Ohio lands would be next. Even before the Virginia cession was completed, the region was settling with "amazing rapidity."[10] (By 1790 the population of the Kentucky District exceeded seventy thousand.) George Washington, an astute observer with an extensive personal interest in the fate of the West, was convinced that the "spirit for emigration" could not be restrained. But if "you cannot stop the road," he told his fellow Virginian Richard Henry Lee, then President of Congress, "it is yet in your power to mark the way; a little while and you will not be able to do either."[11]

1. Enterprise and Expansion

Rhapsodic descriptions of the western lands encouraged thousands of easterners, many suffering the effects of local land shortages, to look westward for new homes. In a typical effusion, soldier-poet David Humphreys held forth on the Arcadian delights of the western country:

> Then let us go where happier climes invite,
> To midland seas and regions of delight;
> With all that's ours, together let us rise,
> Seek brighter plains, and more indulgent skies;
> Where fair Ohio rolls his amber tide,
> And nature blossoms in her virgin pride;
> Where all that beauty's hand can form to please,
> Shall crown the toils of war, with rural ease. [12]

Other writers were at a loss to describe the bounty of western nature: "words would fail to give you a just idea of its riches."[13] According to a report from Kentucky, "any description I can possibly give, would fall infinitely short."[14] A visitor to the Ohio country called on "industrious farmer[s] from the eastern states" to emigrate to "this delightful country": "struggle no longer with the devouring embarrassments of cold and frost, in the barren regions of the north, but embrace the invitations of peace and plenty in a temperate climate."[15]

The western lands promised great things for an enterprising people. In the words of Richard Henry Lee, the western "country is fine beyond description both in soil and climate—abounding with all those primary and essential materials for human industry to work upon, in order to produce the comfort and happiness of mankind."[16] But if these new lands were potentially very productive—crop yields were said to be "amazing"—Lee and like-minded commentators feared that subsistence could be so easily obtained that settlers would have little incentive to be industrious, particularly as long as markets for surpluses remained inaccessible. A little work would go a long way. The West already seemed "a perfect paradise" to one member of the team of surveyors sent by Congress to the Ohio country—though he would recruit "a few select friends" to provide company. And there would be plenty of time to socialize. "The people of this country"—the lands bordering on the national domain—were, he reported, "the most indolent in the world."[17]

Mankind generally—and the United States in particular—stood to benefit little from the spread of subsistence farming and a general regression to semisavage indolence. The lure of fertile land and easy living threatened to draw multitudes from productive pursuits in eastern communities into lives of laziness and sloth. Expansion thus would unleash centrifugal forces that would undermine the prosperity and power of the new republic.[18]

These themes were developed in a satirical blast against pastoralism and republicanism that appeared in the *Connecticut Magazine* in April 1786. "Lycurgus" mockingly claimed that Congress's liberal provisions for territorial self-government constituted a blueprint for "universal liberty and universal poverty." "Embosomed in academic groves, and surrounded by the wild magnificence of nature," old soldiers would "*sit each under his own tree* . . . cultivating peace with the beasts and the savages." Thus would "commence that glorious millenium [*sic*], so often predicted by the American poets."[19] "Lycurgus"'s satire underscored concerns about the character of western settlers and settlements that pointed the way toward a more elaborate scheme of territorial government. He scoffed at the idea of the West as an asylum or refuge, suggesting that the line between civilization and savagery would become dangerously blurred in a pastoral landscape. Once assimilated to his new environment, the refugee would regress to the level of the "beasts and savages," or even to the vegetable condition of "his own tree."

For "Lycurgus," the republican pastorale was nothing less than a formula for dis-uniting the states and betraying the new nation's promise. Strict republicans suspected that the United States was "already much too large": they must also fear, concluded "Lycurgus" in one of his most extravagantly satirical passages, that the new nation might become too prosperous:

> It is evident that the inland parts and western frontiers of the country are by far the most healthful and fertile portion of our dominions; and therefore, if we hold them in possession, they certainly ought never to be settled. Poverty,—hard labour—and shortness of life are essential to the preservation of our liberties.[20]

Disunion, "Lycurgus" suggested, was the logical, republican solution to the danger of American prosperity.

Other, less playful writers also predicted that the new states would break off from the union and, following Vermont's example, become "rich and happy" by escaping the old states' burdens of debt and taxes.[21] Malcontents of all sorts would seek refuge on the frontiers, "Primitive Whig" told readers of the *New-Jersey Gazette*, including those "running away from publick taxes, and private debts." Thus, he concluded, "we diminish our internal strength under the notion of extending our dominion."[22]

Depopulation—the loss of productive workers, taxpayers, and potential purchasers of state lands—was the eastern analogue of western settlement run amuck. Theorists offered reciprocal solutions to both problems. Economic revival in the East would end the "waste of people," banished to the wilderness by lack of work and indebtedness.[23] Meanwhile, development of the productive potential of the West would open up new markets, sustaining the growth of population and prosperity throughout the union. At the same time, frontier development would drive up western land prices, thus blocking the escape of the improvident and unproductive to "free" land, subsistence farming, and a reversion to savagery. A vigorous, integrated national economy would accelerate population growth while attracting industrious immigrants from abroad. According to a writer in the *Maryland Gazette*, a large and growing population was the key to national "strength and riches"—provided the "great majority of those numbers are usefully employed."[24]

II. Squatters

Squatters had already begun moving across the Ohio and forming widely scattered, unauthorized settlements. Intruders on the public lands were encouraged by the return of peace and by the apparent inability of Virginia and then Congress to control their movements. Even if squatters could be made to pay for their lands—a doubtful proposition—dispersed settlement would retard the development of commercial agriculture and discourage further purchasers. Congress would thus lose revenue from land sales while being liable for the costs of defending scattered, strategically vulnerable settlements that were bound to provoke the Indians. Mismanagement of the frontier would jeopardize one of Congress's few likely sources of revenue.

Congress was forced to act quickly because of the anticipated spread of illegal settlement. When federal troops, commanded by Colonel Josiah Harmar, arrived in the Ohio country in early 1785, only a few squatters had ventured across the river, although Harmar was soon persuaded that "the number of settlers farther down the river is very considerable and, from all accounts daily increasing." But the squatter settlements remained sparse, probably never including more than a few hundred hardy souls. Commentators warned, however, that the rapid movement of great numbers across the Ohio was imminent—and would be irresistible.[25] A western Pennsylvanian described the "impatience" of would-be settlers on the Ohio lands who were waiting for Congress to define its land policy. If terms were not attractive, he warned, "Congress will lose the only opportunity they ever will have of extending their power and influence over this new region." Settlers "will go and settle themselves down, and not only locate for themselves, but enter into some sort of covenant to protect each other, and make their new title good." The threat was not an idle one. The writer may have seen a handbill proclaiming mankind's "undoubted right to pass into every vacant country" and challenging Congress's power to sell the Ohio lands.[26] Exploiting the long history of jurisdictional confusion in the region as well as the novelty of congressional pretensions not positively authorized by the Articles of Confederation, the sponsors of this message proposed to organize a new state. Separatist movements elsewhere, notably in Vermont, the Wyoming Valley, and western North Carolina, represented efforts to wrest control of public lands from particular states. Given its notorious weakness, Congress was at least equally vulnerable to separatist agitation. Rhode Island's delegates had made the connection explicit. "Now is the critical juncture," they reported in late 1783: "In the course of a few years the [Ohio] country will be peopled like Vermont. It will be independent, and the whole property of the soil will be lost forever to the United States."[27]

Squatters became a problem as the potential uses and "public" character of the public lands were clarified. Before the Virginia cession, squatting had not been a conspicuous or pressing problem for state authorities who were characteristically intent on promoting westward expansion for commercial or speculative reasons or to pay off state debts. However much they might lament unauthorized settlement, it was often difficult in practice for them to distinguish between legal and illegal settlers. They perceived, or preferred to perceive, no essential difference between squatting and legitimately locating a prospective property holding; squatters simply had not yet perfected their titles by warrant and survey. Given the chaos of overlapping surveys, the courts might find actual purchasers to be "intruders" on lands they had located and developed in good faith.

According to southern practice, good title was the culmination of a series of steps—from location to survey—and of its successful defense against counterclaimants. This was the system, modified to preclude controversy over property lines, that southerners Jefferson and Williamson first proposed to extend across the Ohio. Not surprisingly, Jefferson at this time did not see squatters as a problem; in a sense he did not "see" them at all. He "rather doubt[ed]" that anyone had settled across the Ohio. Even granted that there were such settlers, he continued, "these very people will be glad to pay the price which Congress will ask to secure themselves in their titles to these lands."[28] In other words, squatters could be left in place, to be transformed retroactively into legitimate settlers—the first purchasers of the public domain.

The character and scope of challenges to national property and jurisdiction became clearer in the months between the Jefferson-Williamson proposals and the adoption of a revised land ordinance in May 1785. As congressmen learned more about the frontier, southern and northern views on western policy began to converge. In effect, southerners, particularly influential Virginians, came to accept the necessity of ensuring compact settlement and of maximizing revenue by a more systematic sale of lands than practiced in their own states. The prevailing confusion about land titles in the southern backcountry resulting from indiscriminate locations directed their attention to the need for a rational system of surveys. (One writer noted that in some places in Kentucky there were "8 or 10" overlapping claims: "whoever purchases there, is sure to purchase a lawsuit."[29]) Financial needs and strategic considerations made a coherent, township settlement pattern increasingly attractive. Virginians were also concerned about national indebtedness and, no less, about the vulnerability of the state's Kentucky District to Indian attack.

Jefferson endorsed the new policy orientation embodied in the 1785 land ordinance; his conception of the squatter as imperfect, but perfectible citizen-farmer could not be sustained. The ordinance provided for the prior survey of federal lands, thus avoiding the entire process of title perfection that characterized southern policy. Acknowledging that Congress would have to take a more active role than he had first anticipated in preparing land for sale, Jefferson wrote James Monroe from Paris that the adopted system represented an improvement over his own proposals "in the most material circumstances": "I am much pleased with your land ordinance."[30] Under the Jefferson-Williamson plan, Congress simply would have imposed regularity on unauthorized and undirected settlement. But Congress would take the initiative under the 1785 ordinance: as soon as seven ranges of townships, each six miles square, had been surveyed, commissioners of the continental loan office would offer federal lands for competitive bidding at "public vendues" in each of the old states. "None of the lands" would "be sold under the price of one dollar the acre" in specie or its equivalent.

The cost of federal lands under the 1785 land ordinance would block out poor, lazy squatters; instead, the territory would attract industrious settlers determined to recoup their investment by developing their property and finding markets for their products. Under the new land system, settlers would be clustered in adjacent townships, thus facilitating the development of local markets; internal improvements would link East and West. The shift toward the township form did not mean that southerners were suddenly convinced of the superiority of Yankee civilization. James Madison thought the New Englanders' predilection for reserving town lots for the support of religion smelled "strongly of an antiquated Bigotry."[31] But Virginians and Marylanders intrigued by the lucrative commercial potential of trade links with the Ohio country saw reason to favor a more systematic land policy that would lead to larger, denser, and therefore more productive settlements.

The emphasis on commercial agriculture and economic development reflected Congress's overriding concern with revenue. Its goal was to create a national domain that would produce revenue through land sales. The idea that the sale of the West would help pay for the Revolution became fixed in congressional thinking, particularly as prospects for developing other revenue sources dimmed. Consequently, Congress showed little enthusiasm for proposals that called for extensive, free land grants, even when they promised to satisfy soldiers' bounty claims or secure the frontiers.[32] The commitment to a commercial frontier was incompatible with propositions to rusticate old soldiers, or with pastoral fantasies about sustaining a balance at a "middle stage" between nature and civilization most propitious for the preservation of republicanism. Republican liberty would soon degenerate into licentiousness if the frontiers were opened to lazy, lawless, and improvident squatters. Western policy makers became convinced that republican institutions would only take root where orderly and industrious settlers were organized in compact settlements.

The desire to transform the western lands into valuable property as soon as possible prompted a broad indictment of scattered, illegal settlements. Congressmen recognized, of course, that the market price depended on various factors, including clear title, the supply of land for sale, access to markets, fertility and other intrinsic values. While locating *ad libitum* made sense for individual settlers who, as purchasers, were interested in good lands at nominal prices, it would retard regional economic growth and thus work against the settlers' own long-run interests. The public interest in revenue from land sales and in maintaining a peaceful (inexpensive) frontier thus seemed to converge with the private interests of westerners in the future prosperity of their new communities.

There was no room for squatters in this picture. The squatters' chief sin was their inability—or unwillingness—to pay for their lands. Drafters of the land ordinance were also determined to neutralize the traditional preemptive advantage enjoyed by squatters and speculators: location, survey, and sale were to be rationalized and centralized. Success of the new land policy hinged on the government being able to offer unencumbered titles. This meant clearing squatters off the land, by force if necessary.

Congress's subsequent military operations against illegal settlements beyond the Ohio were justified by conventional ideas about the character of frontier people. Settlers supposedly reverted to barbarism as they pushed beyond the frontiers of civilization: the stages of historical development defined by contemporary social science were reversed when projected across progressively emptier spaces. Thus, according to Benjamin Rush, the "first settler" in a new country "is nearly related to an Indian in his m[a]nners."[33] Such logic could lead Congressman David Howell of Rhode Island to imagine "combinations [of] . . . Indians and disaffected, or corrupted white people" "should depressed and disorderly settlements prevail over these lands."[34] Of course, "disorderly" whites were more likely to be at war with the "savages" and to drag everyone else into their disputes.[35] Such lawless violence threatened the orderly progress of settlement by deterring industrious easterners from purchasing federal lands. In the words of a Boston writer, "the terror of savages would deter the people of *this country* even from Paradise."[36]

The squatters who moved on to the federal lands were easily confused with "savages." One of the federal surveyors wrote from Fort Harmar, at the junction of the Ohio and Muskingum rivers, in July 1786, that this "lawless set of fellows . . . are more our enemies than the most brutal savages of the country." The surveyors anticipated continuing interference "from a few rascally yellow fellows, that are outcasts of all the tribes, and the whites who have been dispossessed of fine bottoms."[37] White intruders in the Northwest were also likened to wild animals, "roaming" or "rambling" across the trackless wilderness. (Speculators seeking out prime sites were like "wolves," Washington wrote.[38]) This characterization was most memorably expressed in Crèvecoeur's *Letters from an American Farmer*: on the frontier men "are often in a perfect state of war" with each other and with "every wild inhabitant of these venerable woods. . . . There men appear to be no better than carnivorous animals of a superior rank."[39]

Warnings about a reversion to savagery reflected the concern that frontier settlers were, in Crèvecoeur's words, "placed still farther beyond the reach of government, which in some measure leaves them to themselves." This lack of restraint clarified the limits of republican liberty. Unflattering images of semisavage settlers and speculators showed the dangers of rampant, unrestrained privatism—the impulse to pursue private interest at public expense, the very antithesis of the new American idea of liberty as a higher synthesis of private and public realms. Private interest and enterprise had to be contained within a context that guaranteed productive activity and mutually beneficial exchange. But the discipline of the marketplace, like the rule of law, barely reached the new settlements. Accordingly, the West provided refuge and new opportunities for "banditties" and "the scum and refuse of the Continent."[40] The predatory impulses of these "Rascals," who survived "by hunting and stealing," were recognizable to civilized easterners, themselves restrained by the accumulated force of law and custom.[41] The lawless West released the selfish impulses held in check in the "civilized" East, thus representing the negation of republican liberty.

Western development thus hinged on Congress's determination to clear the ground of squatters, Indian traders, speculators, and other interlopers with an interest in fomenting "uneasiness" among the tribes.[42] Unbounded privatism was seen to jeopardize the security and prosperity of the new nation. In the unenlightened pursuit of their immediate private interests, frontier people casually ignored laws enacted by their own state governments or by representatives of the states in Congress. To secure dubious land claims or commercial concessions they appeared willing to betray the Revolution itself by erecting their own independent governments or by submitting to British or Spanish imperial authority. The history of frontier politics during and after the war (Vermont was again the most obvious example) convinced congressmen that a vacuum of effective authority in the trans-Ohio region was a standing invitation to enemies of the Revolution, domestic and foreign.[43]

III. Speculators

War against the squatters was imperative. Otherwise, the Virginia delegates predicted in late 1783, the Ohio lands

> wou'd not only remain profitless to the United States, but wou'd become a prey to lawless banditii and adventurers, who must necessarily have involv'd us in continued Indian wars and perhaps have form'd Establishments not only on dissimilar principles to those which form the basis of our Republican Constitutions, but such as might eventually prove destructive to them.[44]

If such "establishments" represented the antithesis of the new American republics, the motivations of their would-be founders were all too familiar. Significantly, the "banditii" who infested the public domain preyed on *lands*: they would make their fortunes by exploiting the demands of bona fide settlers. In polite language, these predators were land speculators, a highly evolved species who ventured into the wilds only because of their prospective market value. Given the expected torrent of emigration, they understood that "very great advantages may be made by those who are early in their adventures and speculations."[45]

Why were policy makers so hostile to speculators? The obvious answer is that speculators threatened to usurp the government's role in the western land market. By preempting prime sites at nominal prices and waiting for rising demand to make them valuable, speculators would be enriched while Congress would gain little return for its investment in organizing and protecting the West. There were political implications to this substitution. If Congress could not create, alienate, and guarantee land titles, it could not, for all practical purposes, govern at all. But the hostility to speculators must be carefully qualified. Framers of congressional western policy were not opposed to private participation in the land market: buying and selling by individuals and companies would necessarily be profit-oriented and to some degree speculative. Policy makers did not expect that purchasers would always be settlers. But they were determined that Congress would control the land market. The dollar-an-acre minimum price precluded extensive speculation; meanwhile, Congress would withhold a vast reserve of lands to be surveyed and brought to market over a long period of time.

The attack on speculators is prominent in the correspondence of George Washington, one of many Virginians heavily involved in western land speculation. It was not enterprise or speculation as such that disturbed Washington. Rather, he was opposed to the headlong pursuit of private advantage at the public expense, and at the expense of the future prosperity of the entire community. In other words, efforts to control western settlement— and thus to restrain land speculation—represented an attempt to balance and reconcile private and public interests, to fashion a working definition of liberty appropriate to a dynamic and expanding political economy. The challenge was not to banish the speculation but rather to direct it toward the public good.

Washington's ambivalent position as a speculator warning against speculation reflected not only his assessment of the contemporary strategic situation but also his state's controversial campaign to cede the Ohio country unencumbered by private claims. Out-of-state land companies, not claims by other states or by Congress, presented the chief challenge to Virginia's western jurisdiction; the state's invalidation of private purchases from the Indians was the stumbling block in resolving the protracted impasse over congressional acceptance of the cession.[46] As a consequence, Virginians were sensitive to the conflict between private speculation and public interest in the ceded area, even though the state's land system made such a distinction impossible where the state retained jurisdiction. The result was that the same sort of activity—squatting, locating prime sites, speculating—seemed perfectly acceptable (or at least unavoidable) south of the Ohio while it was seen as a threat to vital national interests across the river.

Washington warned that Congress should not "suffer" that "wide extended Country to be over run with Land Jobbers, Speculators, and Monopolisers or even with scatter'd settlers."[47] Indeed, the lack of restraint encouraged by the apparently unlimited stock of free land seduced squatters, who otherwise might have been content with eking out a marginal subsistence, into dreaming speculators' dreams. This unrestrained speculative impulse, not the more modest ambition of making a living off the land, best explained the strategically dangerous overextension of white settlement. The "rage for speculating in, and forestalling" Ohio lands was contagious, Washington wrote Jacob Read in November 1784. The upshot was that

> scarce a valuable spot within any tolerable distance of [the Ohio River], is left without a claimant. Men in these times, talk with as much facility of fifty, a

hundred, and even 500,000 Acres as a Gentleman formerly would do of 1000 acres. In defiance of the proclamation of Congress, they roam over the Country on the Indian side of the Ohio, mark out Lands, Survey, and even settle them.[48]

Washington's letter betrayed the anxieties of someone who had achieved the status of a "Gentleman" confronting a mad scramble for wealth in which a man's social standing, and even his capital resources, were of no account. In such a world, there was no difference between settlers and speculators, or between good and bad speculators: everyone was an "adventurer." But Washington and other land policy makers also showed that they understood that the unconstrained pursuit of wealth destroyed wealth. If all the potentially valuable locations were brought to market at once, they would have no value—even for speculators. If, Timothy Pickering wrote, Congress opened up the entire Northwest, permitting "adventurers . . . to ramble over that extensive country"—as they did under the southern system of indiscriminate locations—"the best lands would be in a manner *given away*."[49] Furthermore, in Washington's view, the larger the area opened to settlement, the more "extensive" the "field for Land jobbers and Speculators." The result would be to "Weaken our Frontiers [and to] exclude Law, good government, and taxation to a late period."[50] But "compact and progressive Seating" would discourage speculators and multiply the number of "useful citizens," thus advancing the "public interest."[51]

In order to keep up land values and revenue from land sales, Congress had to regulate the available supply and encourage competition for an artificially scarce resource. But speculators, with ambitions to become "petty princes in the western country," were interested in discouraging potential purchasers of the Ohio lands until they had gained control of extensive tracts.[52] According to "Cincinnatus," reports of savage conditions would "lessen the number of buyers" and thus the "price of [federal] land," and, by emphasizing the need for security, encourage Congress to "grant the lands in that quarter on condition of settlement only." "Cincinnatus" traced a widely published letter warning of the imminence of full-scale conflict with the Indians and criticizing congressional land policy to the machinations of Nathaniel Sackett and a company of New York land speculators.[53] The Sackett group promised to defend the frontier by organizing a new state at its own expense, if Congress would grant them an enormous tract of land bounded by Lake Erie and the Ohio, Muskingum, and Scioto rivers. "Cincinnatus" hoped "Congress and the Savages together, will be able to keep them and all others out."[54]

Congress rejected the Sackett proposal, demonstrating its determination to protect its property interests and implement the 1785 land ordinance. The authors of congressional land policy were determined to prevent widespread speculation in the Northwest. Here, at least, the distinction between private and public interest was apparent: the land had to be kept clear of squatters, speculators, and the claims of other governments so that Congress could bring something of value to market.[55] Policy makers attempted to solve the problem of frontier disorder by driving off squatters and speculators and recruiting orderly immigrants to settle in compact townships. Conversely, the government had to prevent widely scattered settlements that increased the risk of Indian wars. War would destroy the market for federal lands while putting further strain on an empty treasury.

In its deliberations on land policy, Congress was forced to define the role of individual interest and enterprise in developing the West. The stock figures in contemporary accounts of frontier life—semisavage squatters, outlaws, speculators, and other unsavory "adventurers"—represented the dangerous excesses of unrestrained privatism. At the same time, policy makers relied on the properly regulated pursuit of private interest to promote the wealth and power of the American union. The distinction between private enterprise and privatism made it possible to identify a positive relationship between individual liberty and the public good.

IV. Settlers and Settlements

Visions of western economic development were premised on the extension of market relations, transportation routes, and a union of eastern and western interests. These visions precluded conceptions of the West as a refuge for old soldiers or virtuous republicans, or as an "assylum for the poor."[56] Implicit in such conceptions was the idea that East and West were utterly different and distinct places. But development depended on an intersectional harmony of interests and a common commitment to pursue happiness in similar ways. The crucial issue was the westerner's relation to the natural world.

"Cato" warned readers of the *Connecticut Magazine* that it was a great mistake to believe that "the advantages with which Nature blesses an infant empire . . . constitute[d] the sum of its happiness." If this were true, America could turn its back on the world—and Americans could turn their backs on each other—in order to live off the bounties of nature. Instead, "Cato" argued, the gifts of nature

> are the instruments of greatness, and the earnest of future felicity: they form the basis of the glorious edifice. . . . In a people so enlightened as ours, advantages should seem to call forcibly for improvement, and to inspire a generous ambition.[57]

A New Yorker elaborated on this theme in an apostrophe to the new nation's potential for development. The "spectacle" of this "laborious nation" transforming the virgin landscape was "interesting, noble and august." God Himself must be "delighted" to see the Americans "animate, by the invigorating breath of industry, all the regenerating powers of nature," to see them "improve the mysterious system of destruction and reproduction, [and] stir up, enrich, and meliorate the earth, rendering the appearance of nature still more beautiful."[58]

An instrumental attitude toward nature, enlarging "all streams of population, opulence and pleasure," created bonds of interest between easterners and westerners. It also defined the boundary between civilized, enterprising whites and "savages," white as well as red. Indeed, the "higher use" argument for expropriating Indian land depended on the settlers' distinctive capacity to develop its full agricultural and commercial potential. The problem was that white settlers seemed all too ready to revert to savagery and thus fail to exploit "the instruments of greatness" presented for their use.

Congress had to recruit settlers who would be willing and able to develop the region's enormous potential. By setting up land auctions in each of the old states to draw industrious, market-oriented purchasers directly from the sources of population growth, the land system was supposed to promote enterprise and preclude savage indolence. So, too, policy makers hoped to preempt the usual course of lawless landgrabbing that one Kentucky writer characterized as a virtual law of American frontier development. "It is well known," he asserted, that "every part of America that has hitherto been settled, has flowed in blood for a long time."[59] But industrious eastern farmers would be less likely to provoke their Indian neighbors than the semisavage predators who usually arrived first in a new country. At the same time, George Washington confidently predicted, "the gradual extension of our Settlements will as certainly cause the Savage as the Wolf to retire."[60]

The recruitment of worthy settlers continued to be a leading concern of territorial policy makers throughout the Confederation period. Washington, Grayson, and other commentators hoped to see a large influx of foreigners settle the West—thus, incidentally, answering antiexpansionist anxieties about the depopulation of the old states.[61] But the new land system was better designed to exploit the rising demand for lands in the eastern states. Jefferson thought the land ordinance would guarantee that the national domain would be settled by a "proper mixture of the citizens from the different states."[62] In either case, it was agreed that Congress should look beyond the frontier itself for purchasers.

Yet the land system was not simply a means of attracting worthy, easily governed settlers. It was also supposed to be a means of educating new settlers—in the broadest sense—to know and pursue their true private interests while fulfilling their public responsibilities. "We live at the origin of things," wrote "P.W." Every decision respecting the founding of these new western societies, even the choice of their names, would have momentous consequences. "Let us engrave the names of our brave Gallican friends on the first beginnings . . . of our great labour," he counseled, so that future generations would learn from these lasting "monuments of gratitude."[63] The Ohio Associates followed this advice, commemorating French aid in the Revolution by naming their first settlement Marietta, after Marie Antoinette. Similarly, Jefferson hoped to inspire proper republican sentiments by the neoclassical names he proposed for the new states in his draft of the original territorial government ordinance. (These state names are used in Map 2.) At the same time, he thought that the land system presented "an happy opportunity . . . of introducing into general use the geometrical Mile, in such a manner as that it cannot possibly fail of forcing it's way on the people."[64]

The land system itself would teach settlers to "see" the western landscape—and their own opportunities within it—through the pattern of the grid that defined specific property holdings.[65] Rational, systematic settlement would help create enlightened communities. As Manasseh Cutler wrote, shortly after the Northwest Ordinance was adopted, the great advantage of the new territory over any "other part of the earth" was "that, in order to begin *right*, there will be no *wrong* habits to combat, and no inveterate systems to overturn—there is no rubbish to remove, before you can lay the foundation."[66] The land ordinance's provision for the public support of education complemented the rationality of geometrical survey, clear property titles, and predefined boundaries. Settlers on the national frontiers would not be the ignorant, degraded frontiersmen who, by common report, are "every day turning their backs upon all the benefits of cultivated society." Cutler's new westerners were turning their backs on the "rubbish" represented by squatters, not on civilization. The result of a "systematic" territorial policy would be that "the whole territory of the United States [would be] settled by an enlightened people."[67]

The relative compactness of settlement that would result from the sale of land by lot or township was also seen as a crucial means of socializing new settlers. In 1782, well before Congress had any lands to administer, Pelatiah Webster advocated controlled expansion so that "we can *extend our laws*, *customs*, and *civil police* as *fast* and as *far* as we extend our *settlements*."[68] Washington also endorsed the idea of "progressive seating." An artificially limited supply would keep land prices up while extending the benefits, and deriving all the advantages of Law and Government from them at once; neither of which can be done in sparse Settlements, where nothing is thought of but scrambling for Land, which more than probably would involve confusion and bloodshed.[69]

In March 1785, shortly before the adoption of the land ordinance, Timothy Pickering agreed that "dispersed" settlers would be "impossible to govern."[70] Tightly clustered in compact settlements directly contiguous to longer settled regions in neighboring states, settlers on the national frontier would be held in check by common interests and associations. They would soon develop civic competence.

The township system incorporated in the land ordinance appealed to southerners, even though they were accustomed to acquiring lands for themselves by indiscriminate occupation. Not only did townships appear to guarantee a population density that facilitated the maintenance of law and order, they also promised to attract groups of immigrants with prior communal bonds. Thus, Grayson explained to Washington, "the idea of a township with the temptation of a support for religion and education, holds forth an inducement for neighborhoods of the same religious sentiments to confederate for the purpose of purchasing and settling together."[71] Although "support for religion" was eliminated from the adopted land ordinance, and Congress agreed to offer alternative townships for sale by individual lot, the new system was designed to promote group migration. The high price of land would deter land speculation while encouraging potential settlers to pool their resources in order to purchase whole townships.

An orderly frontier thus depended on a land system that directed settlement into neighborhood clusters—imposing order on private initiatives— while inducing existing neighborhoods to relocate from the settled parts of the country. These effects were reciprocal: large numbers of industrious farmers would hesitate to venture into the wilderness without assurances that they would soon enjoy the benefits of local institutions—including courts, schools, and churches—convenient neighbors, and easy access to the outside world.

V. The Land Market

Congressmen were aware that the success of their land policy was by no means inevitable. They were convinced that the economic development of the West and the durability of its connections with the East hinged on drafting and enforcing effective regulations. Congress would have to introduce to the national frontier a new kind of settler-developer, capable of putting his property to immediate productive use and therefore justifying its price. The traditional growth of frontier settlements from semisavage subsistence to commercial farming would have to be collapsed into a single stage: the West would be commercial from the outset.[72] American antipathy to taxation reinforced the commitment to drawing revenue from the public land market instead of waiting for unregulated private initiatives to make land valuable, if this were possible, and hence capable of sustaining public burdens.

It thus becomes clear that the formulation of congressional land policy in 1784–1785 represented an effort to create a national market in western lands. The success of the effort depended on mobilizing national and even international demand for new, potentially productive lands. Congress would have to take an active role, at considerable expense, in guaranteeing that market conditions favorable to its and the nation's interests would prevail. Speculators and squatters were major obstacles to this program because, by claiming or occupying prime sites, they distorted supply and, by clogging the courts with conflicting claims, they scared off potential buyers.

Congress attempted to guarantee a true land market through a variety of related provisions in the May 1785 ordinance. First, it determined to remove its land offices from the frontier, thus neutralizing the advantage enjoyed by nearby settlers and speculators with firsthand knowledge of available lands. This crucial feature of the ordinance survived subsequent revision; a related provision, that federal lands be offered at auctions in each of the thirteen Atlantic states, was abandoned. Critics of this requirement thought that by fragmenting demand it would minimize competition and lower prices; they also feared that multiple markets would be a deterrent to foreign purchasers who would not know "when or where to apply for" lands.[73] But the underlying premise, that Congress should not look to existing western settlements for settlers, was generally accepted. Washington, who knew these frontier people all too well, expected (and probably hoped) to see the West peopled from abroad.[74] Given the chaotic history of their own backcountry, at least some Virginians were predisposed to give New Englanders a preference to their own people as prospective purchaser-settlers.[75] In any case, the guarantee that the eastern purchaser would have a fair chance to bid on western property promised to connect latent demand, where surplus population and wealth sought new opportunities, with an unlimited supply of potentially valuable property.

The most important feature of Congress's new land policy was the requirement of survey before settlement, with property lines following a grid system that made clear title possible. The grid thus helped make land more marketable.[76] Washington thought the marketability of federal lands would be further enhanced by mapping the western territory on the basis of accurate surveys. In late 1784 he wrote Richard Henry Lee, recommending that the United States commission a map:

> The expence attending this undertaking cou'd not be great, the advantages would be unbounded; for sure I am, nature has made such an ample display of her bounties in those regions, that the more the Country is explored, the more it will rise in estimation, consequently, the greater might the revenue be to the Union.[77]

As Washington suggested, the surveys that created the grid and guaranteed clear titles had the further advantage of providing purchasers with valuable information about Congress's lands. Potential settlers would know what they were getting.

To assure that citizens of all parts of the union would have equal access to information about the western lands, the ordinance stipulated that each state nominate a surveyor to join United States Geographer Thomas Hutchins in the field. The result, according to the Connecticut delegates, would be to diffuse "as generally as possible thro' the States a knowledge of the Nature and quality of the Country so that the Citizens in general may be enabled to make their Purchases with Judgment and Discretion."[78] The goal, William Grayson told Washington, was that "the Country . . . be settled out of the bowels of the Atlantic States," each state "contributing it's proportion of emigrants."[79] The surveyors would not only act as the eyes and ears of potential purchasers but would help produce accurate surveys that would supply information about tree types and soil fertility as well as potential routes to markets.

The connection between knowledge and land values was axiomatic. The New Hampshire delegates wrote home shortly after the passage of the ordinance, urging that associations be formed to purchase western lands. "The general opinion of the goodness of the soil in this western country . . . has been increasing with every new investigation of it," they reported.[80] Of course, this "goodness" was a function of the knowledge that such investigations produced. In this sense, the survey of the West would represent an investment by Congress: it would create value by producing knowledge.

The crucial question, then, was access to knowledge. Speculators stood to benefit from general ignorance. A few insiders would monopolize information, either by conducting their own investigations and surveys or by abuse of public office.[81] The lack of specific information would deter purchasers prepared to put their property to productive use, and depressed land values would enable speculators to accumulate vast holdings. Government-run surveys thus were essential for guaranteeing both the public interest in land sales and the fullest possible participation of private purchasers in the western land market.

Contemporaries recognized that this was a critical moment for Congress to define its role in opening and developing the West.[82] Unregulated expansion would play into the hands of speculators who would exploit their local situation and superior knowledge to engross the best lands. Settlement would be retarded. The new nation would forfeit a golden opportunity to discharge its war debts without burdening productive citizens with oppressive taxes. Open, competitive bidding—a true market situation—would be impossible. This was the ultimate problem for western policy makers. Only through the creation of a market in western lands could the United States guarantee economic development and preserve their union. A regime of unchecked privatism characterized by lawless violence, squatting, and land speculation jeopardized the long-term interests of enterprising settlers as well as public revenue. The challenge was to direct private initiatives toward the public good. As Pelatiah Webster wrote in his 1782 essay on the western lands, the "secret art, the true spirit of financiering" is "so to graft the revenue on the public stock, so to unite and combine public and private interests, that they may mutually support, feed, and quicken each other."[83]

VI. The Ohio Company

Between 1784 and 1787 assessments of the demand for national property became less and less optimistic. At the outset, many observers assumed the rapid, continuous flow of settlement. Congress only had to screen out undesirable settlers from this westward flow. The human "torrent" seemed irresistible: in Washington's memorable language, "you might as well attempt . . . to prevent the reflux of the tide, when you had got it into your rivers," as to try to stop it.[84] As the river image suggested, that movement might be channeled—indeed, if it could not be, there was no point in developing a western policy at all.

Images of order imposed on the land by the grid system, reinforced by expectations of rapid and orderly development, were supposed to attract orderly and industrious settlers. It was a neat formula—at least in theory. But it soon became clear that large numbers of foreigners or easterners would not be bidding for federal lands, even when offered for sale at a single site, according to a revision of the ordinance. When lands from the first surveys were finally brought to auction late in 1787, only 72,934 acres were sold, providing the government a mere $117,108.22 in revenue.[85] It became clear that Congress would have to devise other means to attract purchasers if it hoped to reap any benefit from its property. This realization set the stage for congressional negotiations with the Ohio Company.

Agent Manasseh Cutler received a sympathetic hearing when he promised that the Ohio Company would mobilize "an actual, a large, and immediate settlement of the most robust and industrious people in America."[86] Congressmen understood that Cutler was offering to settle the region with New Englanders. (Cutler judiciously confined explicit comparisons between northern and southern settlers to his private correspondence. He wrote Nathan Dane of Massachusetts, one of the authors of the Northwest Ordinance, that northerners were "undoubtedly preferable": "They will be men of more robust constitutions, inured to labor, and free from the habits of idleness."[87]) For his part, Virginia Congressman Edward Carrington was pleased to report that the Ohio Company included "the best men in Connecticut and Massachusetts." Congress's contract with the company "will be a means of introducing into the Country, in the first instance, a discription of Men who will fix the character and politics throughout the whole territory, and which will probably endure to the latest period of time."[88]

Although Congress agreed to transfer a large amount of its property to private hands, the Ohio Company purchase was consistent with the goals of the 1785 land ordinance. The company's offer was predicated on the terms of the ordinance. Congress received considerably less per acre than its asking price: it accepted a first payment of $500,000 (in depreciated continental certificates) in exchange for 1.5 million acres west of the seven ranges, with another $500,000 due when surveys were completed. But immediate payment promised at least some financial relief to an impoverished Congress; congressmen could also look forward to rising demand for additional federal land.[89] Most important, the Ohio Company would supply the kind of settlers who would spur rapid economic growth.

Meanwhile, Congress accepted responsibility for maintaining order in the new settlements. By 1787 it was clear that buyers—including the Ohio Company—would settle for nothing less than a fully developed "colonial" government, qualified by appropriate compact guarantees, during the territorial period. Policy makers agreed that the loose system proposed in Congress's 1784 territorial government ordinance relied too much on settlers to manage their own affairs. Spurred on by Manasseh Cutler, Congress adopted a new plan for governing the Northwest on July 13, 1787.

3.

New States
in the Expanding Union

☆ ☆ ☆

THE TERRITORIAL GOVERNMENT ORDINANCES

Congress's initial program for opening the West was set forth in the territorial government ordinance of April 23, 1784, and the land ordinance of May 20, 1785. Congress would guarantee the eventual equality of new western states and, by laying out their boundaries in advance, preempt future jurisdictional controversy. At the same time, policy makers hoped, the rapid sale of the western lands would help relieve the nation's financial burdens while guaranteeing orderly expansion and economic growth.

Congress faced unexpected obstacles in implementing its program for western development. Delays in completing surveys, illegal settlements, and the continuing threat of frontier warfare threatened to drive away prospective buyers. The western lands offered no immediate financial relief; instead, keeping the national domain clear of squatters and speculators constituted a further drain on the treasury. Meanwhile, critics complained that the government ordinance did not provide adequate guarantees for the preservation of law and order before statehood.[1] Others charged that the high price of federal lands and the requirement of advance surveys would discourage prospective buyers.[2]

Contradictory tendencies in congressional western policy became increasingly apparent as criticism mounted and prospects for brisk sales and rapid settlement dimmed. The authors of the original ordinance for territorial government assumed that westward settlement would continue, regardless of congressional policy. Therefore, they were most concerned with establishing equitable terms of union that would bind new states to the old. The land ordinance would simply help direct the flow of population: new settlers would be prevented from spreading too far and thin by the gradual, progressive survey and sale of national lands. But between 1784 and 1787 it became increasingly clear that the land system alone did not constitute an adequate framework for orderly development. In practice, the implementation of federal land policy retarded settlement and the constitutional questions addressed by the government ordinance became more and more remote and hypothetical. As a result, the original relationship between land policy and territorial government was reversed. Policy makers realized that they could only attract orderly and industrious settlers to the Northwest if they guaranteed law and order—and land titles—from the very beginning of settlement.

Congress could not leave frontier settlers to manage their own affairs until they were ready to join the union. Instead, the establishment of an effective territorial government was prerequisite to land sales and settlement. This realization led to a new conceptualization of western politics. In 1784 and 1785 both present and prospective western settlements were described as "states." The development of distinct frontier communities with their own interests and loyalties was taken for granted. But the recognition of western autonomy and distinctiveness implied by use of the word "state" was incompatible with Congress's expanding role in maintaining order and fostering settlement. Despite their antipathy to imperial rule, congressmen began to talk about the need to establish "colonial" government in the West on a "temporary" basis. By 1787, the distinction between a "territory" governed by Congress and the "state" that would eventually succeed it had become clear.

Congress's revenue needs converged with prescriptions for western economic and political development. The relatively high price of land—set at a dollar per acre in 1785—would screen out speculators as well as poor, subsistence farmers and put a premium on commercial agriculture. Settlers would be clustered into neighborhoods that could be controlled and protected with much less difficulty than scattered settlements. Implementation of the land ordinance would create the conditions that would make territorial government possible. If at first westerners would be governed—and would not govern themselves—Congress did not betray its original promises to prospective settlers. The predetermination of private property lines and state boundaries would eliminate the leading sources of conflict on earlier frontiers and guarantee settlers the fruits of peace and prosperity. Westerners were also assured that as soon as their territories qualified for statehood and membership in the union they would be able to reclaim all the rights of self-governing American citizens.

I. The 1784 Ordinance

Congressmen began serious planning for the future government of the West in early 1784 when they could finally look forward to Virginia's cession of its trans-Ohio claims. A committee headed by Virginian Thomas Jefferson and including Samuel Chase of Maryland and David Howell of Rhode Island submitted a report on March 1 which, after successive revisions, was adopted by Congress on April 23.[3]

The 1784 ordinance specified boundaries for sixteen new states, conforming with the requirement of the Virginia land cession that Congress sponsor the creation of new western states not to exceed 150 miles square each.[4] The proposed new states covered the new national domain north of the Ohio (the so-called "ten new states") as well as the transmontane regions of old states that had not yet relinquished their claims. The ordinance provided that "free males of full age" would be authorized by Congress to establish a temporary government for themselves by "adopting the constitution and laws of any one of the original States." When any one of the new states numbered "twenty thousand free inhabitants" it would be empowered to draft its own constitution. The new states were promised admission to the union when their respective populations equalled that of the smallest existing state.

All of these provisions acknowledged the "statehood" of the territories. Given this fundamental premise, it is not surprising that the ordinance had little to say about how Congress would maintain order before settlers began to govern themselves. A motion that "the said settlers shall be ruled by magistrates to be appointed by the United States in Congress assembled, and under such laws and regulations" as Congress should enact was narrowly defeated.[5] Instead, future congresses would simply adopt whatever "measures" might seem "necessary for the preservation of peace and good order." The complete text of the 1784 ordinance follows.

Report of a committee, on a plan for a temporary government
of the Western territory, adopted April 23, 1784

Resolved, That so much of the territory ceded or to be ceded by individual states to the United States, as is already purchased or shall be purchased of the Indian inhabitants, and offered for sale by Congress, shall be divided into distinct states, in the following manner, as nearly as such cessions will admit; that is to say, by parallels of latitude, so that each State shall comprehend from north to south two degrees of latitude, beginning to count from the completion of forty-five degrees north of the equator; and by meridians of longitude, one of which shall pass through the lowest point of the rapids of Ohio, and the other through the western cape of the mouth of the Great Kanhaway: but the territory eastward of this last meridian, between the Ohio, Lake Erie, and Pensylvania, shall be one State whatsoever may be its comprehension of latitude. That which may lie beyond the completion of the 45th degree between the said meridians, shall make part of the State adjoining it on the south: and that part of the Ohio, which is between the same meridians coinciding nearly with that parallel as a boundary line. [See Map 2.]

That the settlers on any territory so purchased, and offered for sale, shall, either on their own petition or on the order of Congress, receive authority from them, with appointments of time and place, for their free males of full age within the limits of their State to meet together, for the purpose of establishing a temporary government, to adopt the constitution and laws of any one of the original States; so that such laws nevertheless shall be subject to alteration by their ordinary legislature; and to erect, subject to a like alteration, counties, townships, or other divisions, for the election of members for their legislature.

That when any such State shall have acquired twenty thousand free inhabitants, on giving due proof thereof to Congress, they shall receive from them authority with appointments of time and place, to call a convention of representatives to establish a permanent constitution and government for themselves. Provided that both the temporary and permanent governments be established on these principles as their basis:

First. That they shall for ever remain a part of this confederacy of the United States of America.

Second. That they shall be subject to the Articles of Confederation in all those cases in which the original states shall be so subject, and to all the acts and ordinances of the United States in Congress assembled, conformable thereto.

Third. That they in no case shall interfere with the primary disposal of the soil by the United states in Congress assembled, nor with the ordinances and regulations which Congress may find necessary, for securing the title in such soil to the bona fide purchasers.

Fourth. That they shall be subject to pay a part of the federal debts contracted or to be contracted, to be apportioned on them by Congress, according to the same common rule and measure by which apportionments thereof shall be made on the other states.

Fifth. That no tax shall be imposed on lands, the property of the United States.

Sixth. That their respective governments shall be republican.

Seventh. That the lands of non-resident proprietors shall, in no case, be taxed higher than those of residents within any new State, before the admission thereof to a vote by its delegates in Congress.

That whensoever any of the said states shall have, of free inhabitants, as many as shall then be in any one the least numerous of the thirteen Original states, such State shall be admitted by its delegates into the Congress of the United States, on an equal footing with the said original states; provided the consent of

MAP 2: A Map of the United States of N. America. From *Bailey's Pocket Almanac, Being an American Annual Register, for the Year of Our Lord 1787* (Philadelphia: Francis Bailey, 1787). The names of the projected new states were taken from a preliminary draft and are not included in the Territorial Government Ordinance adopted on April 23, 1784. (Courtesy of the American Antiquarian Society)

so many states in Congress is first obtained as may at the time be competent to such admission. And in order to adapt the said Articles of Confederation to the state of Congress when its numbers shall be thus increased, it shall be proposed to the legislatures of the states, originally parties thereto, to require the assent of two-thirds of the United States in Congress assembled, in all those cases wherein, by the said articles, the assent of nine states is now required, which being agreed to by them, shall be binding on the new states. Until such admission by their delegates into Congress, any of the said states, after the establishment of their temporary government, shall have authority to keep a member in Congress, with a right of debating but not of voting.

That measures not inconsistent with the principles of the Confederation, and necessary for the preservation of peace and good order among the settlers in any of the said new states, until they shall assume a temporary government as aforesaid, may, from time to time, be taken by the United States in Congress assembled.

That the preceding articles shall be formed into a charter of compact; shall be duly executed by the President of the United States in Congress assembled, under his hand, and the seal of the United States; shall be promulgated; and shall stand as fundamental constitutions between the thirteen original states, and each of the several states now newly described, unalterable from and after the sale of any part of the territory of such State, pursuant to this resolve but by the joint consent of the United States in Congress assembled, and of the particular State within which such alteration is proposed to be made.

Together with the 1785 land ordinance, the territorial government ordinance provided the basic framework for early American territorial policy. Its promises of statehood and eventual membership in the union remained fundamental. In both form and substance the "charter of compact" between old and new states established the principle that the United States would be a union of equal states.

II. First Principles

In April 1786 James Monroe wrote John Jay, Secretary for Foreign Affairs, that Congress was about to decide whether it would establish a territorial government for the Northwest "upon Colonial principles" before the new states to be organized there were "admitted to a vote in Congress with the common rights of the other States." An acknowledged authority on western affairs, Monroe was the leading member of a committee charged with revising Jefferson's 1784 government plan. Under his mentor's scheme, Monroe wrote, settlers would "be left to themselves" before they joined the union.[6] Given their growing skepticism about westerners' character and loyalties, many congressmen now considered such a liberal policy imprudent. Other provisions of the 1784 ordinance were also coming under attack.

Monroe, for one, thought the proposed new states were too small while the population required for their admission to the union was too low.

The ordinance was challenged by critics who preferred "natural" boundaries or who thought the projected new states "very unequal."[7] Pressure for enlarging the new states and for raising the population threshold increased with Congress's difficulties in organizing land sales and settlement in the national domain. Many congressmen feared that small, lightly populated states would not qualify for admission or that, if they did, they would never equal the original members in population and wealth. The revisions eventually proposed by Monroe and his colleagues—and ultimately incorporated in the Northwest Ordinance—were supposed to attract industrious farmers to the Ohio country and guarantee the orderly expansion of settlement. Policy makers became convinced that the large measure of local autonomy permitted by Jefferson's ordinance was incompatible with these goals. As a result, on July 13, 1786, Congress adopted a report submitted by Monroe's committee, calling for establishment of a "colonial" system for the temporary government of its western lands and repealing the 1784 resolutions.[8]

From Jefferson's vantage point in Paris, Congress's choices on the issue of state size and population and temporary territorial government looked like a rejection of his liberal principles in favor of a more restrictive and conservative system. These polarities have also dominated historical writing.[9] On one hand, Congress could allow settlers to manage their own affairs within relatively small "states" that could anticipate early admission into the union. On the other, it could enlarge the new states to the point of jeopardizing their republican character while, by raising the population requirement, protracting the period of "colonial" control indefinitely.

But if congressional decisions on these issues were to be of far-reaching significance to the future of the republic, they were not particularly controversial at the time. Jefferson worried about how westerners would react to changing state size and to the imposition of a more "strong-toned" territorial government. Monroe and his colleagues were more concerned that the process of settlement might never begin unless changes securing law, order, and land titles were instituted. Given Congress's poor start in promoting western settlement there was also good reason to fear that small states would fail to meet the population requirement, and thus be barred from the union indefinitely. Thus, Monroe reasoned, Jefferson's overarching goal of promoting the expansion of the union on the basis of new state equality would be jeopardized unless his proposals for temporary government and small states were discarded.

The formation of frontier settlements and preparation for statehood presented no problems for Jefferson when he propounded the founding principles of the territorial system in 1784. Impressed with the mushrooming growth of Virginia's Kentucky District, he assumed that the region across the Ohio River would also settle rapidly. As he later told the French encyclopedist Jean Nicolas Demeunier:

> We have seen lately a single person (Daniel Boone) go and decide on a settlement at Kentucky, many hundred miles from any white inhabitants, remove thither with his family and a few neighbors, and though perpetually harrassed by the Indians, that settlement in the course of 10. years has acquired 30,000 inhabitants.[10]

When the Kentucky lands filled up, and Congress opened the national domain to settlement, the frontier would push beyond the Ohio. Then, predicted George Washington, the western country "will settle faster than any other ever did."[11]

Because Jefferson, with other contemporary commentators, assumed the continuing growth and spread of population to the west, he concluded that Congress's main task was to connect old and new settlements on equitable terms. The major contribution of his ordinance was to establish the principle of new state equality. Because it was primarily an act "for laying out into distinct States the western Territory ceded to the Union," the ordinance did not deal with the problem of creating and organizing new settlements.[12] Jefferson thought private initiatives, rationalized and directed by the congressional land system, would suffice.

The scope of the 1784 ordinance suggests that Jefferson did not consider the distinction between unsettled and settled areas significant: he expected new frontier regions to fill in rapidly once opened to settlement. He also expected future state land cessions to establish Congress's jurisdiction over rapidly developing areas that would soon qualify for statehood.[13] A North Carolina writer agreed that further cessions were essential. Western "sons of freedom yet value their privileges too high," he warned, to remain subject to the old states and their "invidious policy."[14] The ordinance set forth the terms on which these areas—most notably Kentucky—would join the union. Separatists advocating the division of the old states subsequently read the 1784 ordinance as an invitation to organize their own new states.[15] Though the separatists overlooked the necessity in Jefferson's scheme for prior jurisdictional cessions by the states and for an amendment to the Articles, they did grasp his central concern: "compacts" between old and new states would preclude an exploitative, colonial regime in the West and thus constitute the basis of an enduring union. The existence of those new states—or of settlements that could plausibly aspire to statehood—was taken for granted. Because Jefferson expected western population to grow rapidly, he saw little reason to worry about how the region was governed in the brief time before settlers adopted their own temporary government. Population growth and self-government were reciprocal. Jefferson's fellow Virginian William Grayson was convinced "the right of forming free governments for themselves" would "ensure a settlement of the country in the most rapid manner."[16]

Jefferson failed to anticipate obstacles Congress would face in organizing new settlements across the Ohio. Assuming the inevitability of frontier expansion, he concluded that settlers would bitterly resist being degraded from self-government to colonial dependency. Far from the United States—and from the complications of congressional politics—Jefferson was also inclined to theorize from republican first principles: thus, he told Monroe, westerners "will not only be happier in states of a moderate size, but it is the only way in which they can exist as a regular society"; only a "tractable people"—which frontier settlers assuredly were not—"may be governed in large bodies."[17] But Monroe was convinced that the new states would have to be enlarged, invoking his own experience during his recent "rout[e]s westward" as well as his reading of the current state of national and sectional politics.[18] Following his lead, Congress resolved in July 1786 to form "not more than five nor less than three" new states in the Northwest, "as the situation of that country and future circumstances may require."[19] This formula was subsequently incorporated in the Northwest Ordinance.

The future development of the Northwest would not follow the pattern of the southern frontier. The requirements of the congressional land system, variations in the quality of the land itself (Monroe predicted that the extensive prairies would remain poor and sparsely settled), and the region's strategic vulnerablity made its prospects uncertain. As Congress faltered in its efforts to implement the 1785 land ordinance, the anticipated emigration of American settlers and formation of new settlements was delayed. Far from being an inducement to the kinds of settlers Congress hoped to recruit, the promise of immediate self-government was probably a deterrent. The only legitimate settlers in the national territory, the Illinois French, showed little enthusiasm for local autonomy. Instead, they pressed Congress to confirm their land titles and establish effective territorial government, complaining about being left "in a state of nature, with[ou]t law government or protection" ever since the Virginia cession.[20]

Jefferson may have overestimated the capacity of frontier settlers to manage their own affairs, but he also expected too much from the new land system. The land and government ordinances were paired in Jefferson's thinking. In 1784 he and Hugh Williamson of North Carolina had been the chief authors of a proposed land ordinance designed as companion legislation to the government ordinance.[21] Though Congress rejected Jefferson's and Williamson's proposals, their idea of organizing the western lands under a grid was incorporated in the ordinance finally adopted in May 1785.[22] The land system was supposed to produce revenue while rationalizing settlement patterns and providing the basis for social order in the national domain. The government ordinance therefore could focus on the rights of these frontier communities in relation to the union and to each other. The delineation of state boundaries would maintain order among the new states just as the definition of property rights in the land ordinance would secure orderly settlement.

The goals of fixing state boundaries and private property lines were intimately related, as geographer William Pattison has demonstrated in his fine study of the origins of the rectangular survey system.[23] State lines would constitute a kind of supergrid: surveys within each new state were supposed to begin at its southeast corner, so providing periodic correction for accumulated deviations from meridian lines (which tended to converge as they ran north). Because each new state had its own grid, the common rights of local property holders would reinforce political divisions. The government ordinance was designed to remove any uncertainty about an area's future jurisdictional status: as congressman David Howell reported, "settlers will always readily know in which of the states they are." The jurisdictional confusion that characterized earlier frontier settlements, jeopardizing national security and the survival of the union, would be avoided.[24] The land ordinance would provide the same certainty and security for purchasers of federal lands. "Emigrants from all parts of the world" would be attracted to the Northwest, William Grayson predicted, because the ordinance guaranteed an "exemption from controversy on account of bounds to the latest ages."[25]

The land and government ordinances thus were intended to be complementary. Early in 1785 Howell, one of the authors of the government ordinance, said he expected Congress would soon be able "to open their Land-office, and to establish some government in the Western wilderness."[26] After passage of the land ordinance in May the two ordinances were transmitted to the states and were subsequently printed together in newspapers throughout the country. This was the first publication of the government ordinance in its adopted form.[27] The link between the land system and provisions for territorial government remained crucial for policy makers after 1785. But the fit between the two ordinances became increasingly problematic. The "invisible hand" in the land market became more and more visible as Congress moved to protect its property from squatters and speculators and to locate legitimate buyers. The surveys required by the land ordinance promised to multiply Congress's costs. Delays in bringing federal lands to market and sluggish sales soon showed that the national domain would not be the hoped-for panacea for an empty treasury. Complaints about the high price of federal land and continuing threats of Indian war discouraged prospective settlers; straggling settlements, lacking numbers sufficient for self-defense or self-government, looked to the national government for protection.

It was clear by 1787 that Congress would not be able to sell its lands unless it could provide "criminal and civil justice," thus securing "Peace and property among the rude people who will probably be the first settlers there."[28] In effect, the relationship that Jefferson had posited between the land system and territorial government was reversed: territorial government facilitated the sales that in Jefferson's scheme would have made government unnecessary. Confronted with new, largely unanticipated complications, policy makers began to come to grips with the contradiction between a "liberal" system of territorial self-government and their plans for orderly expansion and economic development. But changes in western policy should not be seen as a rejection of Jefferson's vision of an expanding union. In May 1786 Monroe assured Jefferson that "the most important principles" of his plan were "preserv'd" in the new "colonial" system for the West.[29] The two leading objects of the Northwest Ordinance, Jefferson was later told, were "establishing a Temporary Government" in the West "and providing for its more easy passage into permanent State Governments."[30]

III. From States to Settlements

Between 1784 and 1787, the ideas of "state" and "settlement" became distinct in American western policy. The two ideas were closely linked in Jefferson's original conception of the territorial system: Kentucky and other existing settlements could anticipate admission to the union at an early date; new settlements, formed according to the pattern set by the land ordinance and within state lines specified by the government ordinance, would soon join them. Thirteen new states would soon be "added to the American Constellation," a New Yorker predicted in February 1785.[31] Shortly thereafter a Richmond writer could refer to Spanish threats against "settlers in the new States," as if those states already existed.[32] In a sense, the attainment of "statehood" was understood to be simultaneous with the process of settlement itself.

But there were problems with imputing social order, political competence, and distinct "state" interests to new frontier settlements. As we have seen, the expansion of settlement in a manner compatible with revenue needs and national security was itself problematic. John Jay had ample reason to "fear" that the "Western Country will one Day give us Trouble—to govern them will not be easy, and whether after two or three generations they will be fit to govern themselves is a Question that merits Consideration."[33] As Congress assumed the responsibility of preparing its land for sale and maintaining law and order thereafter, these concerns became more pronounced and the role of the new "states" correspondingly less apparent. Congress's decision to employ base lines for its surveys independent of the new state boundaries reflected this development.[34] The split between settlement and statehood was completed in the Northwest Ordinance: all the "states" would be governed as one (or two) territories prior to the final stages of state making.

The major contribution of the Northwest Ordinance was to reject the notion of territorial "statehood" that was central to the 1784 ordinance. The state boundaries described in the new ordinance were prospective and (to some, unclear extent) variable: they did not govern the settlement process. In the later history of the Northwest the old idea that the new "states" existed from the founding of the territory was occasionally revived in response to proposed boundary changes. Otherwise, statehood was simply a more or less distant promise: it had no relevance for the organization and government of the first settlements.

The emerging distinction between settlement and state also helped resolve a variety of related misgivings about continental expansion. The question, as James Madison put it to Lafayette, was whether or not "the settlements which are beginning to take place on the branches of the Mississippi, [would] be so many distinct Societies, or only an expansion of the same Society?"[35] As long as it was equated with the addition of new states, expansion seemed fraught with danger. An overextended union might give rise to despotic government, or disintegrate into anarchy and confusion—or both. In any case, the Abbé Raynal warned his American friends, "The tranquillity of empire decreases as it is extended."[36] The same logic applied to the separate states. These "republics" should "never desire an extended dominion," a Philadelphia writer explained, because "it has always proved inconsistent with the preservation of their liberties."[37] Yet it was also true that states could be too small. Another Philadelphian denounced the "baneful influence" of agitation for small, new states.[38] The process of state division tended toward complete atomization and the end of all government. The common ground for both writers was that states—small or large, for better or worse—were conceived of as distinct political societies.

Beginning with the premise that frontier settlements were "states," at some early stage of development, it was logical for Jefferson to worry about their relative size. The same principles that controlled political development elsewhere would operate in the new western states; due regard for these principles was imperative during the period of state founding. If the new states "can be retained til their governments become settled and wise," he told Madison, "they will remain with us always."39

Jefferson's insistence on equitable "compacts" between the original states and the western states as a necessary condition for continuing union also reflected his assumption that new settlements were "states" from the outset. Other commentators, arguing from the same premises, were less optimistic. Living at such a "distance" from the Atlantic states, Monroe concluded, westerners "will necessarily be but little interested in whatever respects us."40 In Rufus King's opinion, "no paper engagements . . . can be formed" which would guarantee union "between the Atlantic States, and those which will be erected to the Northwestward."41 King's pessimism reflected a new awareness of divergent sectional interests. But the way he framed the problem showed that he continued to accept Jeffersonian assumptions about frontier statehood. These assumptions made it difficult to imagine an expanding union.

Madison grappled repeatedly with the dilemmas presented by expansion. In August 1784, in a letter to Jefferson discussing the Mississippi crisis, he wrote of "the danger to the Confederacy" that would result from "multiplying the parts of the Machine."42 Assuming that each new state would represent a distinct new interest, it was difficult not to conclude that the union inevitably would collapse. These progressive complications, he wrote Lafayette a few months later, should teach the Spanish not to fear the growth of new western settlements that free navigation of the Mississippi would encourage. He explained:

> As [settlements] become extended the members of the Confederacy must be multiplied, and along with them the Wills which are to direct the machine. And as the wills multiply, so will the chances against a dangerous union of them. We experience every day the difficulty of drawing thirteen States into the same plans. Let the number be doubled & so will the difficulty.43

Whatever comfort the Spanish might derive from these possibilities, they also suggested strongly that expansion and new state creation were *not* in the new nation's best interests. Given the legendary imbecility of the existing union, Congress might well follow "Lycurgus"'s satirical advice and close off the frontiers altogether: the union was "already much too large" and the western lands "certainly ought never to be settled."44 Otherwise, a British writer predicted, the addition of "ten infant states" and Vermont would surely overtax the feeble machinery of national government: "What degree of unanimity may be expected among such a number of states, may be easily imagined."[45]

But these conceptual difficulties could be cleared away if the collective interests of westerners were distinguished from the separate, disaggregated interests of a large number of new western states. During the mid-1780s, sectional political conflict led many Americans to devalue state interests. Interest, they argued, was not always neatly defined by state boundaries but could be regional—and even continental—in scope. This was clearly true in the West where the phantom new "states" lacked governments, land offices, or any other plausible focus of interest. Transmontane settlers understood their common interests, displaying a highly developed sectional consciousness during the Mississippi crisis. According to one report, the threat of a treaty blocking the Mississippi produced "political phrenzy" across the frontiers. "The general voice of the western community . . . is, EQUAL LIBERTY with the thirteen states, or a *breach of peace*, and a *new alliance!*"[46]

Sectional politics reinforced some of the lessons congressmen had been learning in the process of implementing and revising territorial policy. By necessity, Congress directed more and more attention to selling its lands, recruiting settlers, and organizing new settlements. This reorientation had far-reaching implications. First, the focus on the settlement frontier displaced the earlier concern with the status and interests of new western "states." The maintenance of law and order at the local level, which potential settlers demanded, depended on the effective exercise of national authority: "states" did not figure in the equation, at least until some future date. The problem of territorial government thus was transposed from the level of the "state" to that of the local community. The attainment of statehood—that is, self-government and membership in the union—would mark the culmination of a protracted process of building frontier communities from the ground up. Republicanism would flourish in the West not because the new states were either smaller or larger, but because their foundations—communities of orderly, industrious settlers—were well laid. Without such preliminary regulation, George Washington wrote, the country would "be involved in much trouble and perplexity, before any New State will be well organized, or can contribute any thing to the support of the union."[47]

In seeking to attract settlers, Congress had to respond to the individual and associated interests of prospective purchasers, further undercutting the assumption that the new states, as such, had distinctive interests of their own. As settlers' interests were cut loose from the assumption of parochial, mutually exclusive state loyalties, they could be seen as providing potential connections between frontier settlements and the wider world. The expanding scope of interest thus offered a solution to the conundrum of union: its survival would not have to depend on "paper engagements"—or on the exercise of despotic power—*if* the interests of easterners and westerners were developed reciprocally. This was the implicit message of the Mississippi furor. It was the explicit premise of promoters of internal improvements like Washington who argued that "strong commercial bands" alone could prevent the loss of the West.[48]

IV. The Northwest Ordinance

In September 1786 a new congressional committee, consisting of Nathan Dane of Massachusetts, William Samuel Johnson of Connecticut, Charles Pinckney of South Carolina, Melancton Smith of New York, and William Henry of Maryland, reported an elaborate system for the temporary government of the West. In April and May 1787 the proposed ordinance received two favorable readings but failed to gain final approval as Congress lost its quorum. After a brief recess, Congress appointed Virginians Edward Carrington and Richard Henry Lee and South Carolinian John Kean to join Dane and Smith on yet another territorial government committee. Building on earlier proposals—and probably incorporating suggestions made by Manasseh Cutler, agent for the Ohio Company—this committee quickly produced a new draft. Congress responded with equal (and uncharacteristic) dispatch: after three readings on successive days the Northwest Ordinance was adopted on July 13, 1787. Every state delegation in attendance endorsed the Ordinance; only Abraham Yates, Jr., of New York (who, Dane wrote, "appeared in this case, as in most others, not to understand the subject at all") voted against it.[49]

Whatever credit Cutler and the Ohio Company deserve for the specific provisions—and even the passage—of the 1787 ordinance for territorial government, it clearly was intended to attract "robust and industrious" settlers from New England.[50] Many of these settlers were only willing to venture westward under the company's aegis and with the promises of law and order written into the Ordinance: the inducements to emigrate under the existing land and government ordinances were inadequate. The real issue—for settlers and policy makers alike—was land. The enjoyment and productive use of the land depended on clear title, protection from "savage" neighbors—Indian or white—and access to markets. These conditions required the effective exercise of congressional power during the territorial period. Local autonomy and frontier democracy were not vital issues to potential settlers—at least to those Congress hoped to recruit. The settlers' concern with political rights was prospective: once their new communities were successfully founded, could they look forward to joining the union on an equal footing? In the meantime, provisions for "colonial" government were not only an administrative necessity: they were a necessary inducement to potential settlers.

By clearly distinguishing the first frontier settlements from the states they would eventually become, the Northwest Ordinance reflected a new way of thinking about territorial expansion. Settlement and economic development would come first, enabling Americans to exploit the vast new opportunities opening to their west while promoting the wealth and power of the entire nation. The success of their enterprises—measured by crossing a population threshold now set at sixty thousand—would conjure new states into existence. Then westerners would enjoy the full benefits of American citizenship.

The text of the Ordinance reflects its gradual and uneven development through successive committee drafts—and its hurried completion. The opening section on inheritance elaborates on the September 1786 committee report; the provisions for temporary government are traceable (with significant modifications) from the Monroe committee report of July 1786; and the "compact articles" represent revisions of principles set forth in the 1784 ordinance, notably concerning new state boundaries and qualifications for statehood.

The protracted, incremental composition of the Ordinance has made the question of its authorship perennially controversial. Its haphazard organization has also disguised the document's underlying coherence. But for all its shapelessness, the Northwest Ordinance embodies a unified vision of economic development in an expanding union of states, the culmination of a brief, intensive period of debate and deliberation about the future of the American West. Congressmen reconciled—at least for the time being—the apparently contradictory goals of their western land and government policies. In order to raise revenue from land sales and foster economic development, Congress instituted a system of "colonial" government in the first, scattered settlements. As their numbers grew, settlers would gain a measure of self-determination: the second stage of territorial government, including a popularly elected general assembly, would be initiated when there were "five thousand free male inhabitants of full age" in the territory. Finally, when there were "sixty thousand free Inhabitants" in any one of the planned states, the pioneer settlers of the Northwest could draft their own republican constitution and claim a place for themselves in the American union.[51] The complete text of the Ordinance follows.

An Ordinance for the government of the territory of the
United States North West of the river Ohio.

Be it ordained by the United States in Congress Assembled that the said territory for the purposes of temporary government be one district, subject however to be divided into two districts as future circumstances may in the Opinion of Congress make it expedient.

Be it ordained by the authority aforesaid, that the estates both of resident and non resident proprietors in the said territory dying intestate shall descend to and be distributed among their children and the descendants of a deceased child in equal parts; the descendants of a deceased child or grand child to take the share of their deceased parent in equal parts among them; and where there shall be no children or descendants then in equal parts to the next of kin in equal degree and among collaterals the children of a deceased brother or sister of the intestate shall have in equal parts among them their deceased parent's share and there shall in no case be a distinction between kindred of the whole and half blood; saving in all cases to the widow of the intestate her third part of the real estate for life, and one third part of the personal estate; and this law relative to descents and dower shall remain in full force until altered by the legislature of the district. And until the governor and judges shall adopt laws as hereinafter mentioned estates in the said territory may be devised or bequeathed by wills in writing signed and sealed by him or her in whom the estate may be, being of full age, and attested by three witnesses, and real estates may be conveyed by lease and release or bargain and sale signed, sealed and delivered by the person being of full age in whom the estate may be and attested by two witnesses provided such wills be duly proved and such conveyances be acknowledged or the execution thereof duly proved and be recorded within one year after proper magistrates, courts and registers shall be appointed for that purpose and personal property may be transferred by delivery saving however to the french and canadian inhabitants and other settlers of the Kaskaskies, Saint Vincents and the neighbouring villages who have heretofore professed themselves citizens of Virginia, their laws and customs now in force among them relative to the descent and conveyance of property.

Be it ordained by the authority aforesaid that there shall be appointed from time to time by Congress a governor, whose commission shall continue in force for the term of three years, unless sooner revoked by Congress; he shall reside in the district and have a freehold estate therein, in one thousand acres of land while in the exercise of his office. There shall be appointed from time to time by Congress a secretary, whose commission shall continue in force for four years, unless sooner revoked; he shall reside in the district and have a freehold estate therein in five hundred acres of land while in the exercise of his office; It shall be his duty to keep and preserve the acts and laws passed by the legislature and the public records of the district and the proceedings of the governor in his executive department and transmit authentic copies of such acts and proceedings every six months to the Secretary of Congress. There shall also be appointed a court to consist of three judges any two of whom to form a court, who shall have a common law jurisdiction and reside in the district and have each therein a freehold estate in five hundred acres of land while in the exercise of their offices, and their commissions shall continue in force during good behaviour.

The governor, and judges or a majority of them shall adopt and publish in the district such laws of the original states criminal and civil as may be necessary and best suited to the circumstances of the district and report them to Congress from time to time, which laws shall be in force in the district until the organization of the general assembly therein, unless disapproved of by Congress; but afterwards the legislature shall have authority to alter them as they shall think fit.

The governor for the time being shall be Commander in chief of the militia, appoint and commission all officers in the same below the rank of general Officers; All general Officers shall be appointed and commissioned by Congress.

Previous to the Organization of the general Assembly the governor shall appoint such magistrates and other civil officers in each county or township, as he shall find necessary for the preservation of the peace and good order in the same. After the general Assembly shall be organized, the powers and duties of magistrates and other civil officers shall be regulated and defined by the said Assembly; but all magistrates and other civil officers, not herein otherwise directed shall during the continuance of this temporary government be appointed by the governor.

For the prevention of crimes and injuries the laws to be adopted or made shall have force in all parts of the district and for the execution of process criminal and civil, the governor shall make proper divisions thereof, and he shall proceed from time to time as circumstances may require to lay out the parts of the district in which the indian titles shall have been extinguished into counties and townships subject however to such alterations as may thereafter be made by the legislature.

So soon as there shall be five thousand free male inhabitants of full age in the district upon giving proof thereof to the governor, they shall receive authority with time and place to elect representatives from their counties or townships to represent them in the general assembly, provided that for every five hundred free male inhabitants there shall be one representative and so on progressively with the number of free male inhabitants shall the right of representation encrease until the number of representatives shall amount to twenty five after which the number and proportion of representatives shall be regulated by the legislature; provided that no person be eligible or qualified to act as a representative unless he shall have been a citizen of one of the United States three years and be a resident in the district or unless he shall have resided in the district three years and in either case shall likewise hold in his own right in fee simple two hundred acres of land within the same; provided also that a freehold in fifty acres of land in the district having been a citizen of one of the states and being resident in the district; or the like freehold and two years residence in the district shall be necessary to qualify a man as an elector of a representative.

The representative thus elected shall serve for the term of two years and in the case of the death of a representative or removal from office, the governor shall issue a writ to the county or township for which he was a member, to elect another in his stead to serve for the residue of the term.

The general assembly or legislature shall consist of the governor, legislative council and a house of representatives. The legislative council shall consist of five members to continue in Office five years unless sooner removed by Congress any three of whom to be a quorum and the members of the council shall be nominated and appointed in the following manner, to wit; As soon as representatives shall be elected, the governor shall appoint a time and place for them to meet together, and when met they shall nominate ten persons residents in the district and each possessed of a freehold in five hundred acres of Land and return their names to Congress; five of whom Congress shall apppoint and commission to serve as aforesaid; and whenever a vacancy shall happen in the council by death or removal from office, the house of representatives shall nominate two persons qualified as aforesaid, for each vacancy, and return their names to Congress, one of whom Congress shall appoint and commission for the residue of the term, and every five years, four months at least before the expiration of the time of service of the Members of the Council, the said house shall nominate ten persons qualified as aforesaid, and return their names to Congress, five of whom Congress shall appoint and commission to serve as Members of the council five years, unless sooner removed. And the governor, legislative council, and house of representatives, shall have authority to make laws in all cases for the good government of the district, not repugnant to the principles and Articles in this Ordinance established and declared. And all bills having passed by a majority in the house, and by a majority in the council, shall be referred to the Governor for his assent; but no bill or legislative Act whatever, shall be of any force without his assent. The Governor shall have power to convene, prorogue and dissolve the General Assembly, when in his opinion it shall be expedient.

The Governor, Judges, legislative Council, Secretary, and such other Officers as Congress shall appoint in the district shall take an Oath or Affirmation of fidelity, and of Office,; the Governor before the president of Congress, and all other Officers before the Governor. As soon as a legislature shall be formed in the district, the Council and house assembled in one room, shall have authority by joint ballot to elect a Delegate to Congress, who shall have a seat in Congress, with a right of debating, but not of voting, during this temporary Government.

And for extending the fundamental principles of civil and religious liberty, which form the basis whereon these republics, their laws and constitutions are erected; to fix and establish those principles as the basis of all laws, constitutions and governments, which forever hereafter shall be formed in the said territory; to provide also for the establishment of States and permanent government therein, and for their admission to a share in the federal Councils on an equal footing with the original States, at as early periods as may be consistent with the general interest,

It is hereby Ordained and declared by the authority aforesaid, That the following Articles shall be considered as Articles of compact between the Original States and the people and States in the said territory, and forever remain unalterable, unless by common consent, *to wit,*

Article the First. No person, demeaning himself in a peaceable and orderly manner shall ever be molested on account of his mode of worship or religious sentiments in the said territory.

Article the Second. The inhabitants of the said territory shall always be entitled to the benefits of the writ of habeas corpus, and of the trial by Jury; of a proportionate representation of the people in the legislature, and of judicial proceedings according to the course of the common law; all persons shall be bailable unless for capital offences, where the proof shall be evident, or the presumption great; all fines shall be moderate, and no cruel or unusual punishments shall be inflicted; no man shall be deprived of his liberty or property but by the judgment of his peers, or the law of the land; and should the public exigencies make it necessary for the common preservation to take any persons property, or to demand his particular services, full compensation shall be made for the same; and in the just preservation of rights and property it is understood and declared; that no law ought ever to be made, or have force in the said territory, that shall in any manner whatever interfere with, or affect private contracts or engagements, bona fide and without fraud previously formed.

Article the Third. Religion, Morality and knowledge being necessary to good government and the happiness of mankind, Schools and the means of education shall forever be encouraged. The utmost good faith shall always be observed towards the Indians, their lands and property shall never be taken from them without their consent; and in their property, rights and liberty, they never shall be invaded or disturbed, unless in just and lawful wars authorised by Congress; but laws founded in justice and humanity shall from time to time be made, for preventing wrongs being done to them, and for preserving peace and friendship with them.

Article the Fourth. The said territory, and the States which may be formed therein shall forever remain a part of this Confederacy of the United States of America, subject to the Articles of Confederation, and to such alterations therein as shall be constitutionally made; and to all the Acts and Ordinances of the United States in Congress Assembled, conformable thereto. The Inhabitants and Settlers in the said territory, shall be subject to pay a part of the federal debts contracted or to be contracted, and a proportional part of the expences of Government, to be apportioned on them by Congress, according to the same common rule and measure by which apportionments thereof shall be made on the other States; and the taxes for paying their proportion, shall be laid and levied by the authority and direction of the legislatures of the district or districts or new States, as in the original States, within the time agreed upon by the United States in Congress Assembled. The Legislatures of those districts, or new States, shall never interfere with the primary disposal of the Soil by the United States in Congress Assembled, nor with any regulations Congress may find necessary for securing the title in such soil to the bona fide purchasers. No tax shall be imposed on lands the property of the United States; and in no case shall non resident proprietors be taxed higher than residents. The navigable Waters leading into the Mississippi and St. Lawrence, and the carrying places between the same shall be common highways, and forever free, as well to the Inhabitants of the said territory, as to the Citizens of the United States, and those of any other States that may be admitted into the Confederacy, without any tax, impost or duty therefor.

Article the Fifth. There shall be formed in the said territory, not less than three nor more than five States, and the boundaries of the States, as soon as Virginia shall alter her act of cession and consent to the same, shall become fixed and established as follows, to wit: The Western State in the said territory, shall be bounded by the Mississippi, the Ohio and Wabash rivers; a direct line drawn from the Wabash and post Vincents due North to the territorial line between the United States and Canada, and by the said territorial line to the lake of the Woods and Mississippi. The middle State shall be bounded by the said direct line, the Wabash from post Vincents to the Ohio; by the Ohio, by direct line drawn due North from the mouth of the great Miami to the said territorial line, and by the said territorial line. The eastern State shall be bounded by the last mentioned direct line, the Ohio, Pensylvania, and the said territorial line; provided however, and it is further understood and declared, that the boundaries of these three States, shall be subject so far to be altered, that if Congress shall hereafter find it expedient, they shall have authority to form one or two States in that part of the said territory which lies north of an east and west line drawn through the southerly bend or extreme of lake Michigan [see Map 3]; and whenever any of the said States shall have sixty thousand free Inhabitants therein, such State shall be admitted by its Delegates into the Congress of the United States, on an equal footing with the original States, in all respects whatever; and shall be at liberty to form a permanent constitution and State government, provided the constitution and government so to be formed, shall be republican, and in conformity to the principles contained in these Articles; and so far as it can be consistent with the general interest of the Confederacy, such admission shall be allowed at an earlier period, and when there may be a less number of free Inhabitants in the State than sixty thousand.

Article the Sixth. There shall be neither Slavery nor involuntary Servitude in the said territory otherwise than in the punishment of crimes, whereof the party shall have been duly convicted; provided always that any person escaping into the same, from whom labor or service is lawfully claimed in any one of the original States, such fugitive may be lawfully reclaimed and conveyed to the person claiming his or her labor or service as aforesaid.

V. An Expanding Union

The emphasis on economic development in American thinking about the West made it possible to see territorial expansion as a unifying project. Manasseh Cutler and other publicists claimed that all interests converged in the new settlements: "The advantages of almost every climate are here blended together; every considerable commodity, that is cultivated in any part of the United States, is here produced in the greatest plenty and perfection."[52] These great natural endowments, rightly used, would guarantee the nation's greatness. A New York writer thus chided his countrymen: "all nations but the Americans know the value and abilities of America; we

MAP 3: A Map of the United States compiled chiefly from The State Maps and Other Authentic Information (Detail). By Samuel Lewis (n.p., 1795). Note that projected new state boundaries are not shown on maps of this period. (Courtesy of the American Antiquarian Society)

have those resources within ourselves which no other nation can boast." But, he complained,

> we totter about like infants, afraid to venture beyond the length of our leading-strings. . . . Youth is the time for exertion and enterprise, in the political as well as the natural constitution. The seeds must be sown in infancy, and they will be rooted in age.[53]

Significantly, this writer thought the new nation's "constitution" would be written in the works of enterprising Americans. So too, in pursuit of their own interests, western settlers would advance the interest of all. Prosperity and abundance would be the true cement of union.

In late 1791 Madison returned to the problem of union in an essay on "Consolidation" written for the *National Gazette*. By extricating "states" from distinct, mutually exclusive "interests," he was now able to argue for a stronger union—*and* for states' rights. "If a consolidation of the states into one government be an event so justly to be avoided, it is not less to be desired . . . that a consolidation should prevail in their interests and affections." The states would be bastions of liberty in the continuing struggle against incipient despotism. Yet the states could not survive if guided by "local prejudices and mistaken rivalships." Therefore it was the patriotic duty of all Americans "to consolidate the affairs of the states into one harmonious interest."[54]

Madison's argument may seem disingenuous, or at least paradoxical. But such logic suggested a solution to the problem of the extended republic. Indeed, expansion across space might serve to control and perhaps one day eliminate the factional discord that republicans found so vexing. Inspired by prospects for boundless national wealth and happiness in an expanding union of interests, Americans could also be confident that republican liberty would be well secured in an expanding union of states.

4.

From Territory to State

☆ ☆ ☆ ☆

The hopes of the 1780s were not soon or easily fulfilled. The Ohio Indians remained a formidable presence and the British continued to occupy posts in the Northwest well into the next decade. As a result, potential settlers turned to safer, more attractive destinations to the southwest, and the territory's population lagged. But national policy makers were not devastated by the failure to attract many purchasers to the federal lands. With the union apparently secured under the new federal Constitution, the development of the national domain seemed considerably less crucial than it had in the founding period. Import duties provided a lucrative substitute for revenue from land sales.

During these years of gradual, intermittent growth, the Northwest Ordinance provided the framework for territorial administration under Governor Arthur St. Clair. Only when settlement accelerated in the late 1790s did the pioneer settlers of the region demonstrate much concern about their political future; only then would settlers begin to read the Ordinance closely, particularly its compact articles, in order to determine the extent of their rights. But with the territory's population spurting past forty thousand in 1800, agitation for statehood finally gained momentum. Focusing on the interpretation of the Northwest Ordinance, the resulting controversy illuminated the often contradictory character of the principles on which the American territorial system was founded.

In the Northwest Ordinance the Continental Congress pledged that the territory would be formed into new states and admitted into the union on equal terms with the original states. Compact article V provided that when any of the three to five contemplated states "shall have sixty thousand free inhabitants therein" it could claim admission to the union "on an equal footing with the original States, in all respects whatever." Article IV made it clear, however, that this "equality" would be narrowly defined. In order to protect federal property interests, "primary disposal" of the public lands was secured to Congress and territorial and new state legislatures were barred from taxing "the property of the United States" until it passed into private hands.[1]

The potential conflict between local and national interests and contradiction between the embryonic new state's rights and congressional authority became fully apparent in the Ohio statehood movement. Statehood advocates and their adversaries approached these questions from many angles. Responding to changing political circumstances, territorial Republicans who promoted the change and Federalists who opposed it developed different conceptions of statehood and state equality as well as distinct interpretations of the Northwest Ordinance.[2]

Republicans in the vanguard of new state agitation defined statehood as self-government, contrasting that eagerly anticipated boon with their degraded, dependent condition under the rule of Federalist appointees. Republicans appealed to the Ordinance when they sought to block moves by Governor St. Clair to sustain his unpopular regime. In effect, they invoked the Ordinance's compact articles against the provisions for temporary government under which St. Clair acted. Identifying St. Clair as the chief obstacle to the attainment of equal rights and self-government, statehood proponents cultivated support of the new Republican majority in Congress and welcomed its initiative in organizing a state government: they assumed that Congress would act disinterestedly to implement the Ordinance compacts.

The statehood movement reached its climax in 1802 when national Republicans, eager to consolidate their party's power, pushed an enabling act through Congress calling for a state constitutional convention and prescribing terms for the new state's admission.[3] Federalists launched a vigorous counterattack, blasting local Republicans for their willingness to accept the allegedly unequal conditions set forth in the enabling act. One particularly controversial condition prohibited the new state from taxing federal lands for five years after their sale. (The measure was designed to protect federal revenue interests during the period purchasers on credit completed their payments.) According to Federalist critics, such "invidious" conditions showed that the leading danger to Ohio's rights came from the Republican-dominated national government, not from St. Clair's territorial administration. Though the Federalists did not directly challenge federal property rights, they insisted that Congress could impose no conditions on the new state not already found in the Ordinance. Either the enabling act was redundant, or it was a gross violation of Ohio's rights.

Federalists argued that their opponents were wrong to assume that Congress would act disinterestedly: Congress had an obvious, material interest in altering the Ordinance compacts at the new state's expense. They accused the Republicans of overreacting to the putative excesses of territorial officials—at worst a temporary nuisance—and overlooking the real threats to the new state's rights and interests. Federalists further suggested that Congress encroached on the embryonic state's rights by calling the constitutional convention, thus interfering with this fundamental act of self-government. No such role was specified for Congress, they charged: according to Article V, the free people of the new state "shall be at liberty to form a permanent constitution and State government."

At different times, both Republicans and Federalists presented themselves as strict constructionist defenders of the Ordinance. Within their distinct conceptual frameworks—and political circumstances—both groups confronted the larger, finally unresolvable question in early territorial history: what were the constitutional limits of national authority in the territories? In their efforts to redeem the new states from colonial degradation, Republicans focused on the arbitrary power of territorial officials. Federalists, fighting a desperate rearguard action against the Republican juggernaut, shifted attention to the creation and admission of new states. In doing so, they did not hesitate to expose and exploit the conflicting interests and contradictory principles on which the territorial system itself was founded.

I. Subjects or Citizens

On his arrival in Marietta in 1788, St. Clair told the settlers that the "system" of government "formed for this country . . . is temporary only, suited to your infant situation, and to continue no longer than that state of infancy shall last."[4] St. Clair and his opponents agreed that the Ordinance guaranteed the political future of the territory. Functioning as a kind of territorial "constitution," the Ordinance bridged the gap between dependent colony and independent state: attainment of statehood justified the territory's temporary colonial condition. The provisions for temporary government authorized the (equally temporary) degradation of citizen to stateless subject, but the compact articles guaranteed that the process would reverse itself as the territory crossed successive population thresholds.

Agreement on the eventual outcome of territorial development did not preclude disagreement on basic premises. St. Clair and his supporters insisted that settlers in the Territory were "subjects" of the national government, not true American citizens; his opponents replied that settlers remained citizens, even while agreeing not to exercise their political rights for a limited time. For St. Clair, citizenship only made sense in the context of the gradual development of political community in the Territory. He was convinced the first settlers were politically incompetent, regardless of any "rights" they presumed to claim. In characteristically blunt fashion, St. Clair concluded that "a multitude of indigent and ignorant people are but ill qualified to form a constitution and government for themselves."5 In 1797 Winthrop Sargent, acting governor in St. Clair's absence, thus urged that statehood "be kept distant" until the "first Settlers, or frontier people" were displaced by their more respectable and substantial successors.6

St. Clair linked the condition of individual settlers to that of the larger community. Thus he spoke of the settlers' "infant situation" in 1788, suggesting that they would grow to political maturity under his paternal authority. The analogy of childhood came easily to subsequent opponents of statehood. A writer in the *Ohio Gazette* (published in Marietta) asked,

> Is a young man in a degrading situation under his father or his guardian before he becomes 21 years old? are not we in a comparative situation with him? at a certain age he is admitted to choose his guardian, so we in a middle stage are qualified to choose members of assembly, to make laws for our protection and government, without whose consent no laws can be made.7

Such opponents of statehood urged that the territory remain in a position of dependency until sufficiently mature to assume the responsibilities of political adulthood.

Early in 1801, an antistatehood meeting at Marietta explained why further growth and development were so important. The territory was still a "mixed mass of people, scattered over an immense wilderness, with scarcely a connecting principle." Deficient in population, wealth, and education, the territory was hardly prepared to function as an independent political community. Statehood required a sufficient density and contiguity of settlement, the surplus wealth to support good government, and an educated electorate. The people of the territory and their representatives would have to cope with "abtruse questions of Government and policy"; they would also have to achieve an adequate awareness of the needs and interests of the entire community. The growth and spread of population made possible the "connections" that in turn promoted political development.8

A territory not yet ready for statehood was still a "colony." To St. Clair it was clear that the defective political condition of the territory determined the narrow extent of an individual settler's rights. "The Territories are not States," he wrote Secretary of the Treasury Oliver Wolcott in 1795, "or the inhabitants would be entitled to the same privileges, and participate in all the advantages equally with the other States." The Northwest Territory was a "dependent colony" without representation in the federal Congress or even, at this point, in a local legislature. Therefore, it followed that settlers in the territory "ceased to be citizens of the United States and became their subjects."9 St. Clair's "subjects" bridled at this terminology: while willing to grant that their embryonic "states" temporarily resembled colonies, they denied that as individuals they were merely "colonists," subject to the arbitrary authority of the St. Clair regime. By denominating Northwestern-ers "subjects" or "in a diminutive way . . . Settlers," St. Clair denied their citizenship and appeared determined to perpetuate their degraded, "colonial" condition.10

Statehood agitation in the area that was to become Ohio was closely connected with opposition to Governor St. Clair's territorial government. St. Clair, "with British & princely ideas," was seen as a throwback to the old colonial governors.11 The territory was described as a "colony" with a "government, which no man with the blood of an American in his bosom can contemplate with pleasure."12 During the first phase of territorial government under the Ordinance, the governor and three judges exercised complete authority. Only when the number of free adult males reached five thousand would a general assembly be convened, and even then the federal appointees retained preponderant power. As Thomas Worthington, the leader of Ohio's campaign for statehood, wrote in 1801, the "present arbitrary government [was] better suited for an English or Spanish colony than for citizens of the United States."13

Several criticisms merged in the attacks on the St. Clair regime. Statehood proponents emphasized the "degradation" of settlers from the status of "citizens" in their states of origin to "subjects" under St. Clair's "monarchic system."14 They also chafed at the governor's extensive prerogatives, most notably his unqualified veto power over the territorial legislature, which itself was a belated and halting step toward local self-determination (its first meeting was in 1799). The "subject" settlers confronted the "encroaching usurper" without any constitutional check, or "controling power."15 The degraded and oppressed condition of the individual thus recapitulated that of the territory at large under St. Clair's "colonial, oppressive and unequal government." Judge William Goforth of Columbia (Hamilton County) epitomized the territory's situation in a letter to President Thomas Jefferson in

January 1802: its polity was a "true transcript of our old English Colonial Governments, our Governor is cloathed with all the power of a British Nabob."[16]

What does all this overheated rhetoric signify? The old Federalist St. Clair was often absent from the territory and his autocratic posture may have merited at least some of the abuse. But St. Clair, who enjoyed considerable support in the Cincinnati, Marietta, and Detroit areas, discounted the opposition. "I have but five Enemies in the Territory," he wrote shortly after Goforth had called him a "Nabob." These Republican leaders, with their partisan bombast, may have "misled" a few other impressionable inhabitants ("who probably never saw me").[17]

St. Clair was right to question the extent and depth of popular hostility to his administration, but complaints about the territory's "colonial" condition did strike a resonant chord. Anticolonial—and pseudo-Revolutionary—rhetoric was to become a standard adjunct of statehood movements throughout American territorial history, even where more popular territorial governors supported the change. Use of the term "colony" expressed the chronic ambivalence of frontier communities toward national authority. Comparisons between the Northwest Territory and the American colonies before the War of Independence called up the conventional image of tyranny and bad government—the antitype of the new republics. Yet they also suggested a flattering identification between the future new states and the original thirteen. After all, the Atlantic states had grown powerful and virtuous through protracted colonial apprenticeships. The territories would pass through similar stages of development.[18]

The developmental model, in fact, proved to be central to the very idea of "territory." Territory suggested both "colony"—the beginning point—and "state"—the end. An American colony *became* a state while being administered as a territory. The Northwest Ordinance, with its provisions for progression through stages from colonial dependency to independent statehood, embodied this developmental dynamic. Agitation for statehood—that is, for accelerating this progress—thus did not imply rejection of the Ordinance, even though statehood proponents attacked the territorial government created under its authority. The Ordinance fully authorized the movement toward statehood, clearly mandating the automatic self-destruction of the temporary governments it had called into being.

II. Compact Theories

St. Clair had law and logic on his side when he suggested that full citizenship depended on the attainment of statehood.[19] Though St. Clair's enemies insisted that settlers were "citizens," they acknowledged that the actual exercise of rights was only prospective. Statehood proponents thus issued an "Address to the Citizens" in 1797, calling on Northwesterners to reclaim their rights. Because of rapid population growth, "the happy period is drawing nigh, when the citizens of this Territory shall again be re-instated into those rights and privileges which they formerly enjoyed as citizens."[20] The two uses—and different meanings—of "citizen" in the same sentence reveal the writers' sense of their dynamic political condition: the attainment of *true* citizenship was immanent in the temporarily defective citizenship claimed by territorial "citizens."

The important point was that the settlers' political degradation was only temporary and expedient. St. Clair's bitterest opponents conceded that the national government had to impose law and order on the frontier while it was being settled: lawlessness would deter the orderly and industrious settlers capable of eventually governing themselves. But a temporary "colonial" government was only necessary because small numbers of scattered settlers could not conveniently exercise their rights, not because they were politically incompetent. Though a temporary suspension of rights was necessary to prevent "anarchy" and secure land titles, Congress promised that northwesterners would soon be able to form republican governments consistent with the "principles of the late revolution." "Perhaps with great wisdom," Judge Goforth explained in a 1796 speech, Congress had

> determined it better for the adventurers for a while, to lay aside their rights, not to Alien them, for they are declared to be inalienable, than to go forward destitute of law and government, and held up to the citizens . . . the ordinance in which they divide the territory into States, and pledge the faith of the nation that when any of the said States should have sixty thousand free inhabitants therein such State shall be at liberty, to resume those rights.[21]

Settlers agreed to forego their rights temporarily so that Congress could maintain order and develop the federal lands; in return, the United States pledged to welcome the new northwestern states into the union. In the words of territorial judges Samuel Holden Parsons and James Varnum, the Ordinance was therefore to be viewed "in the light of a compact between the United States and all the settlers."[22]

The "compact" idea enabled theorists to reconcile despotic colonial rule with American conceptions of political rights. St. Clair rejected the equality and reciprocity implicit in this conception, suggesting instead that the Ordinance was more like the old colonial charters in which the British sovereign granted privileges to his subjects. The so-called articles of compact "with much more propriety, may be called the terms on which the colonies shall be settled." The territorial governor was the first of many critics to argue that it was logically absurd to posit a "compact" without distinct parties. The "people of the Territory" did not exist as a separate community, but were instead "comprehended in the whole" American nation: could it then be said that "the United States made a compact with themselves"?[23] Though St. Clair did not discount the compact articles, he insisted that their authority could not derive from any imagined reciprocal engagements. Instead, they represented promises made by the United States government, exercising full sovereign authority over its own property, to encourage settlement in the Northwest.

St. Clair's opponents responded that purchasers of federal lands, as American citizens, could never become "subjects" of Congress and so forfeit their rights to self-government. The rights of American citizens were "inalienable," even in disorderly, unsettled frontier conditions that temporarily prevented their exercise. Defenders of territorial rights argued that their participation in the Revolutionary War effort entitled them to the same rights enjoyed by "our brethren in the Atlantick States." "We have equally contributed in every point of view," Goforth asserted, "either with respect to service or sacrifice, in order to obtain" the blessings of freedom. Self-government was not merely a privilege incidental to membership in particular state communities, but a right that settlers took with them wherever the United States exercised jurisdiction.

If settlers possessed the inalienable rights of American citizens, then they could bargain with their fellow citizens on terms of equality. The authority of the "compacts" in the Ordinance derived from separate engagements between individual settlers and the federal government. In effect, they bound themselves *not* to exercise their rights until their numbers reached designated levels. Thus the "colonial" government authorized by the Ordinance, though it often matched and sometimes surpassed the "tyranny and domination" of British rule, was ultimately based on consent. Every settler "has impliedly assented" to the territorial government, Goforth concluded, and "it is certainly our duty as well as inclination to give it every effect, untill we can constitutionally lay it aside."[24]

The notion of a transcendent American citizenship led statehood advocates in the Northwest to revive the natural rights rhetoric of the Revolutionary era. They saw no conflict between the authority of the national government and the "sovereignty and Independence of the people" in the Territory: these were perfectly reconciled in the Ordinance compacts.[25] An early prostatehood "Address" therefore encouraged northwesterners to "step forward and demand our rights," confident that Congress would "grant them with pleasure."[26] Worthington's brother-in-law (and future governor) Edward

Tiffin of Chillicothe reminded his fellow "Inhabitants" that "we are free men and have rights which the god of nature and the benign influences of the federal constitution is waiting to confer upon us."[27]

Jefferson's election encouraged territorial Republicans in the vanguard of the statehood movement to turn to the national government for support against the Federalist St. Clair. But their faith in Congress and "the benign influence of the federal constitution" also derived from their understanding of the Ordinance. They identified Congress with the compact agreements it was constitutionally bound to fulfill; the provisions for temporary government, under which St. Clair exercised apparently "despotic" power, were merely temporary, expedient means toward the ends specified in the compacts. By this logic, Congress was entitled to interpose its authority to "protect the people in their rights and check an unconstitutional measure, though it should come from so respectable a source as the [territorial] legislature."[28] The government provisions were subordinate to the binding promises of its compacts: territorial officials were constitutionally responsible to Congress, and therefore to the compact agreements that controlled relations between the people of the Northwest and the United States.

The distinction between the two parts of the Ordinance is warranted by its language. Only the compact articles were supposed to "forever remain unalterable." It was therefore logical to conclude that the governmental provisions were not only temporary, but subject to tinkering. St. Clair himself noted that they appeared to be "as much in the power of Congress to alter or repeal as a law which may have passed yesterday."[29] Congressional practice justified the distinction between the parts of the Ordinance: numerous changes in the government provisions were enacted, often in response to popular pressure from the Territory; meanwhile, because the compact articles were largely prospective in scope, Congress had little occasion to tamper with them.[30]

St. Clair's opponents argued that the compact articles set limits on the "time that our submission can be constitutionally called for."[31] Judge Goforth, in his letter to Jefferson, offered the fullest reading of the Ordinance in this vein: "The Confederate Congress who gave existence to the ordinance Government seem to have been conscious that such a Government would not sit well on citizens from the free states and therefore appear to meliorate it by the Solemn and unalterable compact with which they prop it."[32] Its authors, Goforth thought, had intended that the two sections of the Ordinance should balance one another, that the compact articles provide the context in which the government provisions should be read.

The Northwest Territory's "ordinance government" was undoubtedly a necessity in the early stages of its settlement, but the increasingly unpopular

St. Clair administration represented the perpetuation of colonial government beyond its proper time. The attacks on St. Clair suggest that the autocratic powers he claimed were inappropriate to the stage of political self-consciousness attained in the territory. Those who protested against the governor's rule implicitly affirmed their readiness, therefore, to govern themselves. When St. Clair's Republican opponents drafted a state constitution in November 1802 they stripped the governor of much of his power and secured the legislature's supremacy. Invoking the promises of the compact articles, they repudiated the system of territorial government established by the Ordinance.

III. Conditional Statehood

As long as the Federalists retained control of the national government, statehood advocates in the Northwest relied heavily on the Ordinance's constitutional guarantees. They aimed their anticolonial rhetoric at the temporary government provisions while relying on the compact articles to enable them to "throw off the colonial yoke" and break the "chains of aristocracy."[33] With the growth of the territory's population—reported as 45,365 in the 1800 census—residents in the eastern "state" could anticipate soon crossing the sixty thousand threshold and being able to claim admission to the union.[34] But Jefferson's victory, coupled with the Republican ascendancy in Congress, promised to transform the territory's political situation and, coincidentally, partisan attitudes toward the Ordinance. The Republicans were now in a position to accelerate the state-making process—as the Ordinance allowed—without waiting for the eastern state's population to reach sixty thousand. Meanwhile, the new administration allowed St. Clair and his friends to remain in control of the territorial government. As a result, territorial Federalists could present themselves as champions of the Ordinance when Republicans began pushing for statehood, protesting congressional interference in territorial affairs and urging fellow citizens not to sacrifice rights guaranteed by its compacts in exchange for early admission.

St. Clair and his allies argued that the Republicans, in their haste to gain admission for the new state, were running roughshod over rights vested in the people of the Northwest by the Ordinance. Though these arguments left most voters unpersuaded, Federalist opposition to statehood on the basis of strict construction of territorial rights under the compact articles raised important questions about the state-making process. To what extent could Congress determine the timing and terms of admission? Did the Northwestern states have an unconditional right to join the union, regardless of the will of Congress?

In 1801 St. Clair and his allies attempted to change the future state boundaries in the Northwest, obviously intending to keep the territory "in the colonial state" as long as possible. The territorial legislature "consented" to an alteration in boundaries that would have split the territory's prospective eastern state and enlarged the western states, as defined in Article V.[35] According to St. Clair's interpretation of the Ordinance, Congress's subsequent approval of this measure would suffice to alter the compact accordingly. As a Federalist with a dim view of the readiness of the still sparsely settled—and largely Republican—territory for self-government, St. Clair sought to delay the advent of statehood as long as possible. His outraged opponents saw the division act as a blatant partisan move to turn back the clock: statehood had been promised when any one of the embryonic "states" reached a population of sixty thousand, but the promise was meaningless if boundaries could be redrawn at will.

The boundary controversy was a direct prelude to the final push for statehood. One of the leading charges against St. Clair, in a list drawn up by Thomas Worthington, was that he "attempted to effect the dismemberment of the Territory and to destroy its constitutional boundaries."[36] St. Clair's division act focused attention on the specific language of Article V concerning boundaries; petitioners consequently barraged Congress with pleas to vindicate the territory's "constitutional" rights.[37] When the division act passed, a hostile assembly minority report proclaimed that the Ordinance "has ever been considered and acknowledged as the Constitution of this Territory," and that the boundaries "fixed and established" in Article V "must forever remain unalterable, unless by common consent." Of course, the assembly majority did "consent" to these changes. But here is where the minority could turn the defective character of the territorial government—which St. Clair usually was so anxious to emphasize—to its own advantage. Because of limits on suffrage under the Ordinance, the assembly was not truly representative and could not be said to act for the people of the territory as a whole. Further, the minority reasoned, the dependent character of the territory made true consent impossible. Consent presupposed a competence—and freedom of action—that only states could claim. Therefore, "no alteration can take place until the people residing within the boundaries assume a state government; because, if it was subject to an alteration while under a Territorial government, great imposition might be practiced."[38]

While the minority conceded the subordinate, dependent character of the territory under the Northwest Ordinance, it insisted that the people of the territory had a full claim on the rights—that is, to statehood within specified boundaries—set forth in Article V. Neither St. Clair nor his friends in the assembly could diminish those rights; instead, the claims of future states were a constitutional standard against which the territorial government should be measured. When St. Clair's opponents compared him to a British colonial governor and accused him of unconstitutional acts they were, in effect, reading him out of the Ordinance. The authors of the Ordinance had intended that the colonies formed in the national domain would become states; in view of this intention, the specific promises of Article V were controlling. St. Clair had exceeded the authority delegated to him under the Ordinance.

Statehood advocates collected thousands of signatures on petitions designed to show Congress that northwesterners were overwhelmingly opposed to boundary changes. Claiming that the territorial government was arbitrary, oppressive, and unrepresentative, they called on Congress to exercise its authority directly in the Territory. "Any act of the Legislature of this Territory . . . cannot be the will of a majority of the people, four fifths of whom are not represented by them": petitioners therefore were forced to look to Congress "as the only guardians of our rights."39 Congressional Republicans listened attentively to these complaints. They quickly disposed of a resolution offered by territorial delegate Paul Fearing, St. Clair's ally, asserting Congress's right, with the consent of the territorial legislature, to "alter the boundaries of the States" in the Northwest. On January 27, 1802, after perfunctory debate, the House rejected St. Clair's division bill by a decisive 81–5 margin. Interpreting the popular outcry against division as support for statehood, the House and Senate then agreed on an act enabling northwesterners to hold a constitutional convention and stipulating conditions for admission to the union.40

Not only did congressmen turn a deaf ear to the territorial government on the boundary question; they also resolved to bypass the territorial legislature in organizing a state government. The petition campaign convinced Republican representative Robert Williams of North Carolina that "nine-tenths" of the people in the Territory "wished a State government."41 But, added another Republican, Marylander Joseph Nicholson, "if the government of the Territory were to remain organized as at this time, I believe we might wait till doomsday, before we obtained their approbation." If Congress failed to intervene, it would be "in the power of the President," acting through his appointed governor, to thwart the popular will and "keep the district under a territorial government as long as he pleases."42

Republicans justified congressional interference in the state-making process by citing St. Clair's apparent unwillingness to respond to popular sentiment. The governor's authority was constitutionally unlimited: in the words of one newspaper writer, "Being independent of the people for his office, they have no barrier to shield them from his power and encroachments."[43] An "Address" from New Market in Ross County complained that the right of electing representatives under the second stage of territorial government had not "liberated" them from the "galling yoke" of colonial rule. St. Clair's influence corrupted the legislature, leaving the Territory to "groan under the intolerable pressure of despotic imposition."[44] The Republican Corresponding Society of Cincinnati was convinced that "were the preliminary arrangements for a convention, the exclusive province of the territorial legislature, the governor or the council might, by refusing their concurrence, procrastinate the measure for ever."[45] But because St. Clair and his government *were* responsible to Congress, it was incumbent on Congress to uphold territorial rights until statehood enabled northwesterners to protect themselves.

Statehood forces relied on interference by the national government because it was politically expedient. Further, their appeals to Congress and the president were compatible with the idea that northwesterners could claim rights as American citizens, not as citizens of particular states. But Federalists were quick to point out the potential dangers of such appeals. They insisted that it was far more urgent to establish the relative limits of territorial and national authority than it was to restrain the alleged abuses of territorial officials. Properly speaking, the embryonic Northwestern states could claim no "rights" unless Congress scrupulously adhered to the letter of the Ordinance. St. Clair's authority was constitutionally grounded in the Ordinance's provisions for temporary government; he was answerable to his superiors for any dereliction of duty. But if the Ordinance were abandoned, who then would presume to resist the arbitrary, uncontrollable will of Congress?

Congressman Roger Griswold of Connecticut outlined the major arguments subsequently raised by territorial Federalists in opposing the statehood movement. He insisted that, as a corporate entity acting through its existing government, the Territory had rights that Congress was bound to respect. "If . . . you may legislate for these people before they are admitted into the Union, you may also legislate for them afterwards; and if you do not like the constitution they now form, you may pass a law for another Convention." By usurping authority over the state-making process, Congress could delay or prevent admission altogether. And why, Griswold asked, did Republicans assume that Congress was better able to speak for the people of the Territory than their own elected representatives? The will of the people could only be ascertained through regular, constitutional channels: if it would not listen to the legislature, Congress had no other alternative than "going round to every man in the Territory, and obtaining his opinion." But such an arrogation of authority would make a mere cipher out of the government duly organized under the Northwest Ordinance. Here was a dangerous precedent. If Congress were "to interfere with these internal concerns, and to regulate them by a national law," the inevitable result would be the consolidation and destruction of all the States."[46]

Federalists preempted the states' rights arguments usually associated with their opponents. Republicans replied that the equation between the Territory and existing states was utterly inappropriate. Nicholson thought it an "absurd doctrine": "I ask if Maryland can be compared to the Territory?"[47] While statehood proponents in the Northwest asserted that they were ready to reclaim their rights and govern themselves, they agreed with Nicholson that they did not possess the collective identity or political competence of a state as long as they remained under the Ordinance government. Their complaints about St. Clair's despotic rule suggested that the Territory would remain in this debased, dependent condition until redeemed by Congress. As Goforth wrote President Jefferson, "we object not to submit to what may be done by Congress provided we are emancipated from our present anti-revolutionary government."[48] Republicans like James Finley, "considering ourselves as in a minor state," thus were willing to defer to Congress to determine "the mode of calling a convention—the purposes for which it shall be called—the time when, and the place where it shall convene."[49]

Some territorial Republicans had misgivings about leaving the initiative entirely with Congress. Writing from Washington, D.C., in March 1802, Worthington justified the enabling act to his close political ally Nathaniel Massie, founder of Chillicothe:

> You seem to think any interference by the U. S. would injure the republican cause—My Dear sir can you suppose that the great body of people are pleased with our present form of government? I think not. Let us examine how far congress intend to interfere? They say we believe your Government oppressive and that through the artifice of your rulers every attempt you make to change it is defeated[;] we will therefore point out a mode by which to know your real desires—should you prefer a state government we are willing to receive you[;] on the other hand should you prefer your present government you are at liberty to do so.[50]

Congressional interference would facilitate expression of the popular will, thus, in Edward Tiffin's words, emancipating northwesterners from a government under which "we now *breathe,* to one under which we may *live.*"[51]

Federalists were quick to seize on potential problems with the Republican position. They challenged the assumption that Congress's role was "disinterested and friendly" and its "interposition . . . both constitutional and necessary."[52] Negotiations over the terms of admission clearly demonstrated that Congress was very much interested, most notably in securing federal property rights. Because Republicans thought of statehood as liberation from the territorial regime, they were relatively unconcerned about future relations between the state and the union. Yet how could the new state bargain effectively with Congress if the constitutional convention was Congress's creation?

By calling the convention into existence and stipulating admission conditions, Federalists charged, Congress virtually wrote the Ohio constitution. "In the name of Heaven!" exclaimed "Mentor" in the *Ohio Gazette*, "why did they not make a constitution for us at once?" "If there be any act in which the sovereignty of a people ought to be untouched, and sacred," he continued, "it is the one of forming a permanent constitution." Yet, because Congress had specified who would vote for convention delegates, "the very right of citizenship is dependent on the will of a foreign power." Thus "the sources and head springs of its sovereignty, are contaminated by foreign influence. . . . WHERE WILL THIS PRINCIPLE LEAD US?"[53]

Federalists argued that the Territory could exercise state rights before admission. The compact articles of the Ordinance vested specific rights in the projected "states" that Congress could not touch; provisions for temporary government created representative institutions through which northwesterners could express their will and claim their rights. Thus, while their opponents asserted that the compacts set limits to the arbitrary rule of territorial governments, Federalists suggested that it was only by the action of those governments that the compact promises could be redeemed. According to the Federalist account, northwesterners became increasingly politically competent as they progressed through the stages prescribed in the Ordinance. Finally, as Article V stipulated, on attaining a population of sixty thousand, they were entitled to take the last step toward self-government by drafting a state constitution. Only when the new state presented itself for admission did Congress have the right to act, and even then it was strictly bound by the Ordinance.

The crucial question was whether the northwestern "states" could claim the right to admission, regardless of the will of Congress. If they could, Congress's role in organizing new state governments and negotiating the terms of their admission was at the least problematic. Turning anticolonial rhetoric against national instead of territorial authorities, the Dayton Association viewed the enabling act "as bearing a striking similarity to Great Britain, imposing laws on the provinces."[54] A Federalist newspaper writer charged his Republican opponents with aiding and abetting the sacrifice of territorial rights: by submitting to Congress's direction, "they acknowledge" its "right . . . to controul the affairs of our own internal concerns."[55] The danger was that in their eagerness to gain admission, statehood advocates would agree to onerous conditions that would reduce the new state to an inferior, unequal position in the union.

Opponents of the enabling act insisted that the terms offered by Congress were, in the words of Elias Langham, "unfavorable to our interest and a c[u]rb to our liberties, and but an *Indian* gift at best."[56] Most controversial was a provision exempting federal lands from state taxes for five years after their sale; in return, Congress pledged 5 percent of land sales revenue to building roads to the east, the reservation of one section in each township for schools, and state control over a district including the Scioto salt springs. The enabling act also cut off Wayne County from the new state, appending the area to the recently established Indiana Territory. (Federalist attacks on these boundaries, ironically echoing Republican opposition to St. Clair's division bill, are discussed in the next chapter.) Langham thought the school grant was an "Indian gift" because the 1785 land ordinance had already pledged section 16 to support education. Meanwhile, the new state would be deprived of the right enjoyed by every other state to tax private property. In an inflammatory address to the state constitutional convention, St. Clair asked why such conditions are "imposed upon us before we can obtain a right which is ours by nature and by compact?"[57]

Many congressmen appeared to agree with St. Clair that the new state would be able to claim unconditional admission when its population reached sixty thousand. In the House, Nicholson urged quick action: "If we admit them now into the Union, we may make very important terms, which they will observe inviolate, if not lost to every principle of good faith; whereas, if we wait until they shall have acquired the right of admission, without our consent, we can make no terms with them whatever."[58] This being so, replied Federalist Calvin Goddard of Connecticut, why should Congress "precipitate" the enabling act, "when in all probability, before these details can be made, the Territory will have obtained the number of sixty thousand, and be entitled of right to admission into the Union?"[59]

Congress's urgency supposedly betrayed an intention of fastening unequal terms on the new state while it still remained in the territorial condition and under its control. Writing as "Frank Stubblefield," St. Clair's ally William McMillan of Cincinnati charged that Congress sought to negotiate an "advantageous treaty . . . before we might demand admission."[60] A Cincinnati newspaper, the *Western Spy*, published a long letter from an unnamed senator expressing incredulity that the convention could be "so blind to the true interests" of their constituents as to agree to Congress's conditions:

The proposed exemption of the great body of your lands from taxation, for the term of five years, would be degrading to your state, derogatory to your legislature, and burthensome, oppressive and disaffecting to your citizens. Which of the state legislatures of the United States, have ever before been so shackled? How is it possible, that your people can or will submit to such a grievous inequality of contributions, as it would create and fasten upon you?

The senator went on to dismiss land grants to the state as "bribes" that would "soon be yours of course without price or condition." Why, he asked, were statehood advocates so eager to act when in "one year more at farthest you will have the number which entitles you to become a state without consent of the general government, under the ordinance?"[61]

Territorial Federalists elaborated these themes as delegates to the constitutional convention prepared to meet. They now took their stand on the principles of the Ordinance, particularly its promise of new state equality in the union. One writer claimed the Federalists "had too much regard for the sacred rights of freemen, to consent we should be brought into the union under such degrading circumstances as are held out" in the enabling act.[62] To secure equality, a "Friend to Instruction" insisted, it was necessary first to "become independent" and form a state government: then "we can on equal ground treat with Congress on these propositions without endangering our independence."[63] In the words of "Peter Squib," "the people of the territory have the right of forming a constitution for themselves, on the principles of the ordinance, unshackled by the conditions and arbitrary restrictions of congress."[64]

St. Clair took the logic of the Federalist argument to its extreme in his convention speech. Arguing that the territorial legislature was fully adequate "for all internal affairs," he proclaimed the enabling act an arbitrary "interference, . . . in truth a nullity." Therefore, the delegates should ignore Congress's conditions as they drafted a constitution. "Let your representatives go forward with that in their hands, and demand the admission of the Territory as a State. It will not, it can not be refused." If it was, St. Clair continued, the new state was perfectly capable of following the example of Vermont which had remained outside the union "eight years after" the people "had formed their government."[65]

St. Clair made an unconvincing champion of the people's rights under the Ordinance, but, as the Chillicothe newspaper observed, "*Drowning men will catch at straws!*"[66] The governor's well-known aversion to statehood made necessary the very recourse to national authority that he now warned against. After all, Edward Tiffin wrote, "had Congress not interfered, the time so long wished for might have been protracted to God knows what period."[67] The choice between the relatively unrepresentative territorial legislature and the constitutional convention called by Congress also seemed clear enough to Republicans. Nonetheless, St. Clair and his allies raised troubling questions about the state-making process.

The Jefferson administration hesitated to assert that Congress could dictate terms to the new state. It did not appear to Secretary of State Albert Gallatin "that the United States have a right to annex new conditions, not implied in the articles of compact, limiting the Legislative right of taxation of the Territory or new State." Nor was Gallatin impressed with the argument that Congress could impose such conditions as long as the Territory's population remained below sixty thousand: "the United States have no greater right to annex new limitations than the individual State may have to infringe those of the original compact."[68]

Some Republicans, including Gallatin, suggested that departures from the Ordinance could be justified by a process of reciprocal consent. Recalling St. Clair's argument that Ordinance boundaries could be changed by the joint "consent" of Congress and the Territory (acting through the legislature), they argued that the convention was free to "consent" to Congress's conditions. Congress was "one of the parties to this ordinance," according to a writer in the *Ohio Gazette*, and "have most indubitably a RIGHT to *propose* to us the people, who compose the other party, such alterations as they think proper, and we may refuse or accept these offers."[69] Republicans repeatedly appealed to this idea of consent. "We are not . . . for doing anything compulsory," Thomas T. Davis of Kentucky told the House: the convention therefore could do what it liked.[70]

Reciprocal consent implied equal power. But would the new state be able to stand up to Congress? Manasseh Cutler, one of the leading spirits in the original settlement of the Territory, was doubtful. As he wrote his son Ephraim, "You have so humbly submitted to the right which Congress has exercised in making laws for you, should they reject your proposals, you have no ground to complain."[71] Because of the new state's unequal position in petitioning for admission, any deviation from the Ordinance compacts was bound to be disadvantageous. If the Ordinance could be revised at the point of admission, all of its promises—including statehood itself—would be subject to negotiation.

Republicans who recognized the potential pitfalls of the "consent" idea instead argued that the federal Constitution and the Ordinance entitled Congress to lay down certain admission conditions. Anticipating arguments that arose during the Missouri controversy, they asserted that the right of admission necessarily implied the right to impose conditions. They also argued, in the words of Republican leader William Branch Giles of Virginia, that the controversial conditions were simply "made as additional securities for the national property."[72] Article IV of the Ordinance guaranteed federal property interests: the enabling act simply implemented the guarantee. The five year tax exemption, a writer in the Territory noted, "is only explanatory of that part of the ordinance which reserves to the United States the exclusive right of disposing of the soil of the lands of the general government."[73]

Whether or not admission conditions modified or simply "explained" the Ordinance, Republicans effectively acknowledged congressional control over the state-making process. Ironically, those who had invoked the promises of the Ordinance compacts in opposing St. Clair's "colonial" regime now appeared willing to concede that the Ordinance's provisions were not binding on Congress. But Republicans chose not to deal systematically with the constitutional questions raised by their Federalist opponents. Given their dominance in the Territory, Republicans could afford to live with a certain amount of ambiguity. In any case, the constitutional convention acceded to Congress's terms before Ohio crossed the sixty thousand threshold and could claim a right to admission. As a result, the status of the Ordinance as a constitutional document remained unresolved.

IV. Ambiguous Legacies

The subsequent formation of new states in the Northwest did not immediately lay to rest the constitutional questions raised by Ohio Federalists. Statehood advocates in Indiana and Illinois territories neither demanded unconditional admission nor questioned Congress's right to take the initiative in state making by passing enabling acts following the Ohio precedent. Anxious to negotiate the most favorable terms of admission, new state leaders hesitated to challenge congressional supremacy or federal property rights. As a result, admission to the union depended on the practical acknowledgement of new state inequality.

But if political prudence forced northwesterners to accept unequal terms from Congress, the new state equality issue did not long remain submerged. Beginning in the 1820s, the public land states began agitating for the retrocession of public lands to the states, arguing that the continuing federal jurisdiction secured in enabling acts was incompatible with state sovereignty and state equality.[74] Proslavery northwesterners asserted that the congressional ban on slavery (in Ordinance Article VI) constituted a similar infringement on states' rights. Still unresolved questions about the extent of territorial rights were most thoroughly canvassed in the protracted struggle over Michigan statehood. Michiganders questioned Congress's right to lay down conditions—notably with respect to their southern boundary—and asserted their independent right to organize a state government under the Ordinance.

The Ohio Federalists first raised fundamental—and chronically troublesome—questions about the principles of the territorial system and the character of new state-federal relations in the expanding union. The legacy of the Ohio Republicans was no less ambiguous. Subsequent new state proponents may have invoked similar anticolonial rhetoric, but nowhere else was there such a neat fit between the agitation for statehood and opposition to an unpopular, "colonial" territorial government. St. Clair's successors elsewhere were far better politicians. Indiana and Illinois moved rapidly toward admission with territorial officials in the vanguard.[75] Both territories benefited from the "democratization" of territorial government—including broader suffrage and more elected officials—that culminated in the organic act for Wisconsin Territory in 1836.[76] In Michigan and Wisconsin these expanding political opportunities facilitated partisan development in the territorial period. Territorial governors functioned as crucial intermediaries between national parties and their territorial wings. Under these conditions the contrast between "colony" and "state" was no longer compelling. In effect, the text of the temporary government provisions was rewritten by Congress as it exercised a continuing, discretionary authority over territorial administration.[77]

Ironically, the developmental dynamic inherent in the original Ordinance came to be largely vitiated. The territorial condition became easily tolerable—indeed, federal financing of territorial government offered at least one distinct advantage. Although, in an 1816 petition, the Illinois assembly could still speak of the governor's extensive powers as "a badge of Colonial degradation," the conditions that once justified this rhetoric were already rapidly disappearing. Because of the liberalization of territorial government, the territories could claim many of "the same rights & privileges of self government, that are possessed by the respective States."[78] Ambitious politicians, in fact, often found Congress to be more receptive to the political progress of the territories than the people of the territories themselves. As a result, complaints about the territories' "colonial degradation" seem more often intended to raise political consciousness in the territories than to influence Congress. Exasperated by popular resistance to representative government, an 1804 meeting in Knox County, Indiana, urged the territory's freeholders to vote against "remaining in the condition of debased slaves." "There never was a people on earth, not even the Prussians or Turks, in a more humble and degraded condition than we are." Indianans would only have themselves to blame if that condition persisted.[79]

The biggest obstacle to moving up through the stages of territorial government to statehood proved to be popular indifference.[80] But if the leadership ran considerably ahead of public opinion in Indiana and Illinois, the statehood movements in both territories gained easy victories, in 1816 and 1818 respectively. No coherent opposition to the change emerged either at the territorial or national levels. In Michigan, the statehood issue was complicated by a boundary controversy with Ohio and the resulting delays encouraged territorial Democrats to organize a genuinely popular movement for statehood. In Wisconsin, however, large majorities were actively hostile to statehood long after the territory passed the sixty thousand population threshold that qualified it for admission under the Ordinance.[81] References to the territory's "colonial" condition therefore were directed at Wisconsin voters. Statehood proponents hoped to embarrass Wisconsinites into claiming rights "guaranteed to them more than half a century since." According to an 1845 editorial, "it will be her own fault" if the territory, having long since mustered the required population, should "continue to struggle under worse than colonial vassalage."[82]

Statehood proponents sought to sustain—or revive—a reading of the Ordinance that made sense when Governor St. Clair wielded a heavy hand, but which had been subverted by revisions of the provisions for temporary government. Only in Michigan, where the impasse over the southern boundary threatened to keep the new state out of the union, did concern about the territories' "constitutional" rights focus attention on the provisions of Article V. Elsewhere, the people of the Old Northwest could take statehood for granted. In the meantime, the yoke of colonial bondage did not weigh heavily.

5.

Boundary Controversies

☆ ☆ ☆ ☆ ☆

The authors of the Northwest Ordinance hoped to keep the new states free of the jurisdictional controversies that had plagued the old states in the decade after independence.[1] Article V therefore included exact descriptions of boundaries for the first three states to be formed in the southern part of the territory. But because of uncertainty about the region's prospects for population growth, future congresses were left to decide whether to create one or two additional states "in that part of the said territory which lies north of an east and west line drawn through the southerly bend or extreme of lake Michigan." Such discretion seemed necessary in light of the Ordinance's requirement that each new state have a population of sixty thousand "free Inhabitants" before it could claim a place in the union.

Despite Congress's good intentions, the location of new state boundaries in the Northwest periodically became the subject of heated controversy. On these occasions, the determination to fix boundaries in advance proved incompatible with Congress's discretionary authority to change them when forming additional states. Disputes over the boundary provisions in Article V revealed the same fundamental contradiction between territorial rights and national power apparent in the Ohio statehood struggle. The key question was whether or not the Ordinance controlled Congress as well as the people of the Northwest as they set about forming their new states. But the effect of sustained debate over the meaning of Article V was to undercut the Ordinance's constitutional authority. Finally, in resolving the dispute over the Ohio-Michigan boundary, Congress simply ignored the Ordinance altogether. Whatever the validity of its reading of Article V, Michigan was forced to recognize Ohio's claims in exchange for its admission to the union.

A review of boundary controversies in the Northwest enables us to trace the Ordinance's career as a constitutional document. The authors of the Ordinance had had no misgivings about its constitutional standing, particularly when they set forth boundary lines. A key function of colonial charters and state constitutions was to define boundaries; the Northwest Ordinance could be seen as a charter or constitution because it set the limits of new western states and provided for the distribution of their public lands. Settlers would be redeemed from their temporary "colonial" condition by the inevitable growth of population.

Yet to establish new state boundaries over a vast, uncharted wilderness domain was an elusive goal. American policy makers hoped to avoid the confusion of overlapping charter lines characteristic of the British empire in America. But the imperfect state of geographical knowledge (most notably concerning the precise location of Lake Michigan) and unpredictable patterns of settlement and development meant that the Ordinance's projected boundaries were inevitably arbitrary and ambiguous. Northwesterners who stood to benefit from boundary changes often led the attack against these "unnatural" boundaries. But the resulting uncertainty jeopardized territorial rights. The Ordinance was supposed to control development over space and time, and these spatial and temporal dimensions were interdependent. If boundaries were not fixed in advance, the other compact promises would be meaningless: Congress could change a territory's boundaries whenever it threatened to grow large enough to claim membership in the union.

I. Territorial Boundaries

The boundaries set down in the Ordinance were only the latest in a series of proposals for new colonies and new states dating from before the Revolution.[2] A leading feature of these proposals was the emphasis on determinate boundary lines. A remarkable proposal set forth by British radical John Cartwright in the 1775 edition of his *American Independence the Interest and Glory of Great Britain* reflected this concern, anticipating many of the provisions of the later Northwest Ordinance. Cartwright's objective was to preserve "the future balance of power" among the Anglo-American "states." "Might it not be expedient," he asked, "that the limits and boundaries of each, which they should never hereafter pass, should be newly defined by the Grand British League and Confederacy." Cartwright proposed nineteen new colonies, specifying their precise boundaries and giving each a name. When any of these colonies achieved a population of fifty thousand, "they should be entitled and free to erect themselves into an independent political state" on terms of full equality with the other American colonies.[3]

Cartwright's goals and assumptions became familiar ones over the next decade when independent Americans grappled with the western problem. Fixed boundaries were particularly important to the American states as they sought to resolve the many jurisdictional controversies that threatened to undermine their union. Reflecting on the divisive western lands controversy, Congress resolved in 1784 that the time had come when the Confederation should at last "assume its ultimate and permanent form."[4] American statesmen also shared Cartwright's concern that none of the new states "should be too large or too small." State equality was thought to be critical to a "balance of power": the imbalance among the large and small states already in the union was one of its leading liabilities.[5] The balance of power idea was apparent in Congress's 1784 Territorial Government Ordinance. According to what Robert Berkhofer, Jr., has called Jefferson's "ideological geography," the relative sizes of the new states could be manipulated to counter the centrifugal tendencies of an extensive union.[6] The mechanics of the expanding federal system required that new states preserve the interstate balance of power: if they were made too large the union would be jeopardized by dangerous new centers of power.[7]

Most western policy makers agreed on the need for fixed boundaries, small and equal states, and provisions for the orderly distribution and security of national property. But conflicting proposals proliferated because of differences over how to put these principles into practice. Enthusiasm for new states also varied according to how their admission was supposed to affect the sectional balance of power in Congress.[8] The impact of new states could be undercut by making them too large—thus limiting their voting power in Congress—or too small—thus keeping them out of the union indefinitely. Yet there were legitimate reasons for making the new states larger or smaller, depending on different assumptions about the likely future course of western development. After a tour of the Northwest, Monroe was impressed by the "miserably poor" prospects for the region's development. He feared that some of the western states, as defined by the 1784 Ordinance, "will perhaps never contain a sufficient number of Inhabitants to entitle them to membership in the confederacy."[9]

Uncertainty about the future of the West—the impossibility of predicting in the mid-1780s how fast the new states would be settled and of knowing the territorial prerequisites for equality in the union—challenged the wisdom of determining boundaries in advance. The meaning of state "equality" was hardly self-evident. Projections of future development were premised on equations between available land and population and between population and power, but a new state's location, access to markets, resources, and climate were all significant—and at best dimly forseeable—variables. The latent contradiction between the territorial integrity of the new states and the principle of state equality—if equality meant equal potential for development—became manifest in the later history of the Northwest. Speculators and developers frequently invoked the idea of "natural" boundaries in opposition to "arbitrary," predetermined boundaries, insisting that lines should not be fixed until development potential was known.

But the natural boundaries argument could be a Pandora's box. If boundaries were left unfixed, the constitutional rights of territorial "states" would fall to the ground. Fixed boundaries precluded jurisdictional conflicts which would jeopardize the new states as well as the union at large.[10] Most importantly, they created communities capable of enjoying and enforcing claims to political rights that, in the American federal system, could only be exercised collectively. Any challenge to determinate boundaries was thus necessarily a threat to the existence of territorial "states" as political communities.

The boundaries stipulated in Article V of the Northwest Ordinance represented an effort to reconcile the potentially contradictory policy goals of fixed boundaries and new state equality. Congress could form "not less than three nor more than five States," options that reflected misgivings about the development of the Northwest. The framers of the Ordinance wanted it both ways. They wanted to fix boundaries while retaining the flexibility to provide for unforseeable contingencies. But these goals could be contradictory: as a result, opposing constituencies for "strict construction" of the Ordinance and for continuing congressional discretion emerged in the state-making process. Both groups could invoke the ambiguous authority of the Ordinance and the conflicting intentions of its framers. But controversy could not be confined to the interpretation of Article V: its ultimate effect was to call into question the constitutionality of the Ordinance itself.

II. Ohio's Boundaries

As we have seen, the boundary issue first became controversial in 1801 when Governor St. Clair pushed a law through the territorial assembly "consenting" to the alteration of the state lines laid down in the Ordinance.[11] The Federalist governor was clearly determined to keep new Republican states out of the union. As early as 1799, he had warned that if "not divided," the eastern division "must become a State very soon."[12] St. Clair's boundaries would delay statehood for years; they would also produce states of "manageable size." The "principal rivers . . . would run through their . . . centers."[13] This plea for "natural" boundaries gained support from settlers in the Cincinnati and Marietta areas who hoped to improve their commercial and political prospects in the new state or states soon to be formed.[14] A citizens' meeting in Dayton, located near the western border of the first

Ordinance state, insisted that "nature has allotted" the Wabash, Great Miami, and Muskingum rivers "for the centres of states," not their extremes.[15] Furthermore, given its dismal prospects for growth, the far western Ordinance state might not qualify for statehood "in a century." State equality, measured by population, thus dictated inequality in territorial extent. New state boundaries should not be set until their potential for development could be better known.

The predominantly Virginian—and Republican—settlers in the center of the eastern division of the Territory were the leading supporters for statehood under the Ordinance. But the realization that the proposed boundary changes would protract the period of territorial dependency for everyone undercut support for the division law in other areas. St. Clair's attempt to "effect the dismemberment of the Territory and to destroy its constitutional boundaries in order to prevent its advancement to those rights of self-government to which its numbers would entitle it" thus became a leading charge in the brief against him that statehood advocates presented to the Jefferson administration.[16]

Congress rejected St. Clair's division law, instead passing an enabling act that led to the meeting of the Ohio constitutional convention at Chillicothe in November.[17] The badly outnumbered Federalists—who had so recently tried to revise Article V—now presented themselves as strict constructionist defenders of the Ordinance. The Federalists' most effective line of attack was to compare the boundary stipulations in the enabling act with the wording of Article V of the Ordinance. By excluding Wayne County (present-day Michigan) from the new state, Congress evidently was reserving its right to form additional states to the north. The enabling act provided that Congress could annex the north country to Ohio at a future date if population growth proved inadequate to support a separate state. In the meantime, the region was temporarily assigned to Indiana Territory, thus "degrad[ing] these people . . . to a lower state."[18] The substantive complaint was that the five thousand inhabitants of the Detroit area were cut off from membership in the eastern "state" at the very moment the statehood pledge was to be redeemed. Solomon Sibley, a leading spokesman for the statehood faction in Detroit, asserted that Congress had "no authority of passing us into another Territory."[19] As the Dayton Association complained, the Wayne people were transferred "against their consent, from the last step in the second grade of government [with an elected legislature] back into the first [without one], and to another government and another people."[20]

The people of the north country were prepared for statehood as part of one of the "states" described in the Ordinance, only to be turned away at the threshold. Because this reversal of the state-making process was apparently at odds with a strict reading of the Ordinance, the Federalists could make a constitutional argument against the enabling act. Article V permitted the exclusion of the north country from the southern states for the purpose of creating one or two additional "states," not territories. "Mentor" insisted that *"Congress has no right to dismember the territory unless it, does it by forming one or two states north of this line."*[21] According to "Frank Stubblefield" (William McMillan), Wayne County could not be "annexed to Indiana, or seperated from us without mutual consent, for any other purpose than that of increasing the number of independent states."[22] Convinced by such arguments, representatives from Wayne County considered attending the Chillicothe convention, in defiance of the enabling act, but were discouraged by the large Republican majority.[23]

Despite their overwhelming defeat, St. Clair and his allies had raised important questions about the state-making process under the Northwest Ordinance. Specifically, they challenged Congress's right unilaterally to revise or interpret an Ordinance compact article, however much the discretionary authority over Ohio's northern boundary asserted in the enabling act conformed to the spirit or original intention of the Ordinance. Article V left Congress in a quandary. If the eastern state came into the union with the north country, Congress would be precluded from setting off an additional state. Congress had no constitutional authority over state boundaries: to reserve the right to change Ohio's boundaries would violate the principle of state equality. But the north country was hardly prepared for separate statehood—as it turned out, the people of Michigan Territory, organized in 1805, were unwilling to support a territorial assembly until 1824.[24] Simply, a strict reading of the Ordinance suggested Congress only could exercise its discretion to form additional states when the southern states came into the union. Its authority to change new state boundaries was then exhausted.

The debate over Ohio's northern boundary showed how the Ordinance could be invoked as a "constitution" by Federalists who had once opposed statehood as well as by Republican statehood advocates. The upshot of the debate was that while the Republicans grounded their statehood claims in compact articles they also embraced a broad interpretation of Congress's authority to put those compacts into practice. Meanwhile the Federalists subjected the Ordinance to a close documentary analysis that exposed some of its latent defects and contradictions. The subsequent history of the Northwest showed that, because of the disjunction between provisions for temporary government and the compact articles—and the radical distinction and therefore discontinuity between "territory" and "state"—the Ordinance ceased to be very useful in defining the jurisdictional status of the territories. For their compact rights to be meaningful, the people of the territories had to be able to act collectively while still in the territorial condition. If collective existence and action depended on an enabling act, then the new states were simply creatures of Congress. The definition of boundaries was therefore critical in establishing the limits, if there were any, to Congressional authority in the territories: if Congress retained a discretionary authority to change new "state" lines—either because this is what the Ordinance, construed properly, required, or because the Ordinance had no constitutional force—then the people of the territories could only rely on the good will of Congress to redeem the statehood pledge.

The constitutional legacy of the Ohio statehood movement was complex. The authoritative character of the Ordinance was apparently vindicated by the creation of the new state; everyone agreed that the Ordinance was the standard against which the actions of the new state and the national government should be measured. But debate over the interpretation of the Ordinance also showed that it was vulnerable to ambiguities and contradictions that might not be so easily resolved or ignored under different political conditions. These contradictions were rooted in the fundamental dilemma of territorial constitutionalism: how could the territories, as political communities, claim "rights" if Congress was sovereign and its authority unlimited?

The drafters of the Ordinance intended to establish a constitutional regime in the Northwest. They recognized the central importance of fixing new state boundaries in advance in order to create communities capable of exercising the rights specified in the compact articles. But the Ordinance also provided for Congressional discretion, both in defining temporary jurisdictional arrangements and in determining the number and therefore the boundaries of the new states. This flexibility was thought to be necessary because the future development of the Northwest could not be anticipated. The authors of the Ordinance believed that the size, population, and wealth of the new states was critical not only for the success and happiness of these fledgling republics, but also for the survival of a union premised on the "sovereignty" and "equality" of its members. The provision for additional states undoubtedly seemed, when it was devised, an ingenious solution to the potential conflict between the goals of fixed and flexible boundaries. Instead, by leaving Ohio's northern boundary undetermined, it guaranteed jurisdictional confusion that would finally undermine the constitutional authority of the Ordinance.

III. The Toledo War

Ohio came into the union without a fixed northern boundary. Congress's enabling act repeated the language of the Ordinance: the new state was to be bounded "on the north by an east and west line drawn through the southerly extreme of Lake Michigan." But Article VII, section 6 of the Ohio Constitution stipulated that if this line should intersect "Lake Erie east of the mouth of the Miami River of the Lake" (now known as the Maumee River), Ohio's northern boundary should be established—"with the assent of Congress"— by running a line from the bottom of Lake Michigan to the northern cape of Maumee Bay.[25] The state would thus include the future site of Toledo. Controversy focused on whether Congress had "assented" to Ohio's "constitutional line" and if, in any case, it had the authority to deviate from the Ordinance line.

Advocates of the Ohio claim argued that, though Congress did not explicitly endorse Ohio's boundary proviso, it "did assent, by receiving the State into the Union."[26] This was not apparently clear to Congress, however, when it organized Michigan Territory in 1805 with the Ordinance line as its southern boundary.[27] In 1817 Ohio authorized a survey of its "constitutional boundary" (the Harris line), but Michigan responded with a survey of its own (the Fulton line).[28] The Michigan territorial government exercised jurisdiction in the disputed region into the early 1830s. (See Map 4.)

Ohio's designs on Toledo reflected the port's anticipated importance as the terminus of the Wabash and Erie Canal. A local promoter of the state's claims conceded that "so long as this part of the state remained in a wild and unimproved condition, it mattered very little to Ohio, that the public authorities of Michigan should exercise their official functions" in the area.[29] But prospects for rapid economic growth, spurred by canal building, aroused the interest of state leaders in the old claim. A writer in the *Ohio State Journal* rhapsodized, "should the fostering care of the State be extended" over the disputed territory, "a town must inevitably spring up, second to none in importance in the whole Western country"; the town's growth "would be but little short of magic."[30]

Ohio mounted its first effective challenge to Michigan in February 1835 when the legislature ordered a survey of the northern boundary and pledged to uphold its northern claim; in June it organized Lucas County, named after the incumbent governor, Robert Lucas.[31] The Michigan Legislative Council responded with punitive measures designed "to prevent the exercise of a foreign jurisdiction" in the territory.[32] According to the *Detroit Free Press*, the leading Democratic journal, Ohio's attempt to annex federal territory constituted "treason against the United States, . . . a blow upon the Union of these States far more dangerous and destructive to it, than the Nullifiers of South Carolina aimed at."[33] Governor Stevens T. Mason ordered an expeditionary force into the disputed region; his counterpart Lucas responded by assembling troops at nearby Perrysburg. Meanwhile, President Andrew Jackson sent representatives to the region in an effort to prevent bloodshed

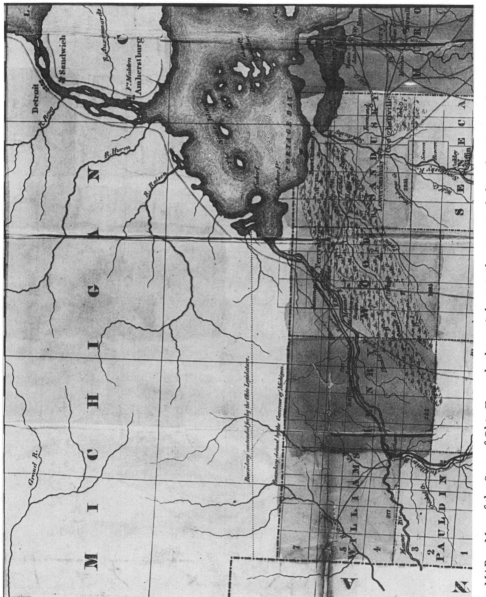

MAP 4: Map of the State of Ohio From the latest & best Authorities; Including the Census of 1830 (Detail). Engraved by A. Reed, East Windsor, Connecticut (Hartford: Silas Andrus, 1835). (Courtesy of the American Antiquarian Society)

and negotiate a settlement. Though the resulting "Toledo War" produced no casualties—only a "great flow of ink," many impassioned speeches, and a few comic opera maneuvers—it was a pivotal episode in the constitutional history of the Ordinance.[34]

The growing sentiment for statehood in Michigan offered Ohio a splendid opportunity to make good on its claims. The Ohio delegation devised the ultimately successful strategy of tying Michigan's admission to a favorable settlement of the disputed boundary. Ohio exploited its advantages as a powerful state with a large congressional delegation and a large bloc of votes in the next presidential election; Michigan was a lightly populated federal territory without voting representation in Congress. Ohio could also count on cooperation from Indiana and Illinois delegates concerned about the implications of Michigan's claims for their own boundaries.

Ohio's political advantages and the apparent weakness of its claims justified the general opinion that Michigan would be forced to sacrifice its rights under the Ordinance to gain admission.[35] Michigan's defenders sought to exploit the sympathy of disinterested observers, defining the issue as a struggle between "expediency" and "right" and portraying their territory as an American "Poland," victimized by its powerful neighbors.[36] But Michiganders, led by their "Boy Governor" Mason, would not submit without a fight. "We are the weaker party," Mason conceded,

> but we are on the side of justice, and with the guidance of HIM who never forsakes the weak, or hesitates to pursue with punishment the unjust, we cannot fail to maintain our rights against the encroachments of a powerful neighboring State.[37]

Short of divine intervention—or resorting to arms—territorial leaders saw their best hope in the adjudication of the conflicting claims before the United States Supreme Court. But in order to have standing before the Court, Michigan would have to be a state: therefore admission should precede resolution of the boundary controversy. Supporters of Michigan's claims were confident that the Court would uphold the Ordinance compacts, the "fixed and irrepealable law of the Land," a "sacred compact" and "solemn pledge."[38] John Quincy Adams told the House of Representatives that the Ordinance was "the constitution of the Northwestern Territory," a "compact as binding as any that was ever ratified by God in heaven."[39]

But the distinction between "right" and "expediency" was not as neat as Michiganders and their friends suggested. The Northwest Ordinance did not define Michigan's boundaries in the same way it did those of Ohio, Indiana, and Illinois. The Ordinance's east-west line was subject to different constructions, depending on whether it was supposed to create "vested" rights in the northern states or to protect the southern states from encroachments: Michiganders maintained that their territorial rights extended to the line, but Ohioans insisted that Congress simply pledged not to interfere with state claims south of the line, while retaining the right to set the boundary anywhere to the north. The underlying question was the extent to which Congress did, or could, exercise its discretion. When did Congress make the decision to form additional states? What rights, if any, were vested in those "states"?

IV. The Case for Michigan

Michigan's supporters insisted that Congress had committed itself to form one or two northern States in 1802 when it authorized only the southern section of the eastern "state" to draft a constitution.[40] The 1805 act creating Michigan Territory reaffirmed the "guarantees, rights, privileges, and advantages" set forth in the Ordinance. Congress "exercised the only discretionary power left" by setting the north-south boundary between the two northern "states."[41] "Any legislation of Congress altering that boundary would be null and void."[42] It followed that Congress "as completely and positively made Michigan a State" on reaching the sixty thousand population threshold "as it then was or is now in [its] power to do."[43] According to this interpretation Congress in 1805 had finished the work begun by the Continental Congress in 1787: if Congress was incapable of such self-limiting acts—at either date— the people of the territories would be left without any constitutional guarantees.

The case for Michigan rested on a distinction between "constitutional" acts or compacts and simple legislation. The distinction began with the two sections of the Northwest Ordinance: though enacted by the same authority as the compact articles, the provisions for government had no constitutional standing. Ohio's "great error," Governor Mason told the secretary of state, was that "she does not separate the first part of the Ordinance of 1787 [the government provisions], from the latter [compact articles] and thus confounds the power possessed by Congress over the first, with that of the second."[44] Michigan's defenders could not argue that Congress had no "discretion" after 1787: the Ordinance clearly left open the question of whether or not to establish additional states. Instead, they argued that Congress's subsequent acts should be interpreted in light of the Ordinance, as fulfilling the original intention of fixing the boundaries of the territorial "states."

The argument for the constitutionality of the Ordinance was strengthened by connecting it with the Virginia cession of 1784 and the resulting "compact between the General Government and the State of Virginia" which gave the United States title in the Northwest and guaranteed the formation of new and equal states.[45] The cession and the Ordinance were linked so often that one Michigan editor could refer to the "Virginian Ordinance of '87."[46] According to the standard argument, the authority of the Ordinance depended on a prior compact and was confirmed and elaborated in subsequent acts of Congress. By virtue of the cession, one writer explained, the United States had become a "trustee, holding the land by a deed of trust for the use of the state of Virginia, the original proprietor, and the other states as copartners." In discharging its resulting obligations, Congress drafted the Northwest Ordinance, thus entering "into a second compact with the settlers of the territory." Because every settler "thereby became a party to the contract," Congress could not tamper with its provisions: "It is a question altogether out of the pale of the legislative expediency."[47] Ohioans who objected to their state's belligerent policy agreed: "This ordinance, being a compact between the old and new states can never be revoked, or infringed."[48]

Inspired by such arguments, territorial Democrats took the lead in promoting Michigan's claims, even to the point of challenging the authority of Congress. "The people of Michigan perfectly understand their rights," the editor of the *Emigrant* proclaimed in September 1834, and they "are perfectly able to assert them. We had rather become a State by our own Sovereign independent act, than under the leading, assisting, moulding hand of Congress."[49] The *Argus* agreed: "every person must be convinced that we had nothing to hope from Congress—that we must depend upon our own exertions to gain admittance into the Union."[50] In just such a defiant mood, delegates convened in Ann Arbor in May 1835 and, without benefit of a congressional enabling act, drafted a constitution and organized a state government.[51]

The key premise of the Michigan claims defense was that there was a necessary and controlling connection among distinct congressional acts over a half century. In this constitutional context, the "ordinance may be considered as it were a part of the federal constitution itself."[52] As the "citizens of the Territory" told Congress in March 1836,

> The people of Michigan have been accustomed to consider the Ordinance of 1787 as their unchangeable and fundamental law. They have been accustomed to look to its provisions as their sufficient guaranty, not only for the protection of all their personal and civil rights, but also, when viewed in connection with the subsequent action of Congress, as their ample pledge for the preservation to them of that southern territorial boundary which its provisions indicate.[53]

Michiganders sought to defend the territorial integrity of their embryonic "state," as it was defined in the territorial organic act of 1805.[54] But what sort of political community was the Territory supposed to be? The citizens of Shelby, Michigan, explained, "although our power is less sovereign and unlike that of an independent State, we have nevertheless vested rights."[55] Therefore, according to "Michigan's Appeal," "as well might Congress change the boundaries of any State in the Union as those of this Territory."[56]

In April 1835, shortly before the first Ann Arbor convention, a writer in the *Argus* asserted that "the people of the Territory have the right *now* to form a constitution and state government; that by the ordinance of '87 this right is secured to them, and that Congress has not the power to abridge it, or to control them in its exercise."[57] Appealing to the authority of the "same excellent ordinance," Michigan Democrats then urged voters to ratify the new constitution and thus uphold the southern boundary. "Our title" to statehood derived from "a right vested in us by the ordinance": Ohio's challenge to the "integrity of our territorial limits forbidding any further delay, the example of Tennessee in analagous circumstances was adopted; and the constitution now presented to your acceptance is the result."[58]

Michigan was in some sense a "state" while still a territory, both by virtue of its predetermined boundaries and because of its automatic right to admission when its population within those limits numbered sixty thousand. According to Governor Mason, the Ordinance gave the people of Michigan "territorial being" and thus authorized them to claim the privileges of statehood.[59] The (unrecognized) Michigan delegation attempted to resolve terminological confusion in a lengthy letter to the Senate Judiciary committee early in 1836:

> It is, then, evident that Congress, in all these resolutions and compacts, have used the phrases "Territory" and "States" as synonomous; that they have spoken of Territories as *States* before they became States in fact, and even before they were divided into specific territorial governments[.] Congress [in the 1805 act] gave a pledge to the people of that Territory, thus specifically bounded by distinct lines, that it should with these boundaries, be a *State*.

The delegates concluded that "Territories, when established with specific boundaries, are incipient States." The argument that Congress had constitutional authority to exercise unlimited power in the territories and over the state-making process was fallacious, and doubly so in "that great territory ceded to the United States upon conditions embraced in the solemn compact making the cession."[60]

From the beginning, statehood advocates recognized that fixed boundaries were the basis of territorial constitutional claims. In 1831 territorial Governor Lewis Cass echoed arguments formerly advanced by Ohioans against Governor St. Clair's attempt to redraw state boundaries in the Northwest: if boundaries could be changed, "our whole country may be thus subdivided, and our admission into the Union indefinitely postponed."[61] The *Michigan Sentinel* warned that "If the claims of Ohio are yielded to, the whole tier of [our] Southern counties . . . will be reduced to a mere skeleton," radically diminishing the territory's resources and population. The result of "such alterations and cutting down," the Monroe editor later concluded, would be that Michigan might never acquire "the population necessary to form a State." This clearly was "not the intention of those who formed the deservedly celebrated ordinance of 1787."[62]

V. The Case for Ohio

Ohioans were insistent that Michigan could enjoy no vested rights under the Ordinance. Congressman Samuel F. Vinton, one of the most vigorous defenders of Ohio's claims, came to the conclusion that the compact articles had no constitutional force: "The ordinance of 1787 is unquestionably an act of legislation"; "so far as it contemplates further and future legislation," it is "the proper subject . . . of legislative discretion."[63] Other Ohioans were reluctant to dismiss the Ordinance so categorically, however, arguing instead that Michigan could claim no benefit from its provisions until admitted to the union. In the meantime, Article V gave Congress discretion over territorial boundaries.

A joint select committee of the Ohio House and Senate conceded the Ordinance "to be unalterable." But it "defines no Territory, and has no application to any power less than an organized State": "Michigan has no boundary but an imaginary one" and therefore no claim to existence as a political community.[64] The Territory did not have the legal standing to claim "rights" of any kind; indeed, Congress still might decide to incorporate it into Ohio, as that state's enabling act provided. Governor Lucas asked, "What Territory was ever found, when a State, with the same boundaries over which the jurisdiction of the Territorial Government was extended?"[65] The answer was none: the relation between a territory and its successor state was not a necessary one and their jurisdictions were never fully coincidental. "Statehood" began when Congress, in its discretionary wisdom, so decided. Only then, the Ohioans claimed, did the compact articles of the Ordinance become effective.

If a territory could claim no vested rights, it had no true corporate identity before statehood. As a result, the *Toledo Gazette* editorialized, Michigan's "present position" was "an enigma." Although "an acknowledged dependent, and an unauthorized agent in the controversy for jurisdiction," Michigan had the temerity to declare "war against a Sovereign State of the Union."[66] Even the editor of the *Cleveland Herald*, an opponent of Governor Lucas's war policy, was appalled at Michigan's presumption:

> She is yet under the pupilage care and protection of the General Government. She is wholly subject to any disposition which congress may feel disposed to make of the Territory, which she claims as her own. For Michigan, then—a Territory which lives merely by permission of the General Government, to attempt by carrying out the principles of nullification and State rights, to enforce her claims to the disputed Territory, is as absurd as it is ridiculous.[67]

Ohioans insisted on the distinction between "territory" and "state" that Michiganders increasingly rejected, particularly after proclaiming their own statehood.

Michigan could have no standing in a judicial proceeding. "Michigan Territory is nothing more than a Corporation, existing by the breath of the General Government," "Citizen" wrote in the *Scioto Gazette*: it lacked the "political character which might give her the right to contest Ohio's claim."[68] Therefore, advocates of Ohio's claims wanted Congress to decide the border dispute as a "political" question, without reference to "right." Congress had absolute authority over the territories: a territory was "a mere *political agency* of the United States," Vinton explained: "It has none of the attributes of independence or sovereignty."[69] Before a territory was formed into a state, Congress could change its boundaries. Furthermore, according to Governor Lucas's reading of Article V, "it is in the power of Congress, at any moment previous to the actual admission of Michigan into the Union as a Sovereign State, to dissolve the Territorial Government, and attach the whole Northwestern Territory to the three States already formed."[70] In other words, the Ohio select committee warned, Congress still could, "by a stroke of the pen . . . blot her out of existence."[71]

Ohioans insisted that the authors of the Ordinance had reserved to Congress a discretionary power over boundaries because of contemporary ignorance about the region's geography and uncertainty about its prospects for development. While the lines separating the three southern states from each other were specified, the location of lines to the north—if any were necessary—was left to the judgment of a later Congress. What then was the point of the controversial east-west line, which Michiganders considered their southern boundary? Ohioans answered that the Ordinance was designed to restrict congressional discretion to interfere with the claims of the new states formed *south* of that line. Without this "prohibition against extending the Northern State or States to the Southward," the jurisdiction—and thus the very existence—of Ohio, Indiana, and Illinois were in continuing jeopardy.[72]

The principle of state equality and the constitutional guarantee of state territory meant that Congress could alter territorial, but not state boundaries.

Ohio's northern boundary had been set forth in the state constitution. Congress reviewed that document before recognizing the new state and admitting its representatives, and thus (at least tacitly) approved the boundary proviso. Governor Lucas had always "been of the opinion that the question was settled when Congress adopted our Constitution without objections to any part thereof."[73] The attempt of the United States to exercise jurisdiction in the disputed district through its territorial government was supposed to be an assault on Ohio's state sovereignty. The Ohio senate protested that, under the federal Constitution, neither the president nor officials acting under his authority in Michigan could "levy war against the people of any State of this Union." The attack on state jurisdiction was "subversive of the rights and liberties of the people."[74] Ohioans argued that Congress had no power to interfere with state boundaries: as the pro-Ohio *Toledo Gazette* proclaimed, if Congress disregarded the "unalienable rights of these states" the effect "would inevitably be, to drive them from the Union."[75] "We will have our rights in spite of all the world," a young Ohioan wrote Governor Lucas: "there is not a single young Buckeye that will not follow you through blood to their eyes."[76]

Ohio's rhetorical bluster matched its belligerent posturing in the "Toledo War." In fact, most Ohioans supported Michigan statehood—if the new state was properly circumscribed. Ohio did "not forget," as a New York paper reminded her, "that she herself had been a territory" and "that the territories are infant States, under the guardianship and protection of the . . . United States."[77] Nor did Governor Lucas and his allies anticipate any sustained conflict either with the territory or the federal government. After all, the goal of Ohio policy—and the point of its bluster—was to convince Congress to confirm its northern boundary claims.

Ohioans generally stopped short of rejecting the Ordinance as a constitutional document.[78] Their key premise—that Congress should continue to exercise its discretion in rearranging new state boundaries—was, after all, compatible with one of the Ordinance's original goals, to guarantee new state equality and the survival of the union. It followed from this interpretation, however, that the boundaries specified in the Ordinance were irrelevant to the present controversy. "In the nature of things as well as by constitutional provision," the *Cleveland Whig* editorialized, "the matter of erecting new states and determining their boundaries, is the business of Congress."[79] Confident Congress would endorse the state's claims, Ohioans disclaimed any intention of "nullifying" national authority. The practical result of their position was to magnify congressional power over the territories while de-priving territorial populations of any effective "constitutional" guarantees.

VI. The Will of Congress

The Michigan-Ohio controversy illuminated the contradiction between fixed and flexible boundaries that was inherent in Article V of the Ordinance. The east-west line through the southerly extreme of Lake Michigan had the virtue of being defined in advance, in unmistakable terms. But in order to secure lake frontage to both Indiana and Illinois, Congress had already revised the line—with the "consent" of those states, although without the consent of the yet nonexistent "states" to the north.[80] Adhering to the Ordinance line would have left Ohio without any access to Lake Erie at all, an embarrassing fact to the Michiganders, who had to disclaim any intention of perfecting their state's "right" to the northern Ohio counties.[81] Such considerations made the natural boundaries argument seem compelling. As the *Indiana Journal* concluded, Congress "cannot fail to perceive the expedi-ency of dividing, as far as practicable, the lake privileges between the several states formed and to be formed in the northwest territory, so that our channels of commerce may not be obstructed by state lines."[82]

The problem with the natural boundaries idea was that it was subject to so many different interpretations and applications. Michigan and Ohio pro-pagandists, for instance, differed on the prospects for Michigan's develop-ment with or without the Toledo strip. Its loss would be "seriously felt," according to the Michigan constitutional convention: "the nature of the country upon her northern frontier, will forever prevent her from being classed among the large states of the union."[83] Michigan would be "reduced to a mere skeleton. . . . [T]he relative importance of the Territory will be lessened" and, of course, "her admission into the Union retarded for a series of years to come."[84] "What security have the smaller states"—like Michi-gan—if large states—like Ohio—may "advance pretensions to the territory of any other, and proceed without obstruction to its forcible possession?"[85] Although already "A state overgrown with almost boundless territory," Ohio was unaccountably "anxious to wrench from little Michigan her rightful soil."[86] Michiganders argued that the principle of state equality was in jeopardy:

> In the future political destinies of the country, it is important that the States formed and to be formed, in the west and northwest, should be as equal as may be in the extent and capability of territory, and in the scale of power and influence.

Insisting that Michigan was in any case "destined always to be the weakest and the most exposed of the Northwestern States," defenders of the territory's claims concluded that the Ordinance line was not only "constitutional" but "far more *natural*" than the one claimed by Ohio.[87]

Ohioans dismissed the idea that Ohio *was* a large state. Vinton pointed out that only two of the sixteen southern and western states were smaller than Ohio. By contrast, "the great difficulty" with the northern part of the old Northwest Territory "will be not in dividing it into two States which shall be *large enough*, but into two *small enough*, having a due regard to the relative extent of the other States in the Union."[88] But was geographical extent an adequate measure of potential population growth and economic development? How could Michigan be made "equal" to Ohio?

Congress's answer, embodied in the Michigan enabling act of June 1836, was to capitulate to Ohio by ratifying its northern boundary claim while compensating the new state by extending its jurisdiction over the Upper Peninsula.[89] According to Michigan hardliners, both changes violated the new state's constitution as well as Article V of the Ordinance. In any case, the "compensation" was practically worthless. The editor of the *Michigan Sentinel* saw the jurisdictional exchange as "the bartering away of our Southern Boundary for the frozen sand hills of Lake Superior."[90] This "cold and inhospitable land, somewhere towards the polar regions" was, in the view of the *Pontiac Courier*, "fit only for the habitation of white bears, frogs, and tortoises."[91] The *Adrian Watch-Tower* wondered whether "it is also contemplated to remove the citizens of Michigan to this . . . *American Siberia*."[92] For their part, the people of the Upper Peninsula had little enthusiasm for being grafted on to the new state: they had long chafed under the "colonial" rule of Michigan Territory and had taken no part in drafting and ratifying the state constitution.[93]

Michigan's defenders challenged Congress's right to add territory to, or subtract it from, the new state.[94] But they no longer entertained hopes that Michigan's rights under the Ordinance would be vindicated. The enabling act "rudely violated the compact of '87" and was therefore an "unconstitutional law."[95] Yet Michigan had no recourse: Congress's action showed that it did not accept the idea that Article V had any constitutional force. If Michigan had "rights" derived from the Ordinance, these rights were no longer "constitutional." Now Michigan would have to vindicate its claims against the United States, not Ohio. As the United States Supreme Court later decided, the question had become political: as far as it was concerned, no rights under the federal Constitution were at issue.[96]

Once Congress had acted to resolve the claims controversy, the practical question became how—or whether—the Michigan constitution would be amended to conform with Congress's will. Snarling Wolverines, "regarding the boundary of the state as inseparable from the constitution," opposed any concession as an "act of self degradation."[97] By accepting Congress's terms and "failing to maintain the rights of the state to sovereignty and to soil" the state's leaders would "place us at once upon a footing infinitely beneath our sister states."[98] Robert Clark, a candidate for the convention called to consider Congress's offer, put the issue neatly: "Michigan as bounded by this [enabling] act . . . is not the Michigan for which our Constitution was formed." If Michigan accepted Congress's definition of its boundaries, "our Constitution will not be one formed by our people, but one imposed upon us by Congress."[99]

Notwithstanding this brave rhetoric, few Michiganders were willing to hold out against Congress indefinitely. The many advantages of statehood outweighed the loss of a few townships.[100] After having inveighed against the Ohio "nullifiers," Michigan's leaders were uncomfortable in their new role as states' rights advocates against the federal government. The status of the new state remained in doubt as long as the territorial jurisdiction remained in force. Urging his colleagues to adjourn, one state senator asserted that "it is the height of absurdity . . . that two independent sovereignties, each supreme in its own authority can exist at the same time in the same State."[101] And many citizens in the disputed territory undoubtedly agreed with "Peace and Union," who did not consider the outcome of the controversy worth "one drop of blood." "What is the difference to us whether we reside in this or that of the five [Ordinance] States?"[102] Michigan Democrats who had formerly promoted the new state's independent assumption of authority, now pushed for a resolution of the boundary question. After another convention refused Congress's terms, a third constitutional convention, meeting at Ann Arbor in December 1836, finally accepted them, and Michigan was admitted to the union on January 26, 1837.[103]

VII. Territorial Constitutionalism

What were the constitutional implications of Michigan's delayed admission? Michigan had drafted a constitution without congressional authorization and had functioned for more than a year as an independent state. Congress finally set the new state's boundaries but required that a convention of the people "assent" to them. Michigan was thus a self-constituted state, following in the footsteps of Vermont and Tennessee and putting into practice what was soon known as "territorial" or "popular sovereignty." At the same time, however, until it was admitted Congress exercised its authority over territorial and new state boundaries. The people were "sovereign," but Congress—by altering boundaries—could determine who the "people" were. This untidy state of affairs was symptomatic of the conceptual muddle that marked the collapse of territorial constitutionalism.

The constitutional future of the territories may have been problematic, but the status of the Northwest Ordinance was not: Congress no longer would consider itself bound by the promises of the compact articles. Whether Article V was dismissed as mere legislation or whether it was interpreted as a mandate for continuing congressional discretion, the result was the same: it did not stipulate "state" boundaries for either of the two northern states and thus did not constitute communities capable of claiming and exercising rights. If the Ordinance still articulated the "principles" of the territorial system, these principles were no longer specific and enforceable. Because a territory could not claim jurisdictional rights before statehood, territorial "rights" were cut adrift from the Constitution. The Northwest Ordinance was not, as Michigan Governor Mason and his allies had once thought, "a part of the federal constitution itself."[104]

Under the Northwest Ordinance, claims to statehood, fixed boundaries, and other constitutional guarantees were designed to constitute a complex of binding promises. As titleholder to the western lands, the United States as embodied in the Continental Congress had had no misgivings about converting its domain into private property. The terms of sale included the promise of eventual statehood: each purchase was in a sense a "compact" reaffirming the Ordinance and through it the original compact with Virginia on which Congress based its title.

The constitutional authority of the Northwest Ordinance as a charter for new western states was probably self-evident in 1787. Its formal defects were not then as clear as they would later become: procedural standards for constitution writing were still ambiguous and were not, in any case, relevant to the case at hand. But the history of state making in the Northwest raised questions about the intentions of the Ordinance's framers and about the interpretation of its specific provisions. The resulting controversies exposed the Ordinance to a scrutiny that finally it could not bear. For instance, the crucial boundary stipulation in Article V could be read in light of the framers' goal of fixing jurisdictional limits in advance. Thus the Michigan Legislative Council concluded that the drafters of the ordinance meant to secure the territorial integrity of the new "states" to be formed in the Northwest:

> when the conditions on which the whole Northwestern Territory was ceded to the Union are adverted to, guarantying, as those conditions do, to every part of that Territory rights and privileges which could be secured only by fixed boundaries, that language does not admit of doubt.[105]

Or the proviso that Congress could form one or two additional states could be read as a mandate for its continuing discretion to secure "natural boundaries" and state equality. Pro-Ohio petitioners from the disputed district insisted that "the power was reserved to Congress to alter or modify the line as to secure to each . . . those advantages which nature seemed to have prepared and designed for the respective divisions to which they belonged."[106]

The constitutional complex thus began to fall apart: compact boundary provisions and the statehood pledge were dissociated. The statehood promise—which was logically empty if boundaries could be changed—was embraced by popular sovereignty theorists and translated from a specific "constitutional" right into the airy realms of higher law. As a constitutional document the Ordinance could not survive the contradictions and ambiguities that became so apparent in the struggle between Ohio and Michigan over the Toledo strip. The Ordinance would no longer "command general assent and respect"; it ceased to function as a constitution for new states.

Yet if the paper war of the 1830s over the meaning and application of the Northwest Ordinance exposed the document's contradictions and limitations, it also provided eloquent testimony to the nearly universal support for the constitutional *ideal* that had guided the American territorial system since its founding. Territories would not be held in perpetual dependency but could look forward to statehood and membership in the union. It was one of the tragedies of American constitutional history that the statehood promise should be cut loose from an authoritative constitutional document, binding on Congress and prospective new states alike. For it was in this constitutional vacuum that the crisis of the union would unfold.

6.

Slavery and Freedom

☆ ☆ ☆ ☆ ☆ ☆

The Northwest Ordinance guaranteed that the territories would be formed into states. But what kind of political communities would emerge in the new states? Here was where the particular concerns of enterprising settlers converged with broader questions of political economy: what were the most propitious conditions for the development of the new states as well as for the success of individual enterprises? In the broadest sense, this was a "constitutional" question: provisions made at the founding of these new states would determine their future growth and prosperity. But, because the debate about the development of the Northwest centered on the authority of the Ordinance compact excluding slavery from the region, it was also a constitutional question in a much narrower sense.

In the protracted controversy over the meaning of Article VI, northwesterners sought to establish both the original intentions of its authors and their authority to bind subsequent generations. The absence of clear testimony by congressmen on the slavery issue and subsequent disagreement about the inviolability of Ordinance "compacts" matched the confusion of conflicting prescriptions for regional development, with or without slavery.[1] As late as the Illinois convention struggle of 1823–1824, slavery proponents could argue plausibly that population grew and the economy developed most rapidly where slavery was legal; at the same time, those who opposed legalization of slavery in the Ordinance states invoked the ideology of private enterprise and free markets—as well as recent census data—to demonstrate the comparative advantages of freedom. Fundamental constitutional and economic issues remained unresolved. As a result, northwesterners could agree neither on what they could do nor on what they should do to guarantee the future wealth and welfare of their rising new states.

I. Prospects for Development

Massachusetts delegate Nathan Dane proposed Article VI just before the final text of the document was adopted. Dane confessed that he "had no idea the States would agree" to the slavery prohibition, the more so because "only Massachusetts of the Eastern States, was present."[2] Dane's surprise betrayed his unfamiliarity with the thinking of his southern colleagues. Even in a period of rising sectional consciousness, southern leaders did not see slavery exclusion as a threat to their vital interests. Instead, northern and southern interests seemed to harmonize in plans for western development.

The idea of excluding slavery from the Northwest had been proposed several times before being incorporated in the 1787 Ordinance. In 1783, Colonel Timothy Pickering included a slavery ban in his proposal for a military colony in the Ohio country.[3] Thomas Jefferson's draft of the 1784 Ordinance for territorial government provided that "after the year 1800 of the Christian aera, there shall be neither slavery nor involuntary servitude in any of the said states." Much to Jefferson's disgust, the failure of one of the two other Virginia delegates (or of North Carolinian Richard Dobbs Spaight) to support his proposal meant that it fell one state short of congressional approval.[4] The idea resurfaced in March 1785 in a resolution offered by Rufus King of Massachusetts that used wording very close to Jefferson's. King called for an immediate ban on slavery, however, while securing slaveowners' interests by providing for the rendition of fugitives. King's resolution was committed, then amended, and finally abandoned altogether as Congress focused its energies on completing the May 1785 Land Ordinance. But King's language, including the fugitive slave clause, was repeated almost exactly in the version offered by his friend Dane in July 1787.[5]

When the Ordinance later became a key text for antislavery constitutionalism, commentators sought to explain this unique triumph for the principles of freedom in the founding era. These writers clearly exaggerated the contemporary importance of Article VI. Despite the obvious links between successive proposals to exclude slavery from federal territory, their authors had little sense of participating in an ongoing, epochal struggle to expand the sway of free institutions. Paul Finkelman, the most careful student of the legislative history of the article, suggests that "the lack of debate . . . or comment" on the exclusion clause shows that "it was not considered particularly important."[6] Subsequent controversy over the authorship of Article VI—Jefferson, King, and Dane were the leading candidates—reflects radically inflated estimates of its significance in later years.

Certainly a sizable number of the American founders were opposed to slavery, on conscientious or prudential grounds. But the idea that there was a coherent group of congressmen working to exclude slavery from the national domain is the invention of nineteenth-century publicists in search of a usable past. Nor was there a proslavery bloc, ready to resist any assault on the institution. In fact, delegates from states with large slave populations, the overwhelming majority in Congress in July 1787, unanimously voted to prohibit slavery in the Northwest.

Early attitudes toward slavery in the Northwest Territory depended on assessments of the future direction of regional development. Southerners were confident that new western states—with or without slavery—would be drawn into their orbit.[7] According to George Washington, Jefferson, and other promoters of western development, the primary bonds between Virginia and the Ohio frontier would be commercial. The "union" between South and West would not be grounded in a common commitment to slavery; on the contrary, because slavery might deter industrious settlers from New England—the best available source—southerners did not hesitate to vote against the extension of slavery across the Ohio.

Southerners could agree to limit slavery for a variety of reasons. Some congressmen were so eager to complete the Ohio Company sale and begin paying off the national debt that they were predisposed to accept last-minute terms proposed by company agent Manasseh Cutler. Some "Southern members," reported Virginian William Grayson, wanted to preempt competition from Northwestern slaveowners cultivating "Tobacco and Indigo"; others may have linked the future of republican government to the spread of grain production and free labor.[8] And Virginians particularly looked to compact, orderly settlement in the Northwest to provide a strategic buffer for the extended, exposed Kentucky frontier. The common ground in each case was a concern with promoting rapid, yet orderly settlement north of the Ohio. Because nature —helped along by proposed improvements in river transportation and canals—decreed that frontier farmers would resort to Alexandria and other Chesapeake markets, western development inevitably would enrich Virginia and Maryland while guaranteeing their enduring economic and political union with the new western states.

In the context of early territorial policy, the slavery issue was only of secondary importance. Rather than being a controversial question of principle or interest separating northerners and southerners, slavery exclusion was subordinate to the overriding concern with development and union. Significantly, debates over what to do with the national domain did not generate alternative visions of frontier development premised on distinctive political economies. The future role southerners projected for the Northwest did not depend on slavery; at the least, their interest in orderly settlement and the spread of commercial agriculture was not incompatible with keeping slavery out of the region. It may be anachronistic to infer a positive preference for free labor in contemporary thinking about western economic development. But slaveholders could accept the ban on slavery as the condition of a process of development north of the Ohio that served their interests. At the same time, of course, slaveholders looking for fresh lands could turn to extensive land reserves where the southern states retained jurisdiction.[9]

The visionary scheme of rapid northwestern settlement and commercial union with the Chesapeake soon foundered. At first, most commentators endorsed the view that the course of empire—and population—was westward. Within limits set by climate, soil quality, and the natural facilities for trade and communication along the "western waters," they predicted that population would spread continuously and evenly across the territory.[10] But until Tecumseh's death in 1813, intermittent Indian wars gave more peaceful frontiers a competitive advantage and retarded population growth and economic development. As a result, slavery exclusion became more and more controversial, with debate centering on whether or not the Northwest would be able to compete successfully against other possible emigration sites for a fair share of the westward flow of population.

During the state-making era in the Northwest, opponents and defenders of the slavery exclusion article alike challenged the assumption that population would grow inexorably toward some inevitable man-to-land ratio. The territory's labor system was a crucial variable. The operative question became: what potential settlers would the exclusion of slavery exclude from the territory? In asking this question, the assumption that emigration was homogenous—or easily homogenized—was also subverted. Participants in the debate were forced to look beyond the territory to the sources of emigration. Their first question would be empirical: how many settlers could be drawn from slave states or free states? Subsequent questions were more obviously value laden: why did or would southerners come to the territory? Did they want to escape slavery or to extend its sway? Implicit in this line of questioning was skepticism about the political character of southerners and their fitness for membership in the new republics forming on the Ohio River, a prejudice amply reciprocated in southern settlers' aspersions on "Yankee" character.

The slavery issue naturally heightened sectional consciousness in the Northwest, both in sharpening the perception of a sectional distinction in the United States generally and in recreating the cleavage in the territory. (It should be emphasized, however, that alignments on the slavery question were not simply determined by place of birth.[11]) Controversy over Article VI also focused attention on the appropriateness of different regions within the Northwest for different kinds of agriculture—and labor systems. Distinctions within the potential emigrant pool were thus mirrored in a fracturing of the homogenous landscape. Different areas would develop differently, both because they were suited to different crops and because slave or free labor was, in turn, supposedly better suited to those crops. The inevitable conclusion was that development could not be assumed: it was contingent and therefore determined by political decisions. And because those decisions depended on how Article VI was read—or rewritten—slavery became a leading constitutional issue in the state-making process.

II. Ohio

"The gradual progress of improvement fills the mind with delectable ideas," Arthur St. Clair told the people of Marietta when he arrived there in July 1788 to assume his duties as territorial governor. The "pleasure" of seeing "vast forests converted into arable fields, and cities rising in places which were lately the habitations of wild beasts" was "something like that" of witnessing "creation" itself. "Situated, as you are, in the most temperate climate, favored with the most fertile soil, surrounded by the noblest and most beautiful rivers, every portion of labor will meet its due reward."[12] As the landscape became transformed, population would grow rapidly and new states would soon be formed. "Candid, well informed & judicious men" were convinced, one western writer claimed in 1789, that within two or three decades "there will be as many inhabitants settled on the western waters" as in the Atlantic states.[13]

The sluggish pace of land sales and settlement soon undermined this optimism. Seeking to explain why it was so difficult in practice to exploit their natural advantages, northwesterners came to radically different conclusions about the proper role of the national government. Federalist supporters of the St. Clair regime complained about Indian depredations, suggesting that a stronger national presence capable of guaranteeing law and order was essential to attracting large numbers of industrious (read: New England) settlers to the region.[14] In response, territorial Republicans, including Virginians settled along the Scioto and in the Virginia Military District, argued that the high-handed St. Clair administration deterred potential immigrants: the region would only develop rapidly when settlers could govern themselves. An attack on the "overbearing and ambitious aristocratic influence" of the territorial government published in Republican editor William Duane's *Philadelphia Aurora* insisted that "many persons residing in the eastern and middle states would long since have added to the number of the inhabitants of the North Western Territory, if they could repose confidence in the government."[15]

The slow pace of population growth focused attention on the sources of immigration. Prescriptions for stimulating settlement reflected the imperatives of partisan competition in the territory as Republicans sought to depose St. Clair and bring on statehood. They also suggested distinctive appeals to potential settlers in different parts of the country. Territorial Federalists sought reinforcement from New England, while Republicans were confident that migration from the middle and southern states would secure their popular preponderance. Federalists raised the slavery issue by charging that their opponents meant to draw southern slaveholders to the territory, rush to statehood and then, under the pretext of the new state's sovereignty, abrogate Article VI.

The authors of congressional western policy had agreed to exclude slavery as part of a larger program for the rapid development of the trans-Ohio frontier. Assuming an insatiable demand for new lands, they set a relatively high price on federal lands in order to raise revenue, while recruiting only the most orderly and industrious settlers to the national domain and preempting the dangerously disorderly and the potentially disloyal.

For at least some early northwesterners, however, the exclusion of slavery was simply another handicap for the region in competing for new settlers. They pressed for land on easier terms both to promote their own enterprises and to attract newcomers. Looking east, they asked how the Northwest could draw away a share of the enormous movement of settlers headed toward the southwestern frontier. One obvious answer was to allow slaveholders to bring their "property" with them across the Ohio. To critics of Article VI the founders' plans for regional development seemed misguided at best. In practice, they concluded, the federal government's selfish and short-sighted goal was to draw as much land sales revenue as possible from western settlers.

Although the impact of slavery exclusion on population growth and economic development was only a minor theme in the Ohio statehood movement, the main lines of subsequent controversy were already apparent. Few northwesterners were prepared to argue openly for legalizing slavery. But supporters of the embattled St. Clair regime sometimes interpreted criticisms of the Federalist governor as covert pleas for legalization. (In light of St. Clair's prior record of upholding slaveholders' claims by insisting on a narrow interpretation of Article VI, these charges are somewhat surprising.) Thus statehood proponent Edward Tiffin was supposed to be advocating slavery when he argued that "men of wealth and independence of sentiment" would be deterred from emigrating to the territory "because they cannot brook the idea of living under a government like ours."[16] Tiffin's premise was that St. Clair's unpopular "colonial" administration put the Northwest at a relative disadvantage in competing with other potential migration sites, both in the United States and in neighboring European colonies; if settlers went elsewhere, population would be retarded and political privileges delayed. But it is not surprising that St. Clair's friends should find a deeper, more sinister meaning in Tiffin's argument. In truth, relatively few settlers worried much about their political "degradation": emigration to the Northwest had been sluggish not because of St. Clair's bad reputation, but because it took so long to pacify the Indian frontier. The only "men of wealth" likely to avoid the territory because of its scheme of government under the Ordinance were slaveholders.

Federalists with misgivings about statehood explicitly connected the slavery issue with the problem of population growth and political development. Answering Tiffin's attack on the territorial government, a "Hamilton Farmer" predicted that if the Virginians succeeded in rushing Ohio toward statehood, "we should have gentlemen enough, and their negroes too." Once they "get their Negroes brought here . . . they would be riding over us with their coaches, and we should be obliged to go out along with their negroes to make roads for them."[17] Rumors circulated that other prominent Republicans also favored slavery. "We have hot times about slavery and Republicanism," Return Jonathan Meigs, Jr., learned from a correspondent in Athens. "News is spreading here that you want such a system adopted." Of course, he added, such rumors were nothing more than "Federal villainy; the party is weak here, but d——d saucy."[18]

Federalists exploited rumors that southern settlers in the Virginia Military District considered the slavery prohibition unconstitutional. "Republicanus" published a fictitious "toast" in the *Ohio Gazette* (Marietta), supposedly by a Republican: give me "forty negro slaves, [and] a good living and I am content."[19] Proslavery elements allegedly argued that legalization of slavery would attract settlers from across the Ohio and "make the State rich."[20] Another writer in the Marietta newspaper had a simple explanation for Republican statehood agitation: "some are sure this is to be a favorable time to introduce slavery into this territory," while others simply wished "to be promoted under the state government."[21]

During the statehood struggle few public figures dared advocate the abrogation of Article VI and the introduction of slaves. John C. Macan, unsuccessful candidate for the state constitutional convention, thought that the principle of state equality demanded that the new state retain the power to decide the issue for itself—"a privilege," he noted, "which almost every state in the union holds as a just right."[22] But most Republicans vigorously disavowed this early nineteenth-century equivalent of "popular sovereignty." Although the constitutional convention narrowly circumscribed the rights of free black settlers, the completed document also incorporated the wording of Article VI on slavery.[23] Deference to the large number of Yankee settlers in the territory as well as their own abhorrence of the peculiar institution precluded any serious attempt to tamper with the article: indeed, fidelity to Article VI became a kind of political litmus test in early Ohio politics. The "freeborn Sons" of Ohio were toasted at an Independence Day celebration in Cincinnati in 1806: "true to the rights of humanity, and the principles of liberty," they would "never permit the foul form of slavery to tread on their sacred soil."[24]

III. Indiana

Pressure for suspension, modification, or abrogation of Article VI was more pronounced in outlying regions of the Northwest Territory. The first petition to Congress for repeal of the slavery exclusion clause was drawn up at Kaskaskia, in the Illinois country, in 1796.[25] The petitioners claimed that the prohibition of slavery was an "*ex post facto*" law, depriving pre-1787 slaveholders of "property" previously secured to them. Insecurity about the status of the so-called "French slaves" had already driven some early Illinoisans across the river to Spanish Louisiana where slavery remained legal. Article VI thus worked not only to deter potential emigrants but perhaps even to diminish the existing population.[26] This concern with population growth—or loss—was heightened by the distance of the Illinois country from the line of settlement and uncertainty about the development potential of the unfamiliar prairie region.

The Kaskaskia petitioners' initiative against Article VI gained momentum as successive divisions of the territory established new governments to the west, beyond Ohio's Yankee frontier. Southerners dominated Indiana and Illinois territorial history, and a sizable number of them, particularly those in leadership positions (including many slaveowners), wanted to open the region to the further importation of slaves. Their petitions betrayed an ambivalent attitude toward the authority of the Northwest Ordinance. Its articles could not be considered true "compacts" because, as the Kaskaskia petition explained, "they were made *ex parte* by the original States only." No one in the territory had consented to these articles: in fact, their spokesmen assured Congress, had the people of the territory been asked for such consent in 1787, they would have refused it. Slavery proponents did not proceed to the logical conclusion that the Ordinance was unconstitutional and therefore void. By the very act of petitioning, successive petitioners deferred to Congress's authority to revise, rescind—or uphold—the Ordinance compacts. But their suggestion that the people of the territory would have favored slavery in 1787, and still did in 1796, implied a more dynamic, "democratic," proto-popular sovereignty conception of consent that became explicit in later proslavery agitation. The Ordinance could be altered if the "parties" to the compacts—the original states, represented in Congress, and the people of the projected new states—consented.

In subsequent years proslavery forces sought to manifest their "consent" to the abrogation of Article VI so that a simple, reciprocal act by Congress could have constitutional effect. Thus, Virginian William Henry Harrison, Indiana's first territorial governor, orchestrated a territorial convention at Vincennes in 1802 that resolved, in the name of the "People of Indiana Territory," to "agree that the operation of the Sixth Article . . . should be suspended for the space of ten years."[27] In 1805, petitioners from Illinois sought a separate territorial government within the boundaries "alloted, in the fifth article of compact . . . to form the western state," while offering their "consent" to a modification of Article VI that would "admit. . . slavery."[28]

Efforts to circumvent Article VI did not overtly challenge its constitutional authority. But the impact of proslavery arguments ultimately proved subversive. Proslavery polemics emphasized defects in the original form of the compacts—notably in the alleged absence of competent parties—and suggested that "consent" could be more authoritatively obtained by referring the question to Congress and to the people of the territory or new state. The significance of the proslavery campaign to rewrite the Ordinance was not so much that it failed to win congressional approval for overturning Article VI, but rather that it promoted the idea that the Ordinance's authority was contingent, not perpetual. The Ordinance's efficacy depended on the present will of the contracting parties. Following this logic, slavery proponents could argue that when the new states drafted their own constitutions, the United States could no longer claim authority under the Ordinance to insist on the compacts without degrading the new states to a level of inequality.

Because Congress proved unwilling to tamper with Article VI, proslavery Indianans sought to circumvent it in practice. Territorial authorities upheld owners' claims to the French slaves, despite the apparently plain language of the slavery exclusion clause.[29] Only the most "metaphysical" sophistry about vested property rights could explain why "the negroes that were in our territory before the passing of the ordinance are retained in absolute slavery since," one critic charged.[30] But legal challenges proved unavailing. The newly established territorial legislature took another bold step toward fully legalizing slavery in 1805 when it passed "An Act concerning the introduction of Negroes and Mulattoes into this Territory." According to this controversial law slaves could be brought into Indiana (as "servants") under supposedly voluntary agreements.[31]

The slavery controversy in Indiana centered on the status of the indenture act until it was repealed in 1810. The act's defenders insisted that the distinction between "servant" and slave was genuine and disclaimed any interest in opening the territory to slavery. They charged that antislavery agitation disguised "sinister [partisan] views," and was simply a "cloak to answer other purposes." After all, "Chrisley Crum" explained in the Vincennes newspaper, everyone knew that "to have slavery admitted into this territory, while it is a territory, is out of the question."[32] Whatever the state of popular opinion in Indiana, assembly candidate Thomas Randolph wrote, "Congress would not give its sanction."[33]

Indianans opposed to slavery took little comfort in these assurances. The institution was well on the way to becoming an established fact, notwithstanding Article VI. The territory's thinly disguised "system of slavery" was "nothing but a shameful usurpation," charged Elias McNamee. The Ordinance was "our constitution" and "paramount to every law, arising from it: . . . any law obviously contrary to it, is null and void."[34] Yet if the indenture act was "contrary both to the spirit and Letter" of Article VI and therefore "unconstitutional," who had the authority to strike it down?[35] Virginia born-and-bred Governor Harrison was supposed to represent federal interests and was empowered to veto improper territorial legislation; but he was also the leader of the proslavery faction. He and his allies knew that Congress would not interfere as long as lip service was paid to the Ordinance and slaves were called "servants." For its part, the anti-Harrison party was convinced that the campaign to legalize slavery would climax with statehood, when the sovereign people of Indiana would cast off the last remnants of colonial dependence—including the Ordinance compacts. If Indianans wanted to hold slaves, Congress would not "attempt to deprive us of [statehood,] our birth-right," the proslavery "Eumenes" boasted: it might as well "attempt to stop the mouths of the Mississippi and drown us!"[36]

Opponents of the Harrison regime finally realized they could not rely on outside authority to enforce Article VI. Pursuing an indirect approach, they could agitate for Harrison's removal from office, but the governor's popularity in the territory and connections in Washington made the success of such a campaign doubtful.[37] The only viable option was to try to gain control of the territorial legislature, repeal the indenture law, and block further efforts to introduce slavery by subterfuge. Slavery would be established in Indiana Territory, antislavery activists warned, unless vigilant voters purged the assembly of Harrison's friends.

The assumption that the effective authority of Article VI depended on the will of the people, even if it was in some sense "constitutional," was shared by enemies of slavery as well as its supporters. In the struggle for public opinion climaxing with the 1809 territorial elections, Harrison's proslavery party enjoyed the initial advantage. Harrisonians could present the legalization of slavery as a reform measure that would stimulate settlement, enrich the territory, and even ameliorate the condition of the slaves themselves: Indianans could choose either freedom from slavery or development. Although opponents of slavery were able to counter these claims separately, they failed to link free institutions and economic development in a coherent or convincing fashion. By 1809, however, the influx of free state immigrants had already begun to transform the character of the Indiana electorate. Opponents of slavery may have been on the defensive in the war of words, but the rapid growth of the native northern population meant that their arguments would be increasingly well received. At the same time, recent settlement patterns provided the best practical refutation of the proslavery argument: Indiana could prosper without slavery.

Because the attainment of statehood depended on crossing the population threshold—sixty thousand free inhabitants—set forth in Article V of the Ordinance, any program for stimulating settlement had political implications. As long as population languished, Indianans would remain in colonial "bondage" to the federal government; they would not be allowed to govern themselves—their "birth-right" as free born Americans. Slavery advocates claimed that the admission of slaveholders and their slaves would accelerate population growth and in turn spur Indiana's economy, thus guaranteeing the embryonic state's future wealth and welfare.

Even opponents of legalizing slavery accepted the premise that the "rapid progress and prosperity of this country" depended "on the emigration from other states."[38] The challenge was to divert a fair share of "the great current of [westward] emigration" to Indiana.[39] Debate centered on the likely impact of slavery on settlement patterns. Assuming that immigrants from free states were more concerned with getting good land than with keeping their distance from slavery, proslavery writers argued that the slavery ban was a kind of unnecessary self-denial.

In 1805 the Indiana representatives cited the excellent "prospects of a speedy & an immense increase in our population."[40] But, in Governor Harrison's opinion, there were impediments. Only when these were removed would "the settlement and improvement of our country . . . correspond with its fertility & highly advantageous situation."[41] Many Indianans would have included the prohibition of slavery among the "embarrasments that have impeded" population. Slavery advocates assumed that "the population west of the Ohio must chiefly be derived from the Southern and Western States where slaves are most numerous."[42] The implications of excluding slaveowners and their chattels were spelled out in a legislative resolution in

1806: "because of its situation," Indiana would have to attract settlers from states where "slavery is tolerated, or for many years remain in its present situation, its citizens deprived of the greater part of their political rights, and indeed, of all those which distinguish the American from the citizens and subjects of other Governments."[43] According to this formulation, white Indianans would remain in political bondage unless they could hold bondsmen of their own. Otherwise, the promise of Article V would be defeated by the restriction in Article VI.

The influx of southerners and their slaves would stimulate the economy as well as population growth. New arrivals drove up land values and stimulated demand for local agricultural production, thus introducing new wealth into circulation; anxious to gain returns on their investments, they would soon produce their own surpluses for insatiable foreign markets. These arguments were most fully developed by "Slim Simon" in the *Vincennes Sun* in February 1809. He set out to refute General Washington Johnston's contention that legalization was an "aristocratic" plot that would reduce nonslaveholding whites to poverty and dependence.[44] "We are all poor," he wrote, "and if we are to be regulated by your principles of political economy, we shall remain so to the end of time." Contrary to Johnston's claim, the price of free labor would not be driven down by competition from slaves. "We have a market for all the surplus produce that can be raised," explained "Slim Simon," and this demand would reward all producers, slaveowning or not, and guarantee high wages for white workers.

General Johnston's pessimistic projections presupposed constant demand in an economy of scarcity. But a slave-based economy was dynamic, "Slim Simon" contended, because it could best exploit growing worldwide demand for agricultural products. He therefore concluded that the Indiana economy was performing well beneath its natural capacity—within the limits set by the potential productivity of the land and market demand—because of artificial obstacles to the growth of the labor supply. But he was not simply content to invoke the (relatively) untapped supply of slave labor and the apparent shortage of free white settlers. He thought it was a mistake to consider black and white labor interchangeable—and therefore competitive: the legalization of slavery would create new and better opportunities for all white workers.

For "Slim Simon" the introduction of slavery was essential to economic progress; it was a labor-saving "improvement" equivalent to the introduction of new technology. General Johnston and other leaders of the party opposed to legalizing slavery would condemn whites to "the menial offices of slaves," under the pretense of defending their interests. "I suppose you will prohibit" the use of spinning machines, "Slim Simon" sneered, "lest it should deprive

16 or 18 poor old women of their employment." "Sir, your ideas are at variance with every innovation of the present, or any past age."

Proslavery writers claimed moral as well as material benefits would flow from opening Indiana to slavery, insisting that the physical condition of slaves brought into the territory would be improved. According to "Slim Simon," "the enquiry for every politician and moralist is, what way are those [slaves] now in the U. States to be disposed of, that they may be least prejudicial to the community at large, most beneficial to their owners, and by which their condition would be most ameliorated."[45] Invoking the key premises of the "diffusion" argument, proponents of slavery argued that legalization would prevent the dangerous concentration of slaves in the South, while securing a more generous subsistence and more humane treatment for the slaves themselves. There was no "safer, surer, or speedier method for softening and ending the rigors of slavery," wrote "Eumenes."[46] Lifting the slavery ban would create no new slaves, but would simply distribute those already in bondage in a way that would enhance their prospects for freedom. In a petition to Congress asking for suspension of Article VI, territorial legislators predicted that "in less than a century the colour would be so disseminated as to be scarcely discoverable."[47] In the meantime, they would be "well fed, and well clothed."[48] "Slim Simon" added the finishing touches to the case for legalization, cleverly identifying the projected diffusion of northwestern slaves with the progress of emancipation in New England. Allow slaves into Indiana, he urged, and "they would be so dispersed, that they could be emancipated with the same ease and safety, that they have been in N. England."[49] Here would be a golden opportunity for Yankee reformers to demonstrate their concern for the slaves' welfare and to take practical steps toward their freedom.

Although they failed to make a coherent case against slavery on economic grounds, antislavery writers effectively countered the spurious moralism of the diffusion argument. Slavery simply was "contrary to equity and republicanism," "Corpus Collosom" told "Eumenes."[50] How could slavery advocates call themselves "republicans," wondered "Citizen," "at the very moment they are exercising the uncontrouled whip of despotism?"[51] Clearly, these writers agreed, legalizing slavery was the entering wedge for aristocracy. "Benevolensus," an Ohio writer, echoed Federalist propaganda in the Ohio statehood campaign, warning that "these mighty men, with their ten thousand slaves, would soon compose the legislative bodies of the Indiana territory."[52]

By 1809 antislavery writers had discovered the most glaring weakness in the diffusion argument. They were willing to concede that slavery would flourish in the territory once it enjoyed legal protection. But improved living conditions would cause the number of slaves to increase. In a reply to "Slim Simon" in the *Vincennes Sun*, "Farmer" wrote that "negroes like every other species of men, when, by what happy causes so ever their condition is rendered more happy, or less deplorable, will proportionately multiply." Granting Indiana's suitability for the production and reproduction of slaves— and, by implication, the temporary advantages of a slave-based economy— "Farmer" called into question the fundamental assumption of the case for diffusion. If, in fact, slavery brought development and prosperity in its wake, it would also increase the total number of slaves, while making them increasingly valuable as property: "it is absurd to suppose that the population of negroes would remain stationary, either in the territory receiving, or the state furnishing the supply, when their condition [in both places] would . . . have been, in some degree, ameliorated."[53] "Farmer" concluded by turning "Slim Simon" on his head: the legalization of slavery would make Indiana more like the South, not New England. When the bountiful subsistence of the frontier era passed, the "fate" of the slave population would be "more and more assimilate[d] . . . to that of the same class of men in the southern states." Indianans knew too well the cruelties practiced on slaves across the river in Kentucky—or on "servants" in their own midst.[54]

In 1809 the production of slaves had a more obvious and direct relationship to the commercial prosperity of the territory than did the growth of a free farming population still primarily concerned with eking out its own subsistence. Antislavery writers therefore could not challenge the short-run material advantages of legalizing slavery. Assembly candidate James Beggs circulated a campaign statement to the voters of Clark County blasting the "violent effort" of the Harrison party to introduce slavery. "They will leap the mighty bulwark of our ordinance," Beggs wrote, and sacrifice the honor of the territory on "the shrine of avarice."[55] Self-interest and "avarice" could not yet be merged with the cause of free soil. But the rebuttal of diffusion did anticipate some of the arguments for a free-labor economy later developed by the anticonventionists in neighboring Illinois. The same conditions that allegedly would ameliorate the condition of slaves—and stimulate their reproduction—would operate on whites, but only if their access to productive lands were not preempted. Slavery and free labor were incompatible: opening the door to slavery would check white migration as well as the rate of white population growth.[56] As a result, the total white population would languish while the number of slaves increased rapidly. These demographic projections, bolstered by each successive United States census, would provide the foundation for the anticonventionists' subsequent identification of freedom with economic development.

Opponents of slavery found that their most effective tactic was to force candidates to take a public stand on the slavery question.[57] Immigrants from free states and southerners opposed to slavery were thus able in 1809 to elect a majority committed to the repeal of the indenture act of 1805. Thereafter, even Indiana politicians who had been in favor of slavery were forced to pledge themselves to oppose the peculiar institution's introduction.[58]

The campaign to overturn Article VI gained new impetus with the creation of Illinois Territory, where southerners remained dominant well after the attainment of statehood in 1818.[59] As in Ohio, although now with better reason, opponents of slavery saw the statehood movement as a proslavery plot. "Caution" warned readers of the *Western Intelligencer* opposed to the "hellish system" to avoid "the fascinating bate [sic] of '*state government*'" while southerners remained in the ascendant. He was confident that within a few years the friends of "humanity and freedom" would become dominant, as they had in Indiana.[60] But the issue remained muted for the time being. While the new state constitution protected slaveholders' existing rights and allowed the temporary importation of slaves to labor in the salt works, statemakers prudently disclaimed any intention of challenging Article VI. Antislavery sentiment in Congress was already building toward the Missouri controversy, and any direct assault on the Ordinance would certainly have thwarted admission.

IV. Illinois

The slavery question emerged fullblown in Illinois in 1823–1824 during the protracted struggle over whether or not to call a new state constitutional convention. The controversy began in earnest in December 1822 when newly elected Governor Edward Coles—a former Virginian who had freed his own slaves on his arrival in Illinois—asked legislators to revise the state's black code and take steps to liberate the French slaves. The proslavery party replied that the "only course" for making such changes would be by calling "a Convention to alter the constitution." Proponents of a convention soon made it clear, however, that they hoped to legalize—not eliminate—slavery in Illinois. In February 1823, at the end of the legislative session, the conventionists gained a narrow victory. With the help of dubious parliamentary tactics, they pushed a bill through the general assembly authorizing a popular referendum to be held in August 1824 on whether or not to hold a constitutional convention.[61] For the next year and a half the convention issue dominated Illinois politics. "It is a dish which is daily nay hourly served up," Horatio Newhall, a young lawyer in Bond County, wrote to his family in Massachusetts. "It furnishes all our food for conversation, for reading and for newspaper scribbling. Party feeling destroys . . . all social intercourse between persons of different parties."[62]

The constitutional status of the Northwest Ordinance and the policy of slavery exclusion were exhaustively debated during the convention struggle. The authority of the Ordinance could no longer be identified or confused with Congress's authority over the territories or with its power to set conditions for the admission of new states. If Illinois was a "free" state simply because of a provision in its own constitution, then it was also entitled to allow slavery by constitutional amendment. Did the Ordinance control the state constitution or had the constitution simply incorporated—and thereby given a new lease on life to—the Ordinance? Courts in the northwestern states were ambivalent on the question, but the climate of opinion in the wake of the Missouri struggle was increasingly congenial to arguments for state sovereignty and state equality that were incompatible with constitutional limitations. Missourians had successfully defied Congress and refused to expunge a clause in their state constitution prohibiting the immigration of free blacks. Their example emboldened proslavery Illinoisans in the ranks of the convention party.[63]

The Illinois conventionists persuasively argued that "the people are the only legitimate source of all political power" and had the absolute and unlimited "right" and even "duty, to amend, alter, or change their form of government." The Ordinance "compacts" could not exceed the reach of the sovereign people.[64] "Congress had no right to, nor ever did, pledge themselves to keep slavery out of this country any longer than the governing power was in their hands," wrote "Truth." Illinois was now "a free and independent state."[65] The conditions set down by Congress in the enabling act were no longer operative: "the dead cannot govern the living, except the living are willing to be governed by the dead."[66] "Shall not the people rule?" asked conventionist editor William Berry. "Is not their will the supreme law of the land?"[67]

Commentators in other states—even in the South—showed little enthusiasm for proslavery agitation in Illinois. But they generally upheld the right of Illinoisans to decide the issue for themselves, without federal interference.[68] In Illinois most anticonventionists recognized the futility of challenging popular authority or states' rights. Although the United States Supreme Court *might* find the admission of slavery an unconstitutional violation of the Ordinance—this was a *"disputed point"*—George Churchill advised his antislavery friends to "rely upon yourselves. The Congress of 1787, with parental solicitude, have confided to you the sacred boon of liberty. It is *your* duty to protect and preserve it."[69]

Many of Churchill's allies were convinced that the legalization of slavery would indeed be "unconstitutional," but it was by no means clear whether federal authorities would be willing or able to do anything about it. Governor Coles, for one, had misgivings about the "policy" of appealing for the "interposition of the Federal Gov't." Such a "dictatorial" strategy, Coles wrote the Philadelphia banker Nicholas Biddle, was "best calculated to arouse the feelings of State pride, and State rights, and that natural love of unrestrained liberty and independence which is common to our countrymen, and especially to our frontier settlers."[70] Not surprisingly, the most elaborate "compact" arguments were put forward by outsiders, not Illinois anticonventionists.[71] Instead, anticonventionists concerted efforts to sway "public opinion," by appealing to the enlightened self-interest and moral sense of Illinois voters.[72] By competing for votes in the referendum set for August 1824, they accepted popular authority as an operational premise. They urged the people of Illinois to exercise their sovereign power to sustain the exclusion of slavery.

The logic of the convention campaign reinforced the conventionists' arguments for popular constitutional authority and thus tended to undercut the authority of the Northwest Ordinance as a constitutional text. Opponents of the Illinois convention movement invoked the Ordinance as a source of moral obligation: it epitomized the wisdom and foresight of the Founding Fathers and was, therefore, an infallible guide for Illinois voters. But the final decision—and the ultimate authority—was theirs.

The larger controversy over Article VI concerned the impact of slavery exclusion on the future development of the Northwest. The proslavery party had always assumed that the region would develop more rapidly if slaveowners were allowed to cross the Ohio. The South was long supposed to be the most likely source of potential emigrants. Slavery advocates could compare the slow growth of the "free" territories north of the Ohio with the rapid settlement of Kentucky and Tennessee, admitted to the union in 1792 and 1796, respectively. If former slaveowners had not remained in the Northwest and if more recent emigrants had not been allowed to bring their slaves into the territory under various pretexts, the contrast would have been still more unfavorable to the "free" frontier.

Conventionists exploited anxieties about Illinois's prospects for development as a free state. Illinois, which had barely qualified for statehood because of its sparse population and only then because of fraudulent census returns, now faced new competition for settlers from Missouri, where slavery was tolerated. Hard times in the aftermath of the 1819 crash emphasized the need for new men, new money, and new crops. Conventionists attributed Illinois's "torpid state" to the slavery ban. Although "Surrounded . . . by the choicest blessings of Providence"—including its situation "between two great navigable rivers," "soil that cannot be equalled by any other state in the Union, or perhaps any other country in the world," and a "climate as agreeable as that of Italy"—Illinois groaned under the "severest dispensations." But with the legalization of slavery, settlers would no longer pass through Illinois on their way to Missouri, and the "flood-gates of emigration" would be opened.[73] Proconvention newspapers published reports that land-hungry southerners were eager to move across the river, including one from a Mercer County, Kentucky, planter who predicted that once slavery was legalized, "the increase of [Illinois's] population will be beyond calculation."[74]

The influx of settlers would guarantee the state's future prosperity. "The tide of emigration . . . would bring with it the wealth of other countries."[75] The crush of new arrivals would bid up the price of improved lands, securing windfall profits to Illinois landowners; they would bring "cash to buy your corn, wheat and bacon to subsist upon" while preparing their own farms.[76] But slavery proponents also anticipated more substantial, long-term benefits from admitting slaves. Slave labor was the key to unlocking the state's natural riches. Slaves were already employed (on a "temporary" basis) in working salt mines in the southern tip of the state: conventionists suggested that they were also better suited to the rich but sickly American bottom lands along the Mississippi.[77] And "why should the prairies of Illinois be excluded from the benefit of their services?" "Yankee" wanted to know.[78] Thomas Burgess toasted the state's fair prospects at a proconvention dinner in Lebanon: "give us plenty of negroes" and nature "will distribute her treasures."[79]

A conventionist writing in the *Illinois Intelligencer* summarized all the good things that the legalization of slavery would bring: "the country would flourish, our state would be more republican, and more populous." Furthermore, the writer explained, slave labor would be better suited to areas that whites found unhealthy: "in sickly season, the sick could have more attention paid them." Finally, "the condition of the slaves [would be] much ameliorated"—the diffusion argument was a perennial favorite of slavery advocates in the Northwest—"and the several churches of Christ would be considerably enlarged."[80] The *Illinois Gazette* concluded, "if slavery was admitted, our country would populate in abundance, wealth would be in our country, money would circulate for a while—it would put a new spring to business."[81]

Was the introduction of slavery the answer to the state's problems? This depended on whether the conventionists' assumptions about development were valid: that the South was the prime source of emigrants, that slave labor would not drive out white workers or deter emigration from nonslaveholding areas, and that, as a slave state, Illinois would be better able to produce more wealth and reproduce its own population more rapidly. But anticonventionists could effectively challenge all these assumptions. The Yankee diaspora was already spreading across the northern frontier. English settlers, led by Morris Birkbeck, the indefatigable liberal promoter, had moved into the prairie region bordering Indiana. These emigrants came to Illinois *because* it was free: the legalization of slavery would cut off these most

promising sources of future population growth.[82] Anticonvention polemicists, led by Birkbeck, argued that slavery and freedom were locally incompatible and that Illinois, therefore, would have to make a choice as to which
emigration to encourage. Legalization would not simply add slaveholders
headed toward Missouri to the immigration from free states. "If slavery was
allowed," wrote Birkbeck (disguised as "Jonathan Freeman"), "free people
would not come to this state, and many who are now here would go away."[83]
As a result, the Monroe County Antislavery Society insisted, "we [would]
surrender the brilliant prospects of having a populous and flourishing free
state, and agree to hang upon the rear of even the poorest slave state."[84]

Recent census data strengthened the case against admitting slavery.
Birkbeck used population figures for slave and free states to blast the argument that slave states grew faster (and therefore produced larger population
surpluses eligible for emigration). He also questioned the central premise of
the diffusion argument, that slave population did not vary according to the
extent of territory in which slavery was permitted. "If Ohio had been a slave
state," Birkbeck calculated, "there would have been, at this time, about two
hundred thousand more slaves in the world—and two hundred thousand
fewer free persons."[85] Like their predecessors in Indiana, defenders of free
soil were willing to grant their opponents' claim that slaves would be better
off in "this land of plenty." But the result would be to accelerate the growth of
the black population: because they would not be "so much crouded as in the
old slave-states," these slave immigrants would be more prolific.[86] Meanwhile, emigration would ease overcrowding for the slaves who remained
behind, and they, in turn, would reproduce more rapidly. These effects were
already apparent south of the Ohio: the total "slave population has increased
in the same proportion as they have been removed to the new states."[87]

The comparison between Kentucky and Ohio was no longer a favorable
one for slavery promoters. Though the two states covered almost exactly the
same extent of territory and enjoyed "equal advantages of climate" and equal
access to the wider world, the 1820 census showed the increase in Ohio's
population over the preceding two decades to be almost 200,000 greater than
Kentucky's. "Laocoon," another anticonventionist, argued that these figures
"must be conclusive against the slave policy, when adopted with a view to the
advancement of population."[88]

Anticonvention writers went on to explain that the white population grew
faster in the northern states because of the superior productivity of free labor
and the more rapid circulation and accumulation of wealth under free institutions. The answer to Illinois's problems was economic development through
manufacturing, internal improvements, and better agricultural tech-
niques.[89] According to "Aristides," "active industry, and an accelerated

circulation of money, always attendant upon it, is always exciting the mass of society in a free state to energy, enterprize, and improvement." Emigrants from the free states "will bring us money and industry," while slaveholders would bring little circulating wealth: their "capital" was tied up in slaves who would displace more productive white workers.[90] "Industry," a "Friend to Freedom" added, would be rendered "unfashionable and disreputable."[91] Those unfortunate whites who still had to work for a living—small farmers and mechanics—"would be degraded and despised, and thrown on the verge of slavery themselves."[92] "We who are not able to hold or own them, will be almost levelled with them."[93]

The choice was clear. Even if the influx of planters and slaves gave a temporary boost to land prices, legalization would destroy the state's brilliant prospects. "Slavery is inimical to commerce, to manufactories, to enterprise of any kind," wrote "Martus": "the man who vests his capital in land and slaves, will not vest it in trade or manufactures."[94] The only trade that slaveholders would promote would be the trade in human flesh. Legalization would not be the step toward gradual emancipation that the advocates of diffusion promised; instead Illinois would become "at once the receptacle and regenerator of slavery." Slave breeding would serve the insatiable needs of southern planters, but it would retard economic development in Illinois.[95] Instead of lasting prosperity, then, "Emigrants from the south" would only "bring us idleness, vanity, luxury, and the slow but fatal disease of slavery"; they would create "an aristocracy of the worst species."[96]

The anticonventionists promised that if Illinoisans chose freedom, "freemen will emigrate, and riches will be the reward of industry."[97] Once the issue was favorably decided, Birkbeck predicted, "true prosperity will begin to beam upon us, and the blessings of heaven will reward our honest industry."[98]

Opponents of the convention campaign were reinforced by the rapid growth of the number of Illinoisans from the free states. One of their most effective tactics was to demonstrate the underrepresentation of the northern, antislavery counties under the existing apportionment scheme. The anticonventionists argued that their antagonists were all for rushing into slavery while they still controlled state politics. "Farmer" had no doubt that a majority in the state were opposed to slavery, "but if we incautiously sanction the call of a convention before a new apportionment is made, there will then be danger that the *minority of the people* will elect a *majority of the convention*; and that the majority so elected, will introduce slavery."[99] This charge was repeated time and time again as the election approached: it provided a popular, democratic rationale for voting against the exercise of popular sovereignty in a constitutional convention. It was just as much the people's right *not* to change as it was to change their constitution. And it soon became clear to the anticonvention managers that they had the votes, malapportionment notwithstanding.[100] Except in the most southern counties the proconvention party was reduced to denying any intention of legalizing slavery. They even suggested that such an attempt would be pointless because it would be "unconstitutional," the very ground that the anticonventionists had, for all practical purposes, abandoned![101]

In this complicated shuffling of arguments and positions, Article VI and the Ordinance generally came to be seen as something more—or something less—than a constitutional text. For the conventionists, eager to overthrow its shackles, it was an "ancient act of one-sided legislation," "an instrument long since out of use in this hemisphere," a "blank sheet of paper."[102] "The *Ordinance* has been held up *in terrorem*," they complained, "as the tutelar god that the people have to worship."[103] There was considerable justification for these charges. Faced with the task of mobilizing votes to uphold the prohibition of slavery, anticonventionists promoted the Ordinance as a kind of higher law, a guide to right action—but not necessarily as an authority in itself: the people gave the Ordinance its authority.

Several lines of argument converged to help transform the Ordinance from a constitutional text into a higher law. Anticonventionists declaimed on the voters' responsibility to the past, to the "sacred Tree of Liberty that was planted by the venerable sages of the revolution, and baptised with the precious blood of our fathers."[104] They also parried conventionist attacks on the tyranny of a musty old "compact" to which the people had never consented by arguing that each new settler's emigration to the territory renewed the Ordinance's authority. The Ordinance set forth the terms of purchase offered by the federal government, the "absolute owners of the soil."[105] The purchase of federal lands thus created duties and obligations in both buyer and seller: every purchaser bought the promise of freedom as well as the soil itself. The Ordinance was a "pledge . . . offered to all persons who should emigrate hither," Alfred Cavarly told an anticonvention crowd at Carrollton. "This public pledge was continued in good faith up to 1818, and was at that date again renewed by congress, in the act enabling the people of this territory to form a constitution of state government, and for the admission of such state into the Union."[106] At that time, "A Citizen of Illinois" explained, "the people of this state . . . in the fullest and most solemn manner, made themselves a party to the ordinance or compact of 1787."[107]

The suggestion that the Ordinance "compacts" expressed the sovereign will of the people as well as the wisdom of the founding fathers intimated that no (earthly) power could now constrain the state. "Common Sense" concluded that though the introduction of slavery would be "illegal" and "a violation of public faith and private right," these were only "reasons why it *ought* not to take place, but are no reasons why it *cannot* take place."[108] But just as any independent state was bound to honor treaty obligations, and to preserve private rights, so Illinois should redeem its promises to those who came before, to Congress, and to the world.[109] The outcome would be of momentous significance for the future of republican government everywhere.[110]

Illinoisans had to keep faith with the Founders by upholding the Ordinance. So, at Sangamo, on July 4, 1823, there were nine cheers for "the Ordinance of '87—Illinois has pledged her faith to support it"; another nine for the "compact made by our fathers, may their children scorn to violate" it; and eleven for the "Tree of Liberty, planted by the ordinance of 1787, nourished by Ohio and Indiana—May Illinois never cut it down."[111] They had to keep themselves free of "that vile prostitute" slavery, another Fourth of July speaker warned, "else depend upon it, she will bring forth a monster to the state, the indignation of God's wrath, and one of the foulest stains upon the American character."[112] "Heaven may withhold the vials of its wrath," an "Old Resident" added, "but it will be in mercy and not in judgement."[113]

Without slavery, Illinois must "become a star of the first magnitude in the American firmament."[114] "What can it require to make Illinois the first state in the union?" asked an editor opposed to the admission of slavery.

> Nothing but the preservation of her free institutions; industry, economy, and good laws. Add these to her superior natural advantages, and she must rise in the scale of states, with a rapidity that the world has never before seen.[115]

But future generations could not claim their inheritance if slavery were permitted. The question, as orator Theodore Cone put it in another Fourth of July speech, was "whether we shall rise to wealth and greatness, and become one of the most powerful states in the Union, or whether distracted by anarchy, we shall sink into insignificance, the scorn and contempt of our sister states."[116] Voters had to keep faith with their fathers, their children, and their God. Mindful of this awful responsibility, Illinoisans rejected the call for a convention by a decisive margin—6,640 to 4,972—in the August 1824 vote.[117]

V. Freedom and Development

When the Northwest Ordinance was drafted the exclusion of slavery was only a subordinate theme in a broad program for western development. Subsequent generations of northwesterners also assumed the primary importance of economic development. But slavery soon came to occupy a central place in debates about the region's future. As a result, the Ordinance was increasingly defined by—and confused with—Article VI.

Proponents of slavery argued that the authors of the Ordinance intended to promote the growth of the Territory's population and economy. Rapid development was essential to fulfilling their promise that settlers would soon enjoy the privileges of self-government and statehood. The exclusion of slavery was supposed to be a means toward these ends, but its inefficacy was soon apparent to some: for them, realization of the goals of the Ordinance was incompatible with strict adherence to Article VI. Spokesmen for opening the region to slavery concluded that the hope of transcending sectional differences—and the need for slavery—in western development was hopelessly visionary.

Slavery advocates developed a notion of "compact" appropriate to their loose construction of the Ordinance. They inveighed against the dead hand of the past, insisting that the Ordinance compacts were renegotiable; the authority of these agreements rested on the continuing will of the contracting parties. And with the attainment of statehood, Congress ceased to be a "party" and the "compact" therefore dissolved. The new states could then incorporate portions of the Ordinance in their own constitutions, but these provisions were like all others, subject to the changing will of the sovereign people.

Emphasis on the region's uncertain material and political prospects gave slavery proponents the early advantage in debates over Article VI. Their appeals to popular sovereignty and states' rights were equally, if temporarily, persuasive. In response, defenders of the article conceded both their opponents' constitutional premises and their focus on political economy. But, most dramatically in Illinois, they overcame these apparent liabilities by promoting a new conception of political obligation—and enlightened self-interest—that stressed the sovereign people's responsibility to past and future generations.

The Illinois anticonventionists warned voters against the "grand temptation" of rising land values legalization would supposedly produce; this "immediate remedy" for hard-pressed farmers "will ultimately be prejudicial to the state and community at large."[118] Yet the lure of "becoming suddenly rich, and of living without labor" was almost irresistible during a period of agricultural depression, even for those "opposed to slavery on principle."[119] Economic hardship and the need for quick relief explained the temporary frenzy that had seized the state. "If ever a change in our constitution is effected for the admission of negroes," "A Farmer" wrote, "it will be because the poverty of the people, and not their will consents."[120] The party opposed to legalizing slavery called on voters to express their "will"—their sense of what would best serve private and public interests over the long run—and not their "poverty." A closer look at the actual impact of slavery on old states like Virginia and new states like Kentucky showed the price the state would pay for the immediate benefits of legalization—if these benefits were not themselves illusory.[121]

Anticonventionists shifted the focus of debate from the present to the future, thus invoking the principle of intergenerational responsibility and accountability. This principle in turn suggested a relationship between the present generation and the founders of the Territory—and of the nation itself. While each succeeding generation was fully sovereign (and so accountable for its acts), it was also entrusted with the hopes and dreams of its predecessors: these enduring ideals constituted a higher law, a transcendent bond between past, present, and future. A vision of future prosperity was integral to this promise, and it was incumbent on today's voters not to foreclose economic development in a paroxysm of shortsighted selfishness.

The authors of the Northwest Ordinance had looked to the future. By embracing their vision and making it their own, northwesterners of succeeding generations could participate in the continuing founding of their rising new states.

7.

From Constitution to Higher Law

☆ ☆ ☆ ☆ ☆ ☆ ☆

In 1887, at a Northwest Ordinance centennial celebration in Marietta, Ohio, Senator George Frisbie Hoar of Massachusetts assessed the impact of the Ordinance on American history. According to Hoar, the principles of the Ordinance had inspired the nation in its epochal struggles for freedom. First, "the men of the Revolution fought that [those] principles . . . might become living realities." More recently,

> the five States of the Northwest sent nearly a million soldiers into the war for the Union. . . . It is this that makes the birthday of Ohio another birthday of the nation itself. Forever honored be Marietta as another Plymouth. The Ordinance belongs with the Declaration of Independence and the Constitution. It is one of the three title-deeds of American constitutional liberty.[1]

In a later celebratory address, a prominent Ohio veteran agreed with Hoar that the moral authority of the Ordinance derived from the heroic deeds of pioneer settlers as well as the sacrifices of those who fought and died to preserve their legacy. "The Ordinance itself was not a living force," Colonel Wager Swayne asserted, "and could not be till its articles of compact were put on as armor by those heroes of the Revolution. They carried its flag into the wilderness." The Ordinance was at the same time both more and less than a constitutional document guaranteeing the creation of free states in the Old Northwest. By itself, it "was not a living force." Only the pioneer settlers who ventured forth "into the wilderness" could give life to its principles: "those men of '76 . . . were the Ordinance." As succeeding generations continued to cherish the Ordinance, so would it endure.[2]

Hoar and Swayne elaborated on themes developed by northwestern writers and orators in the decades before the Civil War. They too moved beyond the text of the document to identify its "living" principles. Antebellum publicists celebrated the conquest of the wilderness and the region's rapid economic development rather than victory on the battlefield. But they also sought to fashion a founding myth that would inspire contemporary sons to uphold the legacy of their revolutionary forefathers. The Northwest Ordinance occupied a central place in this patriotic rhetoric: it constituted a direct link between the first settlers of the region and the national founders; at the same time, the compact articles—notably Article VI excluding slavery—set forth the most advanced Revolutionary ideals. Northwesterners supposedly embraced these ideals and gave them "living force" when they had entered the territory.

Celebrations of the Ordinance emphasized the transcendent principles it expressed as well as the need for successive generations to uphold and renew them. As a result, the legal and constitutional authority of the document itself was discounted. In this respect, Northwestern mythologists simply registered the outcome of sustained controversy in the region over whether the territories and states were subject to specific Ordinance stipulations governing boundaries, the state-making process, and slavery exclusion. Depending on how conflicting interests were affected, the Ordinance was treated reverently by some speakers and writers and dismissed with contempt by others. Promoters claimed that the Ordinance was a constitution for the territories and future states of the Northwest; critics insisted that it had no more constitutional significance than any other act of Congress. Controversy over the meaning of the Ordinance eventually worked to undermine its standing as a constitutional text. Even those who sought to uphold its provisions had to appeal beyond the document—to voters in the territories and new states or to Congress—for support. Implicitly, they conceded the main contention of their opponents, that the continuing authority of the Ordinance depended on the will of the sovereign people or sovereign Congress.

Many commentators challenged the Ordinance's status as a constitutional text, beginning with James Madison who asserted in *The Federalist*, No. 38, that it had been enacted "without the least color of constitutional authority."[3] Later critics also questioned the legitimacy of the Ordinance—its authors' authority. Although it was subsequently reenacted by the new Congress in exercise of its powers under the territorial "rules and regulation" clause of the federal Constitution, the Ordinance henceforth derived its authority from Congress, and could be altered at will: it was not a compact binding on Congress. Further assaults on the Ordinance were made by southerners during the Missouri controversy. Arguing against any constitutional limitations on new states, they insisted that the Ordinance became "utterly void" once the northwestern territories achieved statehood. According to Congressman Philip Barbour of Virginia, "those States might introduce slavery amongst them, if they so willed," notwithstanding the prohibition in compact Article VI.[4] Solicitude for states' rights and state equality ultimately led the Supreme Court to reject the idea that the compact articles had any constitutional force at all. Although "said to be perpetual," they were not incorporated in the Constitution and "they certainly are not superior and paramount to the Constitution."[5]

The most significant challenges to the constitutionality of the Ordinance came from within the Old Northwest itself. Local iconoclasts included the pseudonymous "Yankee" from Illinois who, during the great convention debate of 1823–1824, argued that the "ordinance of '87 has no more effect on the people of Illinois than a blank sheet of paper."[6] In 1848, when Congress debated Wisconsin's boundary claims, Congressman Rudolphus Dickinson of Ohio dismissed the Ordinance: "He did not consider [it] . . . binding." The people of his state "had never regarded the principles of that ordinance since the State was formed; nor was Congress going to regard it; they were going to disregard it now in receiving Wisconsin into the Union." The explanation for these attacks is simple enough. Ordinance provisions or prohibitions favored or penalized specific groups: for instance, those who were for or against slavery, or specified boundaries, or statehood itself. Further, some northwesterners were persuaded by states' rights arguments that limitations on state sovereignty were intolerable, particularly—ironically—as the federal government seemed to fall increasingly under the sway of the "slave power."[8]

Yet if northwesterners objected to specific provisions of the Ordinance, they generally were unwilling to reject the document as a whole. During the Michigan boundary controversy, for instance, Senator Thomas Ewing of Ohio rejected the new state's interpretation of Article V, but added that "next to the constitution itself . . . I hold [the Ordinance] the most sacred among the muniments of our national liberty."[9] This ambivalence reflected a long and controversial history of discourse about Ordinance provisions. The result of these debates was a kind of synthesis: apotheosis and negation alike contributed to the translation of the Ordinance into a "higher law," disconnected from the mundane political world. Indeed, the movement from specific to general and concrete to abstract was as much a result of a long history of criticism of the text of the Ordinance as of claims for its constitutional authority.

Whatever the authority of its specific language, controversy over the Ordinance inspired northwesterners to look back to the founding era to discover the meaning and direction of their own historical experience. The Ordinance thus shaped continuing discussion over first principles, and enabled the people of the Old Northwest to identify the founding of their states with the national founding. Once boundaries were settled, the Ordinance states admitted, and the slavery question definitively resolved by the rapid growth of the free population, the Ordinance could then fill an important need as a symbol of regional distinctiveness.

I. Founding Fathers

Ohioans took the lead in relating the growing prosperity and population of the trans-Ohio region to the Northwest Ordinance. Beginning in the late 1820s, patriotic orators and promoters sought to explain—and sustain—their state's extraordinary development. While fertile soil and easy, natural access to the larger world were frequently cited, the appeal of such explanations declined with the diminishing land supply: settlers intent on fresh land at low prices were already bypassing Ohio en route to newly opened areas to the west. But Ohio continued to thrive, compensating for its natural disadvantages by man-made improvements on the natural landscape. Publicists argued that Ohio's economy was in the midst of a development boom. The capacity of the land to support more people and produce more wealth was vastly increased by the spreading network of canals and the rise of dozens of new towns and cities, bustling with commerce and manufacturing. The key to the extraordinary transformation of this "immense forest" was the Northwest Ordinance.[10]

The free enterprise that enlightened policy encouraged provided the motive force for changes in the landscape and also defined the character of the people who formed the new state. In 1836, at a speech commemorating the forty-eighth anniversary of the settlement of Marietta, state legislator Arius Nye asserted that "*one* common and predominant characteristic [had been] impressed . . . upon the aggregate moving mass and its several individuals" who settled the state, and that was "ACTION, in all the forms by which it is displayed by men in the pursuit of earthly good."[11] Just as nature alone could not explain the state's present prosperity, so too the heterogeneous origins of the first settlers seemed to offer little hope for the development of a distinctive "national character." Ohioans lacked "the homogeneous character of a more ancient and fixed people," conceded Nye. But the very impulse that brought pioneering settlers west transformed them—and their posterity—as it transformed the wilderness. They were an active, dynamic people who founded a new world; because that founding was enacted by the first settlers in their conquest of the wilderness, subsequent generations of Ohioans could share in the founding by continuing their forefathers' improving works.

Ohio publicists defined the state's beginnings in terms that justified and dignified their own "pursuit of earthly good." The first settlers had not been state makers in the classic sense. Though they had taken time off from their private business to draft a constitution in 1802, giving "us a free republican polity, and a government of *laws*," their most important achievement had been to "peril the wilderness and the savage foe" to "purchase a country and a *home* in the west . . . for *us*." Because Ohio's founding was linked to the purchase of government lands, Congress's land and government ordinances of 1785 and 1787 constituted the new state's true organic law.

According to the Ohio historians, purchasers of federal land under the ordinances transcended simple self-interest. Timothy Walker, a prominent young lawyer and writer, told another settlement anniversary crowd at Marietta that the Ordinance had "prepared this then wilderness for social existence, by throwing around it the first protection of law." "The emigrant therefore knew beforehand, that this was a land of the highest political as well as natural promise," and therefore "journeyed with confidence towards his new Canaan."[12] The Ohio pioneers had converted the promise into a sacred, reciprocal obligation. In Salmon P. Chase's words, "the purchaser of land became, by that act, a party to the compact, and bound by its perpetual covenants." As each settler, in taking up federal lands, embraced "the genuine principles of freedom" embodied in the Northwest Ordinance, enlightened private interest and the public good converged.[13]

Chase's "principles of freedom" were set forth in the Ordinance's compact articles, most notably in Article VI, excluding slavery from the territory. By the 1830s, many Ohioans defined freedom both in opposition to slavery and by association with private enterprise. Both senses were evoked when they celebrated the "vigour and spirit of their institutions." With countless other Ohioans, newspaper editor Edward D. Mansfield attributed the "direction" of the "policy and views" of free government in his state to the Ordinance; having established a foundation of free institutions—and having excluded slavery—the Ordinance "has had great, and not less certain because unseen influence, upon the prosperity and happiness of that immense and now populous district."[14]

Freedom and prosperity were inextricably linked. According to another anniversary orator, William M. Corry, the Northwest Ordinance "unsealed those exhaustless fountains of emigration, whose current setting westward, has animated with living streams, so large a portion of this expansive valley." Employing similar imagery, Caleb Atwater, Ohio's first historian, wrote, "we have had flowing towards us, a flood of immigrants who love liberty." Corry and Atwater conceived the true founding of the state to be in the reciprocal action of the settlers' love of liberty and "those excellent laws of Congress," which furnished "a perfect mould for well proportioned republicans."[15] The result, James H. Perkins told the recently formed Historical and Philosophical Society of Ohio, was that "in Ohio . . . was first founded a nearly true democratic community," free of the marks of the "feudal spirit" still apparent in the eastern states and of the "servile element [which] prevented the full operation of the principle of self-rule" in the South. It would not be too much to say, as Perkins did, that Ohio was "the truest democracy which had yet existed."[16] In the same vein, Chase concluded that the freedom established by the Ordinance was a "fit consummation" of the "glorious labors" of the old Congress, "unadulterated by that compromise with circumstances"—that is, slavery—"the effects of which are visible in the constitution and history of the union."[17] Ohio was the freest, most democratic, and thus most truly American state.

Congress could create free institutions in the Old Northwest where, in Walker's words, "all was open and free, as an unsullied sheet, to receive the best impressions of legislative wisdom." In the notion that the principles of the Ordinance were imprinted immediately on nature, the American obsession with written constitutions merged with an organic conception of political community rooted in the soil. "No ancient rubbish had to be cleared away," Walker wrote, echoing language Manasseh Cutler had used fifty years earlier. "The whole region, with some trifling exceptions, was then one continuous solitude, upon which no laws operated but the laws of nature."[18] Because the authors of congressional western policy did not face the same constraints (the "ancient rubbish") facing constitution writers elsewhere, the gap between principles and practice disappeared. As a result, Congress's intentions were translated directly into the free institutions that shaped northwestern development. Subsequent generations could ascertain the guiding principles of the Ordinance without referring to its text: they were clearly apparent in the freedom and prosperity Ohioans so abundantly enjoyed.

The idea of the Ordinance invoked by Ohio orators and publicists was easily detached from the document itself. By emphasizing the transcendent and universal "principles of freedom" embodied in the Ordinance, the Ohioans shifted attention away from the actual text even while celebrating its fundamental importance. This development can be traced in court decisions in Ohio and the other original Ordinance states. Although the Ohio Supreme Court held in 1832 that the Ordinance was "as much obligatory on the state of Ohio as our own constitution," northwestern jurists were divided on whether the specific provisions of the Ordinance were legally binding, particularly when occasional litigants invoked them to gain some practical advantage. It was easier to agree with the Ohioan Walker's assertion in his *Introduction to American Law* (1837) that the compact articles were "paramount to our state constitution" when general principles rather than specific applications were at issue.[19] But the emphasis on principle, notably the guarantee of free institutions, led writers away from a close, legalistic reading of the Ordinance. Ultimately, the transcendent principles expressed in the compacts gave them binding force; the Ordinance did not authorize the principles.

Chief Justice Roger B. Taney and the Supreme Court ruled in *Strader v. Graham* (1850) that the Ordinance was of no constitutional import. As an act of the superseded Confederation government, its continuing life depended on the will of Congress; even then it could not extend beyond the territorial period without reducing the new states to "an inferior condition as compared with the other States." Abolitionist lawyer James G. Birney bitterly rejected Taney's contention that the Ordinance was "merely a secondary or derivative law" and insisted on its "continuing validity." Though he amassed an impressive array of precedents in his lengthy brief against *Strader*, Birney inevitably moved beyond the letter of the law. The "higher law" argument became more and more compelling for defenders of the Ordinance once Taney had made it clear that its text would not be legally controlling. Thus Birney suggested that the Ordinance's principles could not be altered, even by the highest court in the land: "most of the principles established by the ordinance, for all time, as fundamental law, are nothing else than the principles of natural right and justice. There can be no *binding* law—indeed no law—primary or secondary—that opposes these."[20]

Birney's "higher law" version of the Ordinance stood diametrically opposed to Taney's dismissive treatment. Yet both versions moved away from the Ordinance itself as an authoritative text: for Taney, it was a dead letter; for Birney, "principles of natural right and justice" were expressed in the Ordinance, but they did not derive from it. There was a parallel displacement, from the text of the Ordinance to its general principles and their actual operation, in the patriotic effusions of Ohio publicists more interested in explaining the extraordinary development of their state than in locking horns with the Slave Power. According to their accounts, the Ordinance was so much a part of the fabric of their state's political and social life that the text itself easily could be overlooked: this is what Mansfield meant when he spoke of the Ordinance's "unseen influence" upon Ohio's "prosperity and happiness."[21] It was the document itself that was no longer "seen." Yet its beneficent effects were apparent everywhere: Ohioans simply had to look about them to read the living text.

At the 1841 "Buckeye Celebration," commemorating the founding of the state, orator N. C. Read presented a rendition of Ohio's founding conceived as text translated into landscape.

> Whilst yet in her native grandeur, the ordinance of 1787, as she slept in all the magnificence of her wild beauty and unbroken repose, threw over her the splendor of freedom, and consecrated her forever as the home of the free.— Thus, with *the principles of the Revolution mingled with her very soil by the ordinance of '87*—robed in all the spotless purity of free principles—she came into the Union as a State.[22]

Read invited his listeners to imagine the text of the Ordinance actually superimposed on and merged with the territory's "native grandeur" and thus become part of the "very soil" of the state. At the same time, by identifying it with "the principles of the Revolution," he elevated the Ordinance to the same plane as the other great state papers of the founding era. In either case, whether the Ordinance was best known by its fruits or by its essential principles, Read directed attention away from a close reading of the document itself. The text of the Ordinance is, in fact, remarkably complex and incoherent, accurately reflecting the confusion and urgency facing Congress in 1787. But Read and other Ohio publicists were fashioning another, transcendent Ordinance to suit their conception of the state's history.

In its apotheosis, the Northwest Ordinance became more and more of an abstraction, dissolving into other great constitutional documents. According to Atwater, it was "justly considered as the Magna Charta of Ohio, and all of the states northwest of the Ohio river." "That blessed boon," added William D. Gallagher, "sprang from the profound regard of the Fathers of the Republic for the Rights of Man."[23] In a typical gloss of its leading principles, a writer in the *North American Review* called the Ordinance "a national compact, forbidding slavery, securing civil and religious freedom, and all those privileges that others had struggled for through ages of blood and turmoil."[24] Under the Ordinance liberty was secured without bloodshed at the very founding of a new society, thus marking an epoch in world history. Orator Jordan Pugh elaborated this theme: the Ordinance was

> an American production; the offspring of American wisdom and experience. Like the declaration of independence, like the constitution that binds these states together, its language is simple and unostentatious. But how comprehensive is its spirit! How potent are its truths! The west tells its present effect, and the future shadows forth yet mightier results. Its impress is upon our character, and upon our legislation. There it must remain as long as the Saxon race inherits the soil.

In Pugh's inflated rhetoric mere words ("unostentatious language") were discounted while the Ordinance's "spirit" and "truths" were attested by its "comprehensive" and "potent" effects on the people, laws, and landscape. Only "that wondrous prosperity which we now behold" could reveal the Ordinance's true meaning.[25]

Celebrations of the Ordinance thus suggested that the founding fathers of the Old Northwest were none other than the founders of the American nation itself. But the region's settlers were also portrayed as active participants in a continuing process of social and economic development that transformed republican principles into concrete reality. In their own way, the pioneers who landed at Marietta in 1788 and the enterprising legions that followed were also "founders" of Ohio and the other Ordinance states. The result of defining the founding in this double sense was to identify the first Ohioans with the first Americans and thus to establish their republican pedigree. In the same way, causes, the great principles "impressed" on the northwestern wilderness by the Ordinance, were defined by—and easily confused with—their effects, material improvements in a transforming landscape.

II. Authorship and Authority

The growing importance of the Northwest Ordinance as a regional symbol prompted contemporary historians to look beyond the text to try to determine its true authorship. The identity of the document's author—or authors—was by no means self-evident and indeed remains controversial to this day.[26] Differences of opinion often reflected a writer's own background, with ex-southerners promoting the claim of Thomas Jefferson and transplanted Yankees countering with arguments for Nathan Dane of Massachusetts. The answer also depended on how the Ordinance was approached and defined: a close reading, focusing on the text itself and its immediate context, strengthened the case for Dane, whereas an emphasis on the principles behind the text justified the attribution to Jefferson or Rufus King—authors of earlier proposals to limit slavery—or to the Founding Fathers generally.

In his famous exchange with Senator Robert Hayne of South Carolina in 1830, Massachusetts's Daniel Webster celebrated Dane's key contribution as author of the Ordinance in guaranteeing freedom in the Old Northwest. Webster doubted "whether one single law of any lawgiver, ancient or modern, has produced effects of more distinct, marked, and lasting character, than the ordinance of '87."[27] Webster based his claim on Dane's own authority: concerned that southerners might gain credit for a measure that all agreed had "afforded material means in promoting the prosperity and rapid growth of the West," Dane insisted on his own preeminent role, notably in the last-minute insertion of Article VI. Given his ties to Ohio Company investors and his membership on the committee that actually drafted the

Ordinance—the manuscript draft was in his hand—Dane made a strong case for himself. "If there be any praise or blame," he concluded in his influential *General Abridgement of American Law*, "it belongs to Massachusetts; as one of her members [Dane himself] formed it and furnished . . . [most of its] matter."[28]

Throughout the 1830s many northwesterners exalted Dane, "the venerable author of the Ordinance of 1787." In 1833, "Natives of Ohio" toasted his "political wisdom" for securing "the blessings of religion, and learning, and freedom[;] his name will be hallowed forever."[29] Dane's death in February 1835 unleashed a flood of encomiums. William M. Corry asserted that, "Lycurgus-like," Dane had given law to the entire region: "the landmarks of his scheme of government for our territory will only fail with its prosperity, of which they are the permanent foundation." At the same settlement anniversary celebration, the Ordinance was toasted: "may its principles be firmly implanted in our affections, and the remembrance of its author (the venerated Dane) indelibly engraven in the hearts of our children." Later on, perhaps reflecting the influence of previous toasts, Samuel Findlay stretched hyperbole toward impiety. Nathan Dane's "mighty intellect like the sun of Heaven, dawned upon the west, and driving before it the darkness of barbarism, illuminated it with the light of civilization, of science and the arts."[30] In 1837 Timothy Walker brought Dane hagiography to a climax when he called the Yankee jurist "another Moses." "For brevity, comprehension, and forecast," he concluded, the Ordinance "has no superior in the annals of legislation."[31]

These rhetorical flights had little to do with their ostensible subject. Though sober students of the historical record such as Peter Force continued to insist on Dane's authorship, northwesterners soon lost interest in him.[32] It was as hard to see the author in such inflated comparisons as it was to find such sterling literary qualities in the text. Nonetheless, the tributes to Dane are revealing. Northwestern publicists needed a founding father to give mythic resonance to their histories. Therefore, just as the authors of the federal Constitution were considered the nation's founders, Dane, author of the Ordinance, was portrayed as founder of the Old Northwest. But writers and orators tended to identify Dane, the author-founder, with his "works"— the populous and prosperous free states of the West—in the same way they suggested that the true "text" of the Ordinance was imprinted on the landscape. The result was that the image of Dane became lost in the enduring "landmarks of his scheme," in the "light" of progress and "civilization" and in the "principles" that shaped the character of northwesterners.

The apotheosis of Dane was really a celebration of the booming northwestern economy. As Dane himself suggested in 1829, the question of authorship had only become "a subject of particular importance" in recent years when, after decades of erratic growth, the trans-Ohio region finally came into its own. A Cincinnati writer later noted that much of the "reverence and admiration" of the Ordinance "may be attributed to the great prosperity and growth of the States which have grown up under its kindly influence."[33] But because the actual connection between the drafting of the Ordinance and the region's belated ascent to prosperity and power seemed somewhat remote and tenuous, it was unclear how much credit the draftsman deserved. Northwesterners were eager to link their rising fortunes with the national founding, but the weight of Dane's putative achievement proved disproportionately heavy for so modest a figure to bear. The region's historians needed a more plausible founding father, better connected to the national pantheon and equal to the rhetorical task. The solution was to move beyond the text of the Ordinance to identify the author or authors of its guiding principles.

The tendency to emphasize the fundamental principles embodied in the Ordinance—and thus to neglect the document itself—helped bolster the argument for Jefferson. Although it was well known that he was in Europe when the Ordinance was actually adopted, a broader interpretation of congressional western policy credited the Virginian with establishing the principle of slavery exclusion in his original draft of the 1784 ordinance for territorial government. Dane's Article VI simply implemented the Jeffersonian principle. This version of the drafting of the Ordinance proved increasingly attractive in the Old Northwest for several related reasons: a strictly Yankee genealogy for key Ordinance principles would fuel divisiveness in a region heavily settled by southerners and their descendants; Jefferson naturally carried more weight as a putative founder than Dane; and finally, by asserting that they were Jefferson's heirs, northwesterners could portray themselves as authentic American patriots (as against southerners, Virginians included, who had betrayed the founders' noble principles).

Jefferson was presented as an antislavery figure in the Illinois convention struggle of 1823–1824. Anticonventionists sought to convince the state's large ethnically southern population that Jefferson had long been committed to keeping the Old Northwest free.[34] The managers of the anticonvention campaign argued that freedom was secured to the region by enlightened southerners: first, Virginia had magnanimously ceded its western lands to Congress; then Jefferson had taken the lead in establishing new governments on liberal principles—including the prohibition of slavery. In opposing the introduction of slavery into Illinois, the anticonventionists appealed to the intentions of Jefferson and the Founding Fathers, thus setting the Northwest Ordinance in the broader context of the American founding. In later decades, northwesterners opposed to the extension of slavery adopted the same strategy in seeking to forge a regional consensus for freedom and against the Slave Power. As the sectional crisis worsened, politicians and publicists became more and more insistent that the Ordinance was "an *American* production," expressing the most cherished values and goals of the nation's founders.35

In Senate debates over the organization of Oregon and California in 1848, Ohio's Thomas Corwin urged his colleagues to extend the provisions of the Ordinance to the new territories. The Ordinance's "doctrine of free territory is not new; it is coeval with the Constitution, born the same year, of the same parents, and baptized in the same good old republican church." In opposing the machinations of the Slave Power, Corwin took his "stand upon the Ordinance of 1787. There the path is marked by the blood of the Revolution." He chided "southern gentlemen" who would "desecrate the memory of Jefferson," the author of both the Declaration and the Northwest Ordinance, by abandoning his free soil principles:

> When the ample patrimony of Virginia was transferred to the Confederacy [in the 1784 cession], Jefferson, and those of his school, who made this noble donation, at once declared that slavery should not pollute the soil of five rich and powerful new States. Such was Virginian, such was American opinion then.36

The venerable Edward Coles, a native Virginian and the governor of Illinois during the convention struggle, offered the most elaborate argument for Virginia's contribution and Jefferson's authorship in a paper read before the Historical Society of Pennsylvania in 1856. Not only had the Old Dominion ceded the trans-Ohio region to the United States under express conditions, but at the request of Congress she had "formally ratified and confirmed" Article V (altering the size of the new states specified in the Virginia cession) and so "tacitly gave her assent to the whole ordinance of 1787." Coles asserted that Jefferson was the "enlightened and benevolent author" of the Ordinance, basing his claim on the far-ranging operation of his 1784 proposal to exclude slavery from all federal territory after 1800. Even the delayed effect of Jefferson's proposal supposedly revealed a truly antislavery intent: "it is clearly seen that the illustrious author of the ordinance intended it to abolish the then existing state of slavery, as well as to prohibit its ever being tolerated in the country northwest of the Ohio River." By arguing that Article VI represented an expedient and compromised version of Jefferson's more comprehensive and advanced position, Coles could ignore Dane's claims to authorship.

Coles was not simply making Jefferson into an abolitionist—a most unlikely characterization of the owner of more than two hundred slaves. Instead, with Corwin and other northwesterners, Coles insisted that Jefferson was no freak: the founders generally had cherished the goal of securing freedom in the Northwest. "If unanimity of opinion and repetition of legislative action can give weight," Coles argued, "the Ordinance is entitled to even more than the Constitution, which encountered much opposition in the national convention." But, incredibly, the Taney Court had "denounced" the Ordinance "as violating the great principles on which our Government is founded." "What adds to the astonishment is, that this has been done by men professing to be of the Jefferson school of politics."[37]

By the eve of the Civil War many northwesterners had come to see the Northwest Ordinance as one of the great state papers of the founding era, perhaps even—in its guarantees of freedom and civil liberty—the most authentically "American production" of them all. During the Illinois convention struggle a grand jury proclaimed, "if the genius of our national government is to be discovered in any one particular at the time of its formation, it is in the assignment of limits to slavery."[38] Patriotic writers celebrated the Ordinance and its "enlightened and benevolent author" as the ultimate cause of the region's amazing development. Isaac Naylor of Indiana explained his state's "astonishing progress and prosperity"· "the *remote* cause is the 6th article of the Ordinance of '87, prohibiting slavery. . . . The proximate cause is, free men, free thought, free speech, a free press, and free labor." "This article is worth more to Indiana," Naylor concluded, "than all the gold of California, multiplied a thousand times."[39]

As the "author" of Article VI, Jefferson was thus Indiana's true founder. But Naylor carefully distinguished remote from proximate causes: if the principles of freedom could be traced back to Jefferson and the founders, it was the "free men" of the northwestern states who kept them alive. It was this sense of participating in a continuous founding—a vast cooperative enterprise linking contemporary northwesterners to the American Founding Fathers—that most inspired publicists. The people knew what the Ordinance was "worth": its value, like the "gold of California," was embedded in the land itself. In the words of a Pittsburgh editor, "there is no statute or law enacted by any nation ancient or modern whose glorious and beneficial results are so prominently displayed in the very face of the land." The pioneers of Ohio had been drawn to the "boundless wild" land, Arius Nye explained, "devoted and consecrated, by a solemn national act, to the abode of freedom." Free land was the "proximate" cause of free men and in the material abundance that the land afforded, the value of freedom shone forth.[40] When Tom Corwin took his "stand upon the Ordinance of 1787," he had his feet firmly on free soil.

III. Land of the Free

Northwesterners could see the beneficent effects of freedom in the land-scape. In his attempt to describe the character of his rising state, Arius Nye asked his listeners to imagine "an acute and comprehensive observer . . . occupying a position from which he could take, with a *coup d'oeil,* a view of the *state of Ohio, as it is.*" This ideal observer would be rewarded with a panorama "so diversified as, at once, to beautify its aspect to the eye, and to stimulate and reward the industry of its inhabitants"; he would discern "indications of mineral resources and wealth, encouraging, promoting, and rewarding the industry and enterprise of a people, without unduly exciting their cupidity and introducing extravagant adventure, vicious indulgence, and the extremes of luxury and poverty."[41] Here, in short, was a republican landscape, beautiful in its diversity and its busy pursuits, as well as for its ennobling effects on an enterprising citizenry. But another landscape pre-sented itself across the Ohio: there, in Isaac Naylor's words, slavery "stamps sterility upon the soil, and paralysis [upon] the physical, intellectual, and moral power of the people."[42]

As the Civil War impended, the contrasting "look" of slavery and freedom became a stock feature in Republican party rhetoric. But earlier generations of northwestern publicists had had to forge a free soil aesthetic when distinc-tions between North and South were not yet rigorous or clear, and com-parisons that were reported in early travelers' accounts were often unfavorable to the Old Northwest.

The idea that the West, including the states on both sides of the Ohio, constituted a distinct region survived well into the 1830s. According to James Hall's *Letters from the West,* first published in Illinois in the 1820s, it was only necessary to "take the Virginian from his plantation, or the Yankee from his boat and harpoon, or from his snug cottage," for each soon to become "a different man; his *national character* will burst the chains of local habit."[43] But if early travelers in the Ohio Valley generally accepted the idea of a unified West, they did report significant subregional differences. The En-glishman Elias Pym Fordham, though professedly hostile to slavery, found Kentucky with its "refined manners and cultivated minds" a much more attractive place than the free states and territory across the river:

> The question in these wildernesses is this: Shall we have civilization and refine-ment, or sordid manners and semi-barbarism, till time shall produce so much inequality of condition that the poor man must serve the rich man for his daily bread? . . . Servitude in any form is an evil, but the structure of civilized society is raised upon it.[44]

Other Britons, notably Morris Birkbeck, founder of the English Settlement at Albion, Illinois, were more adamantly opposed to slavery but usually agreed that the south side of the Ohio looked more prosperous and civilized. Thus, Adlard Welby, another British visitor, also preferred Kentucky to Ohio: the Kentucky "climate is fine, the land fertile and well cleared, and inclosed; the houses well built, and the landscape as we passed frequently beautiful."[45]

Kentucky was more pleasing to many British visitors because the slave system imposed order and structure on a naturally beautiful landscape: the social inequality essential to civilization was mirrored in the balance between nature and man-made improvements. But the identification of slavery and civilization was hotly disputed by many northerners, particularly in the wake of the Missouri controversy. Bolstered by census data demonstrating more rapid population growth and economic development in free territory, northern writers challenged the visitors' aristocratic assumption that civilization depended on inequality. Instead, proponents of free soil celebrated frontier equality, or what an early orator, Stephen Smith, called "that state of mediocrity in which is to be found the greatest share of happiness." The emphasis on equality reflected the traditional American (republican) aversion to aristocracy but was combined here with a celebration of industry, enterprise, and development. Smith pictured the leveling of forests, "the state everywhere filling with respectable farmers," and countless new towns arising in what was not long since "an absolute wilderness." Smith and his successors saw beauty in dynamic terms, in the transforming hand of man in nature, not in the neopastoral balance traditional social theorists found so appealing.[46]

Because they equated civilization with improvement and development, northern writers were willing—even anxious—to concede the South's natural advantages. The superior fertility of Kentucky's soil was already legendary in the 1780s when John Filson wrote his famous promotional tract. In those years, wrote New Englander George Ogden, Kentucky was like "a garden planted in the wilderness": "all was nature, and all was liberty."[47] But Kentucky squandered these advantages while Ohio, the young giant to the north, surpassed her in wealth and numbers. In the late 1830s Caleb Atwater rhapsodized at length on Virginia's great natural resources, concluding that if "Rufus Putnam and his pilgrims" had

> settled in Virginia [which then included Kentucky], on the same day on which they did in Ohio, and under the same law, which he and they followed here, prohibiting slavery forever in that state, Virginia would now contain five millions of white freemen; and in the next fifty years, Virginia would contain twenty millions of happy human beings.

But the Old Dominion's natural attractions had been forfeited, while "the broad and deep streams of wealth, numbers, enterprise, youth, vigor, and the very life blood of the slave holding states" were "now rolling into Ohio like mighty floods."[48] For Atwater and other promoters of freedom, natural abundance represented a potential for development that could only be fulfilled—and made beautiful—by enterprise and industry. An alternative aesthetic was implicit in this premise: a beautiful landscape was dynamic, homogeneous, and man-made.

Canals and other internal improvements organized the countryside, facilitating private pursuits and bringing northwesterners closer to each other and to the larger world. "We seem to live at a more rapid rate than formerly," Timothy Walker said in 1837: "Society itself sweeps forward with a velocity unknown before." Indianan John H. Farnham exulted in "the spirit of *Internal Improvement* [that] has caused these vast Western forests to bow to the genius of Civilization."[49] Ohioans believed that better transportation combined with technological innovations—notably in steam power—and industrial development would sustain their state's rapid strides toward preeminence in the union. After reviewing the state's many advantages, Atwater confidently concluded that Ohio would soon "be the very first state in this Union, in numbers, wealth and power."[50]

Ohio's greatness depended on the heroic efforts of its own people, not simply on nature's bounties. Patriotic orators linked individual enterprise and social and economic progress with the "principles of freedom" set forth by the founders. At a settlement anniversary in 1833, Judge John Milton Goodenow celebrated the effects of "Liberal Principles": "Like steam engines and rail-roads in the material world—may they continue to remove every mountain and all distance in our social and intellectual state."[51] For Goodenow the transforming landscape mirrored man's moral and intellectual progress. The spirit of enterprise and "ACTION" also strengthened the American union. "Commerce," Atwater explained, "produces a healthy action in the body politic: it leads to industry, to enterprise, and they again lead to competency, comfort, and happiness. Mutual wants produce mutual dependence; and thus an union of interest forms a cement, a bond of union, which no one but a nullifier would ever wish to withdraw from our political fabric."[52]

Atwater's conception of union was a familiar one by the 1830s. Ever since the 1780s prodevelopment theorists had argued that interlocking interest was the best guarantee of intersectional harmony and union; westerners from free and slave states alike were enthusiastic proponents of internal improvements that would bring them closer to eastern markets. But Atwater's discussion reflected a growing sense of regional distinctiveness: for him, the principle of union was best exemplified *within* Ohio and the other free states of the Old Northwest. Ohio's ascent to national leadership in wealth and population demonstrated the superiority of free institutions in encouraging private enterprise and commerce. By contrast, slavery stifled industry, retarded population growth, and thus undermined "union" both within the slave states and between North and South.

Union depended on the common interests of enterprising individuals in what Arius Nye described as the "aggregate moving mass." The history of the Old Northwest demonstrated that enterprise flourished best where the "curse of slavery" was excluded. Therefore, Ohio, "the truest democracy which had yet existed," provided a model not only for other, less enlightened states but also for the union as a whole. Ohio would be first in the union; in order to survive, the union would have to become more like Ohio.[53]

The identification of Ohio with the union helped promote the apotheosis of the Northwest Ordinance. Northwestern publicists linked the opening of the West to the birth of the nation by depicting the Ordinance as one of the founders' central achievements. The Founding Fathers' commitments to freedom and enterprise became manifest in the new world created by enterprising northwesterners at the same time slaveholding southerners and their northern allies were abandoning them.

In an essay on the *General Character, Present and Future Prospects of the People of Ohio* (1827), Atwater showed how the idea of state founding merged with the celebration of economic development. Pioneer settlers, constitution writers, and canal builders all participated in a continuous founding. Thus, Atwater suggested, the landscape itself, properly viewed, should inspire state pride and patriotism. Atwater advised his fellow citizens to

> be prepared for celebrating the final completion of the grand works, now in successful and rapid progress in this State. While the Erie rolls its waves, while the Ohio and Mississippi pour their floods, these works shall remain, MONU-MENTS of the patriotism, of the enterprize, of the energy and wisdom of the founders of this great and growing community.

In a sense, internal improvements, like the grid pattern of the land system, were imprinted on what Timothy Walker called the "unsullied sheet" of the northwestern wilderness. Clearly, Atwater had this broad idea of "authorship" in mind when he promised the "early authors of Ohio" a "rich harvest of fame": antiquarians, authors in the conventional sense, would memorialize the pioneer settlers by assembling "fragments of history"; "men of science" (by reading in "the great book of nature . . . every where, presenting its opened, expanded volume, to his anxious and enquiring eye") would shed new light on the state's bountiful resources, while men of action would erect "the grand works" that would ever remain "MONUMENTS" of the "founders." "Millions on millions shall yet read their writings with filial reverence and affection."[54]

Atwater's conceit would be flattering to the many leading Ohioans, including Atwater himself, busily involved in all these activities. But the broad definitions of authorship and state founding moved beyond self-congratulation to embrace a broader vision of northwestern history in which the authority of the American founders merged with the moral authority of the people of the Old Northwest acting according to the timeless and transcendent principles of freedom.

IV. Sectionalism and Union

Northwesterners came to see the rapid settlement and development of their new states as natural and inevitable. In 1832 a Michigan editor applauded the "spirit of enterprise" so evident in the recent "tide of immigration" from "the old and populous states." Here was a

> demonstration, that a tract of country, extensive, fertile, and, in general, healthy as is this, was never intended to remain in a state of nature, wild, uncultivated, the mere play-place of savages, and the haunts of beasts, but to become subject to the exclusive control of a public-spirited and improving population.[55]

Destined for higher uses, the bountiful natural landscape inspired settlers to fulfill their own potential as productive citizens.

But what prevented this vast westward movement from weakening the union and overextending the republic? In the 1780s danger was seen in the depopulation and impoverishment of the old states and in the unpredictable loyalties and interests of semisavage frontiersmen. By the 1820s, the conquest and "improvement" of nature seemed more certain and the reversion to savagery less likely. Instead, the problem "in a republick so extensive as ours" was that sectional differences would grow increasingly intractable. For one western writer, "the conclusion is reasonable, nay irresistible, that when its different sections become thickly populated, jealousies will arise which will disturb its peace and endanger its liberties."[56]

Beginning in the 1780s, advocates of internal improvements argued that turnpikes and canals offered the antidote to sectionalism. "What stronger bond of union can be invented," asked Robert Fulton in his *Treatise on Canals*, "than those which enable each individual to transport the produce of his industry, 1200 miles for sixty cents the hundred weight?" Building a network of rivers and canals was "a certain method of securing the union of the states, and rendering it as lasting as the continent we inhabit."[57] Improved transportation brought Americans closer together, making the union itself as "natural" as western development. Author John Pendleton Kennedy of Maryland thus celebrated "the romantic, but no longer impracticable exploit of annihilating time and space."[58] In 1835 an Ohio editor repeated the familiar formula: "construction of great and splendid works of internal improvement" would help bind "the separate portions of the nation indissolubly together. . . . A common interest will promote a common feeling, as certainly as facility of intercourse and an interchange of productions will create a common interest."[59] Accompanied and facilitated by internal improvements, westward expansion would strengthen the union. Advocates of improvements proclaimed that a "community of interest" and "mutual dependence" would come into being in the West—if it was properly developed—enabling Americans to transcend sectional differences.[60]

Yet, naturally enough, the gospel of development was appropriated by westerners to promote their own distinctive, sectional interests. Over time, in historian Frederick Jackson Turner's words, "the full influence" of "geographic peculiarities," "special interests," and "developed ideals" was felt.[61] Although northwesterners continued to embrace a vision of union through material progress, they began to define "union" in a way that excluded the slaveholding South. This definition reflected an emerging sense of distinctive "ideals" that had developed during the state-making era in the Old Northwest.

The Northwest Ordinance came to symbolize the region's abiding commitment to what northwesterners believed were fundamental American principles. The authors of the Ordinance, with their "sagacious forecast," had provided for an expanding union, grounded in freedom and common interest. But, northwesterners claimed, this promise had been betrayed by promoters of slavery: only in the free West was the vision of union through development fulfilled. Living under free institutions and enjoying the fruits of unprecedented economic growth, northwesterners had been amply rewarded for their fidelity to the founders' ideals. The "first cause of our wonderful progress is undoubtedly to be found in the character and position of our soil," Walker conceded. But when the potential "settler turned from the contemplation of the soil" to the Northwest Ordinance, "the first fundamental law by which his rights would be determined, the inducement [to emigrate] was multiplied ten fold."[62] The Ordinance, one anniversary celebrant concluded, was "the charter of our social and political prosperity."[63]

Walker and other northwestern orators and writers duly acknowledged their indebtedness to the Founding Fathers. Along with congressional provisions for the sale and survey of public lands, beginning with the Land Ordinance of 1785, the Northwest Ordinance provided a blueprint for future communities, images of an organized landscape and constitutional environment in which individuals could freely pursue their own goals. Yet northwesterners also emphasized that the prosperity that vindicated free principles could only have been achieved by the enlightened enterprise of northwesterners themselves. Thus, in their own way, the pioneers who exploited natural advantages and promoted the rapid growth of wealth and population were also founders of free and powerful new states and authors of their own destiny. The appeal of the Northwest Ordinance as a regional symbol was based on this sense of reciprocity and connection between past and present generations. Northwesterners could see themselves as the founders' true legatees.

As northwesterners contemplated their future prospects, the freedom secured by the exclusion of slavery by Article VI became increasingly important. So, in comparing the prospects of Indiana and Kentucky, one writer began with the usual invocation of natural abundance: Indiana's "wealth"—as Kentucky's had been—was "in her forests, and in her fields." But free soil Indiana's "strength will be in her enlightened citizens and splendid public works made by the State. She is not cursed with that incubus slavery which weighs against the enterprise of her neighbor."[64]

Indiana's material advantages were inextricably tied to the superior morality of free institutions. For Abraham Lincoln and many of his contemporaries, the moral issue became preeminent. "Lincoln was certain," explains political theorist Harry V. Jaffa, "not that the Northwest Ordinance as such had excluded slavery from the territory north of the Ohio, but that the moral condemnation of slavery which demanded and was embodied in the ordinance had kept it out." The Northwest Ordinance may not have had constitutional force—it was up to the people to keep slavery out of the region. But the Ordinance made higher claims on the "moral sense of the people" than could any law or constitution.[65] As northwesterners reimagined their own and the nation's founding, they infused the idea of union with moral purpose as well as material promise. Turning south and preparing for the impending sectional conflict, thousands of them—like Lincoln or Senator Thomas Corwin—took their "stand upon the Ordinance of 1787."

NOTES

Introduction

1. John Gardiner, *An Oration, Delivered July 4, 1785.* . . . (Boston, 1785), 35.

2. For elaboration of this point, see Cathy Matson and Peter Onuf, "Toward a Republican Empire: Interest and Ideology in Revolutionary America," *American Quarterly*, 37 (1985), 496–531.

3. See Clinton Rossiter, ed., *The Federalist Papers* (New York, 1961), 238, for James Madison's contention that the Ordinance was enacted "without the least color of constitutional authority." Congress's constitutional incapacity is also cited by Nathan Dane, one of the Ordinance's authors. Nathan Dane to Samuel Phillips, Jan. 20, 1786, Nathan Dane Miscellaneous Manuscripts (Library of Congress). The best recent account of the history of the Ordinance is in Jack Ericson Eblen, *The First and Second United States Empires: Governors and Territorial Government, 1784–1912* (Pittsburgh, 1968); but see also Paul Finkelman, "Slavery and the Northwest Ordinance: A Study in Ambiguity," *Journal of the Early Republic* (forthcoming). For an exhaustive discussion of constitutional issues, see "Introduction," in Francis Philbrick, *The Laws of the Illinois Territory, 1809–1818* (Springfield, 1950).

4. Act of Aug. 7, 1789, in Francis Newton Thorpe, ed., *The Federal and State Constitutions*, 7 vols. (Washington, 1909), 2:963–64.

5. Gordon S. Wood, *The Creation of the American Republic, 1776–1787* (Chapel Hill, 1969), 259–305; Donald S. Lutz, "From Covenant to Constitution in American Political Thought," *Publius*, 10 (1980), 101–30.

6. Speech of March 30, 1802, in *Annals of the Congress of the United States, 1789–1824*, 42 vols. (Washington, 1834–56), 7 Cong., 1 Sess., 11:1103. For a much later formulation of the same argument, see Governor Stevens T. Mason, Message to the Senate and House, Feb. 1, 1836, in George N. Fuller, ed., *Messages of the Governors of Michigan*, 3 vols. (Lansing, 1925–27), 1:164.

7. King to Elbridge Gerry, June 4, 1786, in Edmund Cody Burnett, ed., *Letters of the Members of the Continental Congress* (hereafter *LMCC*), 8 vols. (Washington, 1921–36), 8:380–82.

8. Jefferson to James Monroe, July 9, 1786, in Julian P. Boyd et al., eds., *The Papers of Thomas Jefferson*, 22 vols. to date (Princeton, 1950–), 10:112–13.

9. Peter S. Onuf, *The Origins of the Federal Republic: Jurisdictional Controversies in the United States, 1775–1787* (Philadelphia, 1983), 127–45, passim. See also Frederick Jackson Turner, "Western State-Making in the Revolutionary Era," *American Historical Review*, 1 (1895–96), 70–87, 251–69.

10. For a typical expression of the expectation that the people of the territories could look forward to being "reinstated into those rights and privileges which they formerly enjoyed as citizens" when they achieved statehood, see "Address to the Citizens" of a meeting in Hamilton Co., Cincinnati, Dec. 6, 1797, reprinted in Randolph Chandler Downes, *Frontier Ohio, 1788–1803* (Columbus, 1935), 183–84. On state and federal citizenship, see James H. Kettner, *The Development of American Citizenship, 1608–1870* (Chapel Hill, 1978), 248–86.

11. Report of May 10, 1786, in Worthington C. Ford, ed., *Journals of the Continental Congress*, 34 vols. (Washington, 1904–37), 30:251.

12. For "tonic," see Richard Henry Lee to William Lee, July 30, 1787, in Burnett, ed., *LMCC*, 8:629–30. The word "colonial" was frequently used in reference to territorial government. See, for examples, James Monroe to John Jay, April 20, 1786, and Timothy Bloodworth to Richard Caswell, Sept. 4, 1786, in ibid., 8:342, 462.

13. Wood, *Creation of the American Republic*, 268–69.

14. Onuf, *Origins of the Federal Republic*, 131–35. The quotation is from Ethan Allen and Jonas Fay, *A Concise Refutation of the Claim of New Hampshire and Massachusetts-Bay to the Territory of Vermont* (Hartford, 1780), 27.

15. St. Clair's Address, May 29, 1795, in William Henry Smith, ed., *The St. Clair Papers: The Life and Public Services of Arthur St. Clair*, 2 vols. (Cincinnati, 1882), 2:353–63, at 356.

16. *Report of Committee to Prepare Memorial to Congress*, March 5, 1834, 23 Cong., 1 sess., S. Doc. 235 (Serial 240), p. 4.

17. Onuf, *Origins of the Federal Republic*, 24–29; Bernard Bailyn, *The Ideological Origins of the American Revolution* (Cambridge, 1967), 224–25 and passim.

18. The quotation is from "The Case of Michigan," *National Intelligencer* (Washington, D.C.), Dec. 5, 1835.

19. William Rawle, *A View of the Constitution of the United States of America* (1829; New York, 1970). See also Joseph Story, *Commentaries on the Constitution of the United States*, 2 vols. (1833; 5th ed., Boston, 1891), 2:197.

20. *Hogg v. Zanesville Canal & Mfr. Co.*, 5 Ohio 410 (1832), 416–17. For a review of state court responses, see Walter C. Haight, "The Binding Effect of the Ordinance of 1787," *Publications of the Michigan Political Science Association*, 2 (1896–97), 343–402.

21. Arthur Bestor, "Constitutionalism and the Settlement of the West: The Attainment of Consensus, 1754–1784," in John Porter Bloom, ed., *The American Territorial System* (Athens, Ohio, 1973), 13–44, at 21.

22. *Strader et al. v. Graham*, 10 Howard 82 (1850), 96. *Strader* elaborated the position taken by the Court in *Pollard's Lessee v. Hagan*, 3 Howard 212 (1845), 223. See the discussions in Philbrick, *Laws of the Illinois Territory*, ccxvi–ccxxii; and Edwin S. Corwin, *The Constitution and What It Means Today*, revised by Harold W. Chase and Craig R. Ducat, 14th ed. (Princeton, 1978), 261–66. For an excellent discussion of constitutional issues in antebellum territorial history, see Don E. Fehrenbacher, *The Dred Scott Case: Its Significance in American Law and Politics* (New York, 1978).

1. Liberty, Development, and Union

1. On the "critical period," see Peter S. Onuf, *The Origins of the Federal Republic: Jurisdictional Controversies in the United States, 1775–1787* (Philadelphia, 1983), 173–85. See also Frederick W. Marks III, *Independence on Trial: Foreign Affairs and the Making of the Constitution* (Baton Rouge, 1973).

2. The literature on republicanism is voluminous. See particularly Gordon S. Wood, *The Creation of the American Republic, 1776–1787* (Chapel Hill, 1969); and J. G. A. Pocock, *The Machiavellian Moment* (Princeton, 1975).

3. Benjamin Franklin, "Consolation for America, or remarks on her real situation, interests, and policy," *American Museum*, 1 (Jan. 1787), 7. My discussion of attitudes toward economic development relies heavily on Michael Lienesch, "Development: The Economics of Expansion," a chapter in *New Order of the Ages: The American Constitution and the Making of Modern Republican Thought* (forthcoming). See also John Robert Van Atta, "Securing the West: Public Lands and Political Economy in America, 1784 to 1841" (Ph.D. diss., University of Virginia, 1982), esp. chaps. 1–3; Drew R. McCoy, *The Elusive Republic: Political Economy in Jeffersonian America* (Chapel Hill, 1980), for a fine treatment of the relation between expansion and republican ideology; and Major L. Wilson, *Space, Time, and Freedom* (Westport, 1974), for an analysis of development themes in antebellum political ideologies.

4. "Introductory Remarks" to [David Humphreys], "The Happiness of America,"

Columbian Magazine, 1 (Oct. 1786), 67. Joyce Appleby provides a useful analysis of contemporary notions of "liberty" in *Capitalism and a New Social Order: The Republican Vision of the 1790s* (New York, 1984), 16–23. My interpretation of American liberal thought relies heavily on Appleby's writings. Marshall Berman, *All That is Solid Melts into Air: The Experience of Modernity* (New York, 1982) has helped me see "development" as an act of imagination, or "dream." For a discussion of early attempts to define the new American character, focused on *Columbian Magazine,* see Lawrence J. Friedman, *Inventors of the Promised Land* (New York, 1975), 3–43.

5. [Anon.], "Oration delivered at Commencement, in the University of Philadelphia, May 7, 1784," *Columbian Magazine,* 1 (Oct. 1786), 84, 85.

6. On "commercial republicans," see Ralph Lerner, "Commerce and Character: The Anglo-American as New-Model Man," *William and Mary Quarterly* (hereafter *WMQ*), 36 (1979), 3–26.

7. For treatments of European perceptions of Revolutionary America, see Durand Echeverria, *Mirage in the West: A History of the French Image of American Society to 1815* (Princeton, 1957); and Horst Dippel, *Germany and the American Revolution, 1770–1800,* trans. Bernhard Uhlendorf (Chapel Hill, 1977).

8. For Thomas Jefferson's interest in developing commercial links between Virginia and the West, see his letters to James Madison and George Washington, Feb. 20 and March 15, 1784, in Julian P. Boyd et al., eds., *The Papers of Thomas Jefferson,* 22 vols. to date (Princeton, 1950–), 6:547–48, 7:25–27. Joyce Appleby emphasizes Jefferson's role as "an early advocate of the commercial exploitation of American agriculture" in "What is Still American in the Political Philosophy of Thomas Jefferson?" *WMQ,* 39 (1982), 287–309, quotation at 295. Virginian expansionists are discussed in Marc Egnal, "The Origins of the Revolution in Virginia: A Reinterpretation," *WMQ,* 37 (1980), 401–28.

9. The ordinance is printed in Worthington C. Ford, ed., *Journals of the Continental Congress* (hereafter *JCC*), 34 vols. (Washington, 1904–37), 28:375–81. For discussions of its legislative history, see Payson J. Treat, *The National Land System, 1785–1820* (New York, 1910), 15–40; and Paul W. Gates, *History of Public Land Law Development* (Washington, 1968), 59–74. William D. Pattison, *Beginnings of the American Rectangular Land Survey System, 1784–1800* (Chicago, 1957), is particularly useful in clarifying the differences between the 1785 ordinance and prior proposals. Malcolm Rohrbough, *The Land Office Business: The Settlement and Administration of American Public Lands, 1789–1837* (New York, 1968), 3–25, offers a good introduction to the history of the ordinance in practice.

10. Richard Henry Lee to Samuel Adams, May 20, 1785, in Edmund Cody Burnett, ed., *Letters of the Members of the Continental Congress* (hereafter *LMCC*), 8 vols. (Washington, 1921–36), 8:122. Though Virginians were unusually sensitive to the debt issue, a broad consensus supported this use of the national domain. A writer in the *Independent Chronicle* (Boston), April 14, 1785, thought land sales revenue would help provide tax relief for manufacturers. See also "An honest chearful citizen," "A word of consolation for America," *American Museum,* 1 (March 1787), 188.

11. Washington to Henry Knox, Dec. 5, 1784, in John C. Fitzpatrick, ed., *The Writings of George Washington,* 39 vols. (Washington, 1931–44), 28:4.

12. Letter from M. Turgot to Dr. Price, March 22, 1778, appendix to Richard Price, *Observations on the Importance of the American Revolution,* 2d ed. (London, 1785), reprinted in Bernard Peach, ed., *Richard Price and the Ethical Foundations of the American Revolution* (Durham, N.C., 1979), 215–24, quotation at 222. This letter— and the Price pamphlet—were widely excerpted in contemporary American newspapers.

13. Item d. New-York, Nov. 4, 1785, *Virginia Journal* (Alexandria), Nov. 17, 1785.

For similar comments, prompted by the commercial convention at Annapolis, see another item d. New York, Aug. 29, 1786, *New-Jersey Gazette* (Trenton), Sept. 11, 1786.

14. "Observator," no. 3, *New-Haven Gazette*, Oct. 27, 1785.

15. "Candidus," *London Evening Post*, n.d., reprinted in *Pennsylvania Gazette* (Philadelphia), July 21, 1784. This theme is discussed further in Peter S. Onuf and Nicholas G. Onuf, "American Constitutionalism and the Emerging World Order," paper delivered at Organization of American Historians meeting, Minneapolis, April 1985.

16. Enos Hitchcock, *A Discourse on the Causes of National Prosperity* (Providence, 1786), 24.

17. Virginia separatists told Congress that "the Western inhabitants can no longer be safe, or useful in Society, without the protecting arm of the federal government." Charles Cummings to President of Congress, April 7, 1785, item 48, f. 97, Papers of the Continental Congress (National Archives, Washington). See the discussion in Onuf, *Origins of the Federal Republic*, 38–40.

18. Count de Mirabeau, *Reflections on the Observations on the Importance of the American Revolution* [by Price] (Philadelphia, 1786), 2.

19. Price, *Observations*, in Peach, ed., *Richard Price and the American Revolution*, 208. The Abbé de Mably warned Americans against allowing "wealth" to "usurp an absolute empire" in the New World: avoid European manners, "vices," and "politics." The new republic must not become another Carthage, "at once *commercial and warlike.*" Gabriel Bonnot de Mably, *Observations on the Government and Laws of the United States* (Amsterdam, 1784), 120–21 (my emphasis). For similar sentiments, see letter from Turgot to Price, March 22, 1778, in Peach, ed., *Richard Price and the American Revolution*, 222. On "agrarianism," see Lienesch, *New Order of the Ages*, 3–11; and, on the idealization of the middle stage of social development—and the "middle landscape"—see Leo Marx, *The Machine in the Garden* (New York, 1964).

20. Particularly Jack Ericson Eblen, *The First and Second United States Empires: Governors and Territorial Government, 1784–1912* (Pittsburgh, 1968), 17–51. But see Onuf, *Origins of the Federal Republic*, 166–71; and Onuf, "From Constitution to Higher Law: The Reinterpretation of the Northwest Ordinance," *Ohio History*, 94 (1985), 5–33.

21. Jefferson to Madison, Jan. 30, 1787, in Boyd et al., eds., *Jefferson Papers*, 11:93.

22. Madison to Marquis de Lafayette, March 20, 1785, in Robert Rutland et al., eds., *The Papers of James Madison*, 15 vols. to date (Chicago and Charlottesville, 1962–), 8:251.

23. Item d. Alexandria, Nov. 15, 1784, *Virginia Journal*, Nov. 25, 1784. See also George Washington to Knox, Dec. 5, 1784, in Fitzpatrick, ed., *Washington Writings*, 28:3. It was widely agreed that "nothing cements mankind together firmly so much as mutual interest." Item d. Charleston, S.C., May 2–8, 1786 (concerning trade policy), *New-Jersey Gazette*, May 29, 1786.

24. Freneau, "On the emigration to America," *American Museum*, 1 (Feb. 1787), 159; Humphreys, "A poem on the happiness of America," ibid. (March 1787), 249. For an excellent study of these and other writers (including Joel Barlow), emphasizing their adaptation of traditional rhetoric to a new vision of secular progress and commercial expansion, see Mason I. Lowance, Jr., *The Language of Canaan: Metaphor and Symbol in New England from the Puritans to the Transcendentalists* (Cambridge, 1980), 208–46.

25. *American Museum*, 1 (Feb. 1787), 160.

26. Item d. Trenton, April 13, 1784, *Virginia Journal*, April 29, 1784.

27. "Farmer," "To the INHABITANTS of POTOMACK RIVER," ibid., Aug. 19, 1784.

28. "Lycurgus," "OBSERVATIONS on the PRESENT SITUATION and FUTURE PROSPECTS of THIS and the UNITED STATES," no. 1, *New-Haven Gazette and Connecticut Magazine*, Feb. 16, 1786; reprinted in *Connecticut Courant* (Hartford), Feb. 27, 1786, and *Maryland Gazette* (Baltimore), March 24, 1786.

29. Cutler, *An Explanation of the Map which Delineates . . . the Federal Lands* (Salem, 1787), reprinted in William Parker Cutler and Julia Perkins Cutler, *Life, Journals and Correspondence of Rev. Manasseh Cutler, LL.D.*, 2 vols. (Cincinnati, 1888), 2:400.

30. Jonathan Loring Austin, *An Oration, Delivered July 4, 1786* (Boston, 1786), 15. The same language was used by a "correspondent," d. New York, Nov. 3, 1785, *Connecticut Courant*, Nov. 7, 1785. the efforts of pioneer settlers "will change" the West "from a savage wilderness, to a civilized field that shall blossom like the rose." The biblical reference is to Isaiah 35: "The wilderness and the solitary place shall be glad for them; and the desert shall rejoice, and blossom as the rose."

31. *Maryland Gazette* (Baltimore), April 17, 1787.

32. Coxe, "An address to an assembly of the friends of American manufactures," *American Museum*, 2 (Sept. 1787), 255.

33. "Americanus" [William Barton?], "On American Manufactures," *Columbian Magazine*, 1 (Sept. 1786), 27. Both "Americanus" and Barton cited Birtish economist James Anderson. See note 35 below.

34. "An American" [William Barton], *The True Interest of the United States, and Particularly of Pennsylvania* (Philadelphia, 1786), 11.

35. "Americanus," "On American Manufactures," 27n, citing Anderson, *Observations on the Means of Exciting a Spirit of National Industry* (Edinburgh, 1777), letter IV.

36. "A Plain, but Real, Friend to America," *Maryland Journal* (Baltimore), Aug. 16, 1785.

37. Jefferson believed that it was America's destiny to spread its people across the New World, thus "doubling the numbers of mankind, and of course the quantum of existence and happiness." Jefferson, Observations on Demeunier's Manuscript [1786], in Boyd et al., eds., *Jefferson Papers*, 10:57.

38. David Howell to Jonathan Arnold, Feb. 21, 1784, in William R Staples, *Rhode Island in the Continental Congress*, ed. Reuben Aldridge Guild (Providence, 1870), 479.

39. Humphreys, "Poem on the happiness of America," 249, 251.

40. Jefferson, *Notes on the State of Virginia*, ed. William Peden (1954; New York, 1972), 164–65.

41. Jefferson to Washington, March 15, 1784, and to G. K. van Hogendorp, Oct. 13, 1785, in Boyd et al., eds., *Jefferson Papers*, 7:26, 8:633.

42. Jefferson to Washington, March 15, 1784, ibid., 7:26. For a plan to build a canal through New York, see Christopher Colles, *Proposals for the Speedy Settlement of the Waste and Unappropriated Lands on the Western Frontiers of the State of New-York, and for the Improvement of the Inland Navigation between Albany and Oswego* (New York, 1785).

43. McMechen was parrying criticism of his vote in favor of the company in the Maryland Assembly. McMechen to Electors of Baltimore-Town, Sept. 20, 1785, *Maryland Journal*, Sept. 23, 1785.

44. Washington to Gov. Benjamin Harrison, Oct. 10, 1784, in Fitzpatrick, ed., *Washington Writings*, 27:480. See also Washington to Knox, Dec. 5, 1784, ibid.,

28:3–5. Washington warned against allowing the "commerce of that country" to "embrace" the Mississippi route: "experience has taught us . . . how next to impracticable it is to divert it." Washington to David Humphreys, July 25, 1785, ibid., 205.

45. "Extract of a Letter from Alexandria, to a gentleman of Wilmington," *Freeman's Journal* (Philadelphia), Aug. 23, 1786.

46. Manufactures would come "sooner to perfection" because of the expense of imported goods. "Letter from an officer of distinction to a gentleman in Carlisle," d. banks of the Ohio, Oct. 12, 1785, *Connecticut Courant*, Dec. 26, 1785.

47. T[ench] C[oxe], "An Enquiry into the Principles on which a Commercial System for the United States should be founded," *American Museum*, 1 (June 1787), 499. For another invocation of the harmony of interests, see New York [City] Chamber of Commerce, *Gentlemen, The Interest of the Landholder. . . . ,* broadside (New York, 1785): "By the union of the farmer, the merchant and mechanic" the new nation had withstood "the open force of our enemies."

48. "Farmer," "To the Inhabitants of Maryland," *Maryland Journal*, Feb. 17, 1786. See also "One of the People," *New-Jersey Gazette*, Sept. 20, 1784: "annihilate commerce, and you effectually ruin the landed interest by sinking the value of lands."

49. "Introductory Remarks" to [Humphreys], "Happiness of America," 67.

50. Barlow, oration to Society of the Cincinnati, *American Museum*, 2 (Aug. 1787), 138.

51. Murray, "Political Sketches" [written 1784–85], ibid. (Sept. 1787), 237, 238, 233, 234.

52. "Hear the Other Side of the Question," *Pennsylvania Gazette* (Philadelphia), Sept. 8, 1784.

53. "Negative Arguments on the Question, whether sumptuary laws ought to be established in the United States," *New-Haven Gazette*, Oct. 12, 1786. For further discussion, see Cathy Matson and Peter Onuf, "Toward a Republican Empire: Interest and Ideology in Revolutionary America," *American Quarterly*, 37 (1985), 496–531.

54. Gardiner, *An Oration, Delivered July 4, 1785. . . .* (Boston, 1785), 35.

55. "Observator," no. 1, *New-Haven Gazette*, Aug. 25, 1785.

56. Barlow, oration to Society of the Cincinnati, 138. For similar rhetoric, see Amicus Reipublicae, *Address to the Public. . . .* (Exeter, N. H., 1786), 35.

57. Item d. Worcester, Mass., Nov. 17, 1785, *New-Jersey Gazette*, Nov. 28, 1785. For a similar prediction, see "COLLECTIVE OBSERVATIONS [on the American states]," *Connecticut Courant*, June 5, 1786: "were agriculture and manufactures attended to, our navigation would revive, commerce flourish, and *produce* and *cash* would be returned to us from abroad for *produce only.*"

58. Washington emphasized the "political importance" of establishing "strong commercial bands" between East and West and thus strengthening the union but conceded that the "commercial advantages"—to Virginia and Maryland—would be "immense." Washington to Knox, Dec. 5, 1784, in Fitzpatrick, ed., *Washington Writings*, 28:4.

59. Washington to William Grayson, June 22, 1785, ibid., 172–73. Washington thought it would be a mistake for Congress to select a "*permanent* seat . . . at this time."

60. These misgivings are discussed in Washington to Grayson, April 25, 1785, ibid., 136–39; and Archibald Stuart to Jefferson, Oct. 17, 1785, in Boyd et al., eds., *Jefferson Papers*, 8:646. See also Onuf, *Origins of the Federal Republic*, 159–60.

61. Madison to Jefferson, Aug. 20, 1784, in Rutland et al., eds., *Madison Papers*, 8:108. See also Madison to Lafayette, March 20, 1785, ibid., 250–55. On the threat of depopulation, see "Primitive Whig," no. 5, *New-Jersey Gazette*, Feb. 6, 1786; and "Amicus," *Freeman's Journal*, Dec. 13, 1786 (decrying "this waste of people").

62. Monroe to Patrick Henry, Aug. 12, 1786, in William Wirt Henry, *Patrick Henry: Life, Correspondence, and Speeches*, 3 vols. (New York, 1891), 2:297; Monroe to Madison, Aug. 14, 1786, in Rutland et al., eds., *Madison Papers*, 9:104–105. See also Timothy Bloodworth to Governor Caswell (of North Carolina), Aug. 28, 1786, in Burnett, ed., *LMCC*, 8:455.

63. Rufus King to Elbridge Gerry, June 4, 1786, in Burnett, ed., *LMCC*, 8:380. For a discussion of Massachusetts's interest in preventing emigration to the Ohio region, see Rufus Putnam to Washington, April 5, 1784, in Cutler and Cutler, *Life of Cutler*, 1:174–76.

64. "Extract of a letter from a gentleman in Maryland to his friend in Philadelphia," *Independent Chronicle* (Boston), Sept. 8, 1785.

65. Grayson told Washington that some congressmen thought it "true policy to get the money with[out] parting with inhabitants to populate the Country." Grayson to Washington, April 15, 1785, in Burnett, ed., *LMCC*, 8:97. "Primitive Whig" also favored giving "the greatest possible encouragement to the influx of foreigners." *New-Jersey Gazette*, Feb. 6, 1786.

66. Ezra Stiles, *The United States Elevated to Glory and Honour*, 2d ed. (Worcester, 1785), 60 (my emphasis). For the best introduction to contemporary population theory, see James Russell Gibson, "Americans Versus Malthus: The Population Debate in the Early Republic" (Ph.D. diss., Clark University, 1982), esp. chap. 1. See also Drew R. McCoy, "Jefferson and Madison on Malthus: Population Growth in Jeffersonian Political Economy," *Virginia Magazine of History and Biography*, 88 (1980), 259–76.

67. "Extract of a letter from Davidson County, North-Carolina," *Virginia Journal*, Feb. 15, 1787.

68. Madison to Jefferson, Aug. 20, 1784, in Rutland et al., eds., *Madison Papers*, 8:108. Madison argued at the Constitutional Convention that American populations would tend to equalize. Speech of July 11, 1787, in Max Farrand, ed., *The Records of the Federal Convention of 1787*, 4 vols. (New Haven, 1911–37), 1:585–86.

69. "A Citizen of Pennsylvania" [Benjamin Rush], "Account of the Progress of the Population, Agriculture, Manners, and Government in Pennsylvania," *Columbian Magazine*, 1 (Nov. 1786), 121. For reports on the "astonishingly great . . . emigrations from the different States" to the Ohio Valley, see "Extract of a letter from Fort McIntosh," *Connecticut Courant*, Nov. 7, 1785; and "Extract of a letter from a gentleman in Kentucky, to his friend in Philadelphia," *New-Jersey Gazette*, Feb. 5, 1785.

70. William Barton, *Observations on the Progress of Population* [read before American Philosophical Society, March 18, 1791] (Philadelphia, 1791), 1. Barton cited Richard Price: "The encouragement of population ought to be one of the first objects of policy, in every State."

71. "Strictures on Abbe Raynal," *Columbian Herald* (Charleston, S.C.), June 6, 1785. "Celadon" wrote, "This continent is the largest, and will be the most populous empire upon earth." *The Golden Age; or, Future Glory of North-America Discovered* (n.p., 1785), 9.

72. T[ench] C[oxe], "Enquiry into the Principles," 514. Joel Barlow asserted that "the blessings of a rational government will invite emigrations." Barlow, oration to Society of the Cincinnati, 142. Lord Sheffield claimed that the Americans' "numbers . . . are certainly much decreased by the war and emigration." Lord Sheffield [John B. Holroyd], *Observations on the Commerce of the American States*, 2d ed. (London, 1783), 105n.

73. Washington to Knox, Dec. 5, 1784, in Fitzpatrick, ed., *Washington Writings*, 28:4.

74. Washington to Lafayette, July 25, 1785, ibid., 206.

75. Williams, "On the Fallacy . . . that Civil Liberty can only exist in a Small Territory," *Columbian Magazine*, 6 (March 1791), 144.

76. For further discussion, see Matson and Onuf, "Toward a Republican Empire," 496–531.

77. Webster, "Essay on the Extent and Value of Our Western Unlocated Lands," April 25, 1782, reprinted in *Political Essays on the Nature and Operation of Money, Public Finances, and Other Subjects* (Philadelphia, 1791), 485–500, quotations at 498, 497.

2. Squatters, Speculators, and Settlers

1. The text of the land ordinance, excerpted below, is taken from Worthington C. Ford, ed., *Journals of the Continental Congress* (hereafter *JCC*), 34 vols. (Washington, 1904–37), 28:375–81. The committee was named March 16 and reported a draft ordinance on April 12. Ibid., 165, 251–56. For subsequent proceedings (April 14–15, 20, 22–23, 26–29, May 2, 4–6, 18–19), see ibid., 264, 268n, 285, 290–96, 298–303, 309–10, 316–17, 319, 322–23, 335–37, 339, 340, 342–43, 365, 370–73.

2. For the legislative history of the land ordinance, see Payson J. Treat, *The National Land System, 1785–1820* (New York, 1910), 15–40; and Paul W. Gates, *History of Public Land Law Development* (Washington, 1968), 59–74. William D. Pattison, *Beginnings of the American Rectangular Land Survey System, 1784–1800* (Chicago, 1957), is particularly useful in clarifying the differences between the 1785 ordinance and prior proposals. For the history of the ordinance in practice, see Malcolm Rohrbough, *The Land Office Business: The Settlement and Administration of American Public Lands, 1789–1837* (New York, 1968), 3–25; and Joseph W. Ernst, "With Compass and Chain: Federal Land Surveyors in the Old Northwest, 1785–1816" (Ph.D. diss., Columbia University, 1958), esp. 33–125.

3. See the brief discussion in Francis Paul Prucha, *The Sword of the Republic: The United States Army on the Frontier, 1783–1846* (1969; Bloomington, Ind., 1977), 6–11. The most thorough treatment is Andrew Robert Lee Cayton, "The Best of All Possible Worlds: From Independence to Interdependence in the Settlement of the Ohio Country, 1780–1825" (Ph.D. diss., Brown University, 1981), esp. 1–24 on squatters. "In almost every respect," Cayton suggests, "the Land Ordinance was the direct antithesis of squatting tactics"; "the basic assumption" of congressional policy was "that the actual settlers in the West were incapable of governing themselves and that educated, responsible easterners were better equipped to guide the development of society." Ibid., 47, 52–53.

4. The Virginia cession, accepted by Congress on March 1, 1784, is reprinted in Clarence E. Carter and John Porter Bloom, eds., *The Territorial Papers of the United States*, 28 vols. to date (Washington, 1934–), 2:6–9. See the discussion in Peter S. Onuf, *The Origins of the Federal Republic: Jurisdictional Controversies in the United States, 1775–1787* (Philadelphia, 1983), 75–102.

5. The report, drafted by a committee also including David Howell of Rhode Island, Elbridge Gerry of Massachusetts and Jacob Read of South Carolina, is in Ford, ed., *JCC*, 26:324–30. On the authorship question, see Pattison, *American Rectangular Land Survey System*, 38–39; and Hugh Williamson to Gov. Alexander Martin, July 5, 1784, in Walter Clark, ed., *State Records of North Carolina*, vol. 17 (Goldsboro, N.C., 1899), 80–83.

6. William Grayson to Timothy Pickering, April 27, 1785, in Edmund Cody Burnett, ed., *Letters of the Members of the Continental Congress* (hereafter *LMCC*), 8 vols. (Washington, 1921–36), 8:106. Grayson's correspondence gives the fullest account of these discussions. See also his letters to George Washington, April 15,

May 8, ibid., 95–97, 117–19; and to James Madison, May 1, 28, in Robert Rutland et al., eds., *The Papers of James Madison*, 15 vols. to date (Chicago and Charlottesville, 1962–), 8:274–77, 284–85.

7. Jedidiah Morse, *Geography Made Easy* (New-Haven, 1784), 112. Pelatiah Webster called them "the richest wild lands in the world." Webster, "Essay on the Extent and Value of Our Western Unlocated Lands," April 25, 1782, reprinted in *Political Essays on the Nature and Operation of Money, Public Finances, and Other Subjects* (Philadelphia, 1791), 485–500, quotation at 490.

8. John Filson, *The Discovery, Settlement and Present State of Kentucke* (Wilmington, 1784).

9. "Extract of a letter from a gentleman in the western country," *Maryland Journal* (Baltimore), April 4, 1786.

10. William Ellery and Howell to Gov. William Greene, Sept. 8, 1783, in William R. Staples, *Rhode Island in the Continental Congress*, ed. Reuben Aldridge Guild (Providence, 1870), 447.

11. Washington to Richard Henry Lee, Dec. 14, 1784, in John C. Fitzpatrick, ed., *The Writings of George Washington*, 39 vols. (Washington, 1931–44), 28:12.

12. David Humphreys, "Address to the armies of the united states of America" [1782], *American Museum*, 1 (March 1787), 238.

13. "A letter from a gentleman in the western country, to his friend in Connecticut," *Maryland Gazette* (Baltimore), Feb. 28, 1786.

14. "Extract of a letter from a gentleman in Kentucky, to his friend in Philadelphia," *New-Jersey Gazette* (Trenton), Feb. 7, 1785.

15. "Extract of a letter from a gentleman in the western country, to his friend in Connecticut," ibid., May 8, 1786.

16. Lee to John Adams, May 28, 1785, in Burnett, ed., *LMCC*, 8:128.

17. "Extract of a letter from a gentleman in the western region to his friend in Boston," *New Haven Gazette and Connecticut Magazine*, Sept. 28, 1786. For a brilliant analysis of contemporary attitudes toward natural abundance, see Lester H. Cohen, "Eden's Constitution: The Paradisiacal Dream and Enlightenment Values in Late-Eighteenth Century Literature on the American Frontier," *Prospects*, 3 (1977), 83–109. Cohen writes, "the hopes and expectations of settlers and promoters were 'utopian.' But 'utopian' ought not to be construed as a synonym for 'Edenic' and 'paradisiacal,' implying the centrality of nature." They saw "nature as a field of opportunity—not for its own sake, but for exploitation." Ibid., 93, 92.

18. Writing as "Nestor," Benjamin Rush asserted that "there is but one path that can lead the United States to destruction; and that is their extent of territory. It was probably to effect this, that Great Britain ceded to us so much waste land." *Independent Gazetteer* (Philadelphia), June 3, 1786. See the discussion in Onuf, *Origins of the Federal Republic*, 159–60.

19. "Lycurgus," no. 10, *New Haven Gazette and Connecticut Magazine*, April 20, 1786.

20. "Lycurgus," no. 2, ibid., Feb. 23, 1786. "Lycurgus"'s first number [ibid., Feb. 16, 1786], a straight argument for development, was picked up by other papers (*Connecticut Courant* [Hartford], Feb. 27; *Maryland Gazette* [Baltimore], March 24). The *Connecticut Courant* reprinted the satirical no. 2 on March 8, but as far as I can tell, no other numbers—all in the satirical mode—were reprinted.

21. *Maryland Gazette* (Baltimore), May 4, 1787; *Independent Chronicle* (Boston), April 19, 1787. For discussion of the connection between Vermont and the western settlements, see also Madison to Washington, March 18, 1787, in Rutland et al., eds., *Madison Papers*, 9:314–17; and Washington to Madison, March 31, 1787, in Fitzpatrick, ed., *Washington Writings*, 29:188–92.

22. "Primitive Whig," no. V, *New-Jersey Gazette*, Feb. 6, 1786.

23. "Amicus," *Freeman's Journal* (Philadelphia), Dec. 13, 1786. See also "A Plain, but Real, Friend to America," *Maryland Journal* (Baltimore), Aug. 16, 1785.

24. *Maryland Gazette* (Baltimore), April 17, 1787.

25. Col. Josiah Harmar to President of Congress, May 1, 1785, cited in Prucha, *Sword of the Republic*, 8.

26. News of Congress's land ordinance evidently had not reached the writer. "P. W., " " Extract of a letter from Bedford, Pa.," *Independent Chronicle*, Aug. 25, 1785; advertisement signed by John Emerson, March 12, 1785, in William Henry Smith, ed., *The St. Clair Papers: The Life and Public Services of Arthur St. Clair*, 2 vols. (Cincinnati, 1882), 2:5n.

27. Ellery and Howell to Gov. Greene, Sept. 8, 1783, in Staples, *Rhode Island in the Continental Congress*, ed. Guild, 447.

28. Thomas Jefferson's comment [May 4, 1784] on G. K. van Hogendorp, "On Western Territory," in Julian P. Boyd et al., eds., *The Papers of Thomas Jefferson*, 22 vols. to date (Princeton, 1950–), 7:220n.

29. Extract of a letter, Dec. 22, 1785, *Maryland Journal*, April 4, 1786.

30. Jefferson to James Monroe, Aug. 28, 1785, in Boyd et al., eds., *Jefferson Papers*, 8:445.

31. Madison to Monroe, May 29, 1785, in Rutland et al., eds., *Madison Papers*, 8:286.

32. Rudolph Freund, "Military Bounty Lands and the Origins of the Public Domain," in Vernon Carstensen, ed., *The Public Land: Studies in the History of the Public Domain* (Madison, 1963), 15–34. See the new state plan devised by Rufus Putnam and associates in Octavius Pickering, ed., *The Life of Timothy Pickering*, 4 vols. (Boston, 1867–73), 1:457–59, 546–49.

33. "A citizen of Pennsylvania" [Benjamin Rush], "Account of the Progress of the Population, Agriculture, Manners, and Government in Pennsylvania," *Columbian Magazine*, 1 (Nov. 1786), 120. Also see item in *Freeman's Journal*, May 24, 1786, citing Abbé Raynal on the degeneration of "Europeans . . . when arrived at the regions of the new world." The theme is elaborated in Roy Harvey Pearce, *Savagism and Civilization: A Study of the Indian and the American Mind* (Baltimore, 1965; orig. pub., Baltimore, 1953, as *The Savages of America*), esp. 53–104; Ronald Meek, *Social Science and the Ignoble Savage* (Cambridge, Eng., 1976); and Michael Lienesch, "Development: The Economics of Expansion," a chapter in *New Order of the Ages: The American Constitution and the Making of Modern Republican Thought* (forthcoming).

34. Howell to Gov. Greene, Feb. 1, 1784, in Staples, *Rhode Island in the Continental Congress*, ed. Guild, 472.

35. Webster, "Essay on Western Lands," in *Political Essays*, 495; Washington to James Duane, Sept. 7, 1783, in Fitzpatrick, ed., *Washington Writings*, 27:133–40; report of congressional committee on West, Oct. 15, 1783, in Ford, ed., *JCC*, 25:693–94. In 1787 John Matthews predicted that the "present inhabitance" of the Ohio country would be chronically embroiled with the Indians: "the truth is they are both saviges." Quoted in Cayton, "Best of All Possible Worlds," 53n.

36. Item from *Boston Gazette*, Feb. 27, 1786, reprinted in *Maryland Gazette* (Baltimore), March 24, 1786.

37. "Extract of a letter from a gentleman at Ft. Harmar . . . to his friend in this town [Boston]," *New Haven Gazette and Connecticut Magazine*, Oct. 5, 1786.

38. For typical comments on the effects of unrestrained movements of squatters and speculators, see Washington to Read, Nov. 3, 1784, in Fitzpatrick, ed., *Washington Writings*, 27:486; and Pickering to Gerry, March 1, 1785, in Pickering, ed.,

Life of Timothy Pickering, 1:505. The Washington quotation is from Washington to Williamson, March 15, 1785, in Fitzpatrick, ed., *Washington Writings*, 28:108.

39. J. Hector St. John de Crèvecoeur, *Letters from an American Farmer* (1782; New York, 1957), 42–43.

40. Washington refuted characterizations such as this, often found in contemporary British writings. Washington to Rev. William Gordon, April 10, 1787, in Fitzpatrick, ed., *Washington Writings*, 29:200. Contemporary American attitudes toward westerners are briefly assessed in Robert F. Berkhofer, Jr., "The Northwest Ordinance and the Principle of Territorial Evolution," in John Porter Bloom, ed., *The American Territorial System* (Athens, Ohio, 1973), 45–55, at 50–51.

41. "Extract of a letter from Louisville," *Maryland Journal*, March 1, 1785.

42. "A letter from a gentleman of eminence in the state of Connecticut . . . to his friend in Chesterfield," d. May 15, 1786, *New-Jersey Gazette*, July 3, 1786; Nathan Dane, Address to the Massachusetts House [Nov. 9, 1786], in Burnett, ed., *LMCC*, 8:503.

43. "The authority of the Congress, can never be maintained over those distant and boundless regions," the English Lord Sheffield predicted in 1783: "her nominal subjects will speedily imitate and multiply the examples of independence." Lord Sheffield [John B. Holroyd], *Observations on the Commerce of the American States*, 2d ed. (London, 1783), 104–105. The British press gleefully reported pervasive "anarchy" throughout America after the peace. Letter from Suffolk, Va., June 1, 1785, *London Chronicle*, Aug. 6, 1785, reprinted in Samuel Cole Williams, *History of the Lost State of Franklin* (New York, 1933), 87–88; "Sketches of the Present Times," *Times* (London), Feb. 2, 1786. For a discussion of American anarchy by a Jamaican writer, see *Falmouth Gazette* (Portland, Mass.), Sept. 10, 1785.

44. Delegates to Gov. Benjamin Harrison, Nov. 1, 1783, in Burnett, ed., *LMCC*, 7:365.

45. "Extract of a letter," Dec. 22, 1785, *Maryland Journal*, April 4, 1786. On the role of "land jobbers" in creating the new state of Franklin, see Extract of a letter from Washington Co., Dec. 15, 1784, *Freeman's Journal*, Feb. 2, 1785. On land speculation and separatism generally, see Thomas Perkins Abernethy, *Western Lands and the American Revolution* (New York, 1937), passim.

46. Onuf, *Origins of the Federal Republic*, 75–102.

47. Washington to Duane, Sept. 7, 1783, in Fitzpatrick, ed., *Washington Writings*, 27:133.

48. Washington to Read, Nov. 3, 1784, ibid., 486.

49. Pickering to Gerry, March 1, 1785, in Pickering, ed., *Life of Timothy Pickering*, 1:505.

50. Washington to Sec. of War Henry Knox, June 18, 1785, in Fitzpatrick, ed., *Washington Writings*, 28:168.

51. Washington to Williamson, March 15, 1785, ibid., 108.

52. "Primitive Whig," *New-Jersey Gazette*, Feb. 6, 1786.

53. Nathaniel Sackett et al., *A Memorial, &c* [to Congress] (New York, Sept. 27, 1785), item 41, IX, f. 349, Papers of the Continental Congress (National Archives, Washington, D. C.); read in Congress, Aug. 23, 1785, in Ford, ed., *JCC*, 29:651n.

54. "Cincinnatus," *Massachusetts Spy* (Worcester), Feb. 16, 1786, also printed in *New Haven Gazette and Connecticut Magazine*, March 9, 1786. "Cincinnatus" questioned the authenticity of a "Letter from a gentleman in the Western country," December 1785, first printed in New York in early January 1786 and republished throughout the country (including *Pennsylvania Gazette*, Jan. 11; *Columbian Herald* [Boston], Jan. 19; and *Massachusetts Spy*, Jan. 26, 1786).

55. A congressional proclamation warning squatters off federal lands was published

in *Independent Journal* (New York), July 2, 1785; and *Freeman's Journal*, Aug. 17, 1785. See note 3 above.

56. Jonathan Loring Austin, *An Oration, Delivered July 4, 1786* (Boston, 1786), 15. See also "Celadon," *The Golden Age; or, Future Glory of North-America Discovered* (n.p., 1785), 9, for an elaboration of the asylum theme: "The poor, the oppressed, and the persecuted will fly to America as doves to their windows.—This Western-World will be the dernier resort, the last refuge, and asylum for afflicted merit."

57. "Cato," "To the Public," *New Haven Gazette and Connecticut Magazine*, Jan. 25, 1787.

58. Item d. New York, July 20, 1786, *Freeman's Journal*, July 26, 1786.

59. "Extract of a letter from a gentleman residing in Kentucky to his friend in Chester co.," ibid., April 11, 1787.

60. Washington to Duane, Sept. 7, 1783, in Fitzpatrick, ed., *Washington Writings*, 27:140.

61. Washington to Knox, Dec. 5, 1784, and to Lee, Aug. 22, 1785, ibid., 28:4, 231; Grayson to Washington, April 15, 1785, ibid., 8:95–97, and to William Short, June 15, 1785, in Burnett, ed., *LMCC*, 8:141–42. On the eastern states' fears of depopulation, see Rufus Putnam to Washington, April 5, 1784, in William Parker Cutler and Julia Perkins Cutler, *Life, Journals and Correspondence of Rev. Manasseh Cutler, LL.D.*, 2 vols. (Cincinnati, 1888), 1:174–75; and Rufus King to Gerry, June 4, 1786, in Burnett, ed., *LMCC*, 8:380–82.

62. Jefferson to David Hartley, Sept. 5, 1785, in Boyd et al., eds., *Jefferson Papers*, 8:482–83.

63. "P. W.," "Extract of a letter from Bedford, Pa.," *Independent Chronicle*, Aug. 25, 1785.

64. Jefferson to Francis Hopkinson, May 3, 1784, in Boyd et al., eds., *Jefferson Papers*, 7:205.

65. John R. Stilgoe, *Common Landscape of America, 1580 to 1845* (New Haven, 1982), 99–107, passim.

66. Manasseh Cutler, *An Explanation of the Map which Delineates . . . the Federal Lands* (Salem, 1787), reprinted in Cutler and Cutler, *Life of Cutler*, 2:393–406, quotation at 404.

67. Item attributed to a "physician of some eminence," *Maryland Gazette* (Baltimore), March 13, 1787; Cutler Journal, July 21, 24–25, 1787, reprinted in Cutler and Cutler, *Life of Cutler*, 1:296, 299.

68. Webster, "Essay on Western Lands," in *Political Essays*, 495.

69. Washington to Read, Nov. 3, 1784, in Fitzpatrick, ed., *Washington Writings*, 27:487. See also Washington to Williamson, March 15, 1785, ibid., 28:107–108.

70. Pickering to Gerry, March 1, 1785, in Pickering, ed., *Life of Timothy Pickering*, 1:505.

71. Grayson to Washington, April 15, 1785, in Burnett, ed., *LMCC*, 8:95.

72. This point is also developed in Andrew R. L. Cayton, "Planning the Republic: The Federalists and Internal Improvements in the Old Northwest," paper delivered at Organization of American Historians meeting, Minneapolis, April 1985.

73. Washington to Lady Huntingdon, June 30, 1785, in Fitzpatrick, ed., *Washington Writings*, 28:181. For the amendment to the land ordinance, stipulating that a single auction would be held at the seat of Congress, see resolution of April 21, 1787, in Ford, ed., *JCC* 32:226; and Madison to Randolph, April 22, 1787, in Rutland et al., eds., *Madison Papers*, 9:397.

74. "More than probably," the western population "will be composed in a great degree of Foreigners." Washington to Lee, Aug. 22, 1785, in Fitzpatrick, ed., *Washington Writings*, 28:231.

75. Edward Carrington to Monroe, Aug. 7, 1787, in Burnett, ed., *LMCC*, 8:631.

76. Stilgoe, *Common Landscape*, emphasizes the artificiality of imposing "urban" forms on the western lands. Of course, this artificiality was the key to the transformation of land into property. For a stimulating essay on perceptions of the landscape, see Hildegard Binder Johnson, "Perceptions and Illustrations of the American Landscape in the Ohio Valley and the Midwest," in *This Land of Ours: The Acquisition and Disposition of the Public Domain* (Indianapolis, 1978), 1–38.

77. Washington to Lee, Dec. 14, 1784, in Fitzpatrick, ed., *Washington Writings*, 28:9. Washington told Filson that "it has long been my wish to see an extensive and accurate Map of the Western territory . . . founded upon actual surveys and careful observations." Letter of Jan. 15, 1785, ibid., 30.

78. Delegates to Gov. Matthew Griswold, May 27, 1785, in Burnett, ed., *LMCC*, 8:124.

79. Grayson to Washington, April 15, 1785, ibid., 96.

80. Delegates to Pres. Meshech Weare, May 29, 1785, ibid., 130–31.

81. For apposite comments on the poor prospects for farmers, as opposed to speculators, under Pennsylvania's land system, see "A Little Land Jobber," "A few Short Hints," *Freeman's Journal*, March 23, 1785.

82. Pickering to Gerry, March 1, 1785, in Pickering, ed., *Life of Timothy Pickering*, 1:504.

83. Webster, "Essay on Western Lands," in *Political Essays*, 499.

84. Washington to Grayson, April 25, 1787, in Fitzpatrick, ed., *Washington Writings*, 28:138.

85. *American State Papers: Documents, Legislative and Executive of the Congress of the United States*, 38 vols. (Washington, 1832–61), *Public Lands*, 3:459.

86. Cutler Journal, July 21, 1787, in Cutler and Cutler, *Life of Cutler*, 1:296; Grayson to Monroe, Aug. 8, 1787, in Burnett, ed., *LMCC*, 8:631–32.

87. Cutler to Dane, March 16, 1787, in Cutler and Cutler, *Life of Cutler*, 1:194.

88. Carrington to Monroe, Aug. 7, 1787, in Burnett, ed., *LMCC*, 8:631.

89. Grayson to Monroe, Oct. 22, 1787, ibid., 659; and Carrington to Jefferson, Oct. 23, 1787, in Boyd et al., eds., *Jefferson Papers*, 12:252–57. For a concise account of these complicated transactions (including an option for an additional 5 million acres for the Scioto Company, headed by William Duer, secretary of the Board of Treasury), see Reginald Horsman, *The Frontier in the Formative Years, 1783–1815* (New York, 1970), 36–37. On the Ohio Company, see also Shaw Livermore, *Early American Land Companies: Their Influence on Corporate Development* (1939; New York, 1968), 134–46; and Cayton, "Best of All Possible Worlds," 61–71.

3. New States in the Expanding Union

1. Congress received frequent complaints from settlers in the Illinois region who "wish to be under the protection" of the United States. Extract of a letter, d. New York, June 22, 1785, *New-Haven Gazette*, Sept. 8, 1785. See also Secretary of Congress to Kaskaskia Inhabitants, Aug. 24, 1786, in Edmund Cody Burnett, ed., *Letters of the Members of the Continental Congress* (hereafter *LMCC*), 8 vols. (Washington, 1921–36), 8:450, promising that Congress would soon adopt a new "plan of a temporary government."

2. For instance, Letter from a gentleman in the Western Country, December 1785, published in newspapers throughout the country, including *Pennsylvania Gazette* (Philadelphia), Jan. 11, 1786; *Maryland Gazette* (Baltimore), Jan. 20, 1786; and *Massachusetts Spy* (Worcester), Jan. 26, 1786. According to George Washington, in a letter to Lafayette, July 25, 1785, in John C. Fitzpatrick, ed., *The Writings of George Washington*, 39 vols. (Washington, 1931–44), 28:208, "Many think the price which

they have fixed upon for the Lands too high" and that the sale by townships would be "a great let to the sale."

3. The April 23, 1784, Ordinance is in Worthington C. Ford, ed., *Journals of the Continental Congress* (hereafter *JCC*), 34 vols. (Washington, 1904–37), 26:274–79. It is reprinted in its entirety below. For the drafting of the ordinance, see the documents and notes in Julian P. Boyd et al., eds., *The Papers of Thomas Jefferson*, 22 vols. to date (Princeton, 1950–), 6:599–605; and the excellent analysis in Robert F. Berkhofer, Jr., "Jefferson, the Ordinance of 1784, and the Origins of the American Territorial System," *William and Mary Quarterly*, 29 (1972), 231–62.

4. The Virginia cession, March 1, 1784, is reprinted in Clarence E. Carter and John Porter Bloom, eds., *The Territorial Papers of the United States*, 28 vols. to date (Washington, 1934–), 2:6–9.

5. Vote of April 21, 1784, in Ford, ed., *JCC*, 26:259–60.

6. James Monroe to John Jay, April 20, 1786, in Burnett, ed., *LMCC*, 8:342.

7. Arthur Campbell to Arthur Lee, Oct. 18, 1784, in Paul P. Hoffman, ed., *The Lee Family Papers, 1742–1795* (microfilm ed., Charlottesville, 1966), reel 7, frame 411; Timothy Pickering to Rufus King, March 8, 1785, in Octavius Pickering, ed., *The Life of Timothy Pickering*, 4 vols. (Boston, 1867–73), 1:508–509.

8. Committee reports of Feb. 14, March 24, May 10, July 13, 1786, in Ford, ed., *JCC*, 30:68–70, 131–35, 251–55, 402–406. See the account of these deliberations in Jack Ericson Eblen, *The First and Second United States Empires: Governors and Territorial Government, 1784–1912* (Pittsburgh, 1968), 28–32.

9. Notably Eblen, *First and Second United States Empires*, 17–51; and Andrew Robert Lee Cayton, "The Best of All Possible Worlds: From Independence to Interdependence in the Settlement of the Ohio Country, 1780–1825" (Ph.D. diss., Brown University, 1981). The historiography is discussed in Ray Allen Billington, "The Historians of the Northwest Ordinance," *Illinois State Historical Society Journal*, 40 (1947), 397–413; and Philip R. Shriver, "America's Other Bicentennial," *Old Northwest*, 9 (1983), 219–35.

10. Jefferson, Observations on Demeunier's Manuscript [1786], in Boyd et al., eds., *Jefferson Papers*, 10:57.

11. Washington to Henry Knox, Dec. 5, 1784, in Fitzpatrick, ed., *Washington Writings*, 28:3–4.

12. Secretary of Congress to Certain States, May 28, 1785, in Burnett, ed., *LMCC*, 8:128.

13. Jefferson's Answers to Demeunier's First Queries, Jan. 24, 1786, in Boyd et al., eds., *Jefferson Papers*, 10:14. See also Jefferson to Madison, April 25, 1784, ibid., 7:118; and Madison to Jefferson, March 16, 1784, in Robert Rutland et al., eds., *The Papers of James Madison*, 15 vols. to date (Chicago and Charlottesville, 1962–), 8:9; and the discussion in Peter S. Onuf, *The Origins of the Federal Republic: Jurisdictional Controversies in the United States, 1775–1787* (Philadelphia, 1983), 161–62.

14. "Extract of a letter from a gentleman of North-Carolina to his friend in the Western Country," d. Hillsborough, June 2, 1784, *Virginia Journal* (Alexandria), Aug. 5, 1784.

15. Petition to Virginia Assembly, n.d., reprinted in *Freeman's Journal* (Philadelphia), Jan. 12, 1785; Address to the Western Inhabitants, enclosed in Charles Cummings to the Pres. of Congress, April 7, 1785, item 48, f. 289, Papers of the Continental Congress (National Archives, Washington); extract of a letter from a gentleman in Frankland, Aug. 17, 1785, *Times* (London), Dec. 31, 1785; "Impartialis Secundus," *Falmouth Gazette* (Portland, Mass.), July 9, 1785.

16. William Grayson to Washington, April 15, 1785, in Burnett, ed., *LMCC*, 8:95–97.

17. Jefferson to Monroe, July 9, 1786, and to Madison, Dec. 16, 1786, in Boyd et al., eds., *Jefferson Papers*, 10:112, 603.

18. Monroe to Jefferson, Jan. 19, 1786, ibid., 9:189.

19. July 7 resolution and votes, in Ford, ed., *JCC*, 30:390–94; Secretary of Congress to Gov. Patrick Henry, July 11, 1786, in Burnett, ed., *LMCC*, 8:403, asking Virginia to revise its cession act accordingly. At this point the population threshold was undecided. Monroe was convinced that easterners who meant to keep new western states "out of the confederacy altogether" would attempt to raise the population requirement to one-thirteenth of the free population of the United States, a prohibitively high level. Monroe to Jefferson, July 16, 1786, ibid., 403–405. This requirement was recommended in a subsequent version of the government ordinance. Report of Sept. 19, 1786, in Ford, ed., *JCC*, 31:669–72.

20. According to Grayson's report, in a letter to Lt. Gov. Beverley Randolph, June 12, 1787, in Burnett, ed., *LMCC*, 8:610.

21. Report of April 30, 1784, in Ford, ed., *JCC*, 26:324–30. See the discussion in William Pattison, *Beginnings of the American Rectangular Land Survey System, 1784–1800* (Chicago, 1957), 38–39.

22. Jefferson considered the revised land ordinance an improvement on his own proposals "in the most material circumstances." Jefferson to Monroe, Aug. 28, 1785, in Boyd et al., eds., *Jefferson Papers*, 8:445.

23. Pattison, *American Rectangular Land Survey System*, 15–36, 53–55.

24. David Howell to Gov. Jonathan Arnold, Feb. 21, 1784, in William R. Staples, *Rhode Island in the Continental Congress*, ed. Reuben Aldridge Guild (Providence, 1870), 480.

25. Grayson to Washington, April 15, 1785, in Burnett, ed., *LMCC*, 8:95–97.

26. Howell to Gov. William Greene, Feb. 9, 1785, ibid., 24–26.

27. The report of March 1, 1784, in Ford, ed., *JCC*, 26:118–20, including Jefferson's suggested state names, was widely published in 1784 as "Resolutions of Congress." See for instance, *Virginia Gazette* (Richmond), May 15, 1784; and *Virginia Journal*, June 3, 1784. The adopted government ordinance and land ordinance were printed in *New-Jersey Gazette* (Trenton) and *Connecticut Courant* (Hartford), both June 6, 1785; *New-Haven Gazette*, June 9; *Salem Gazette* (Salem, Mass.), June 14, 21; *Independent Chronicle* (Boston), June 23; *Columbian Herald* (Charleston, S.C.), June 27, 29, July 1. *Gazette of the State of Georgia* (Savannah), July 21, 1785, published the land ordinance only.

28. Madison to Edmund Randolph, April 22, 1787, in Rutland et al., eds., *Madison Papers*, 9:397; Richard Henry Lee to William Lee, July 30, 1787, in Burnett, ed., *LMCC*, 8:629. As Richard Henry Lee explained, the Northwest Ordinance established a "temporary Government . . . preparatory to the sale of that Country" to the Ohio Company. Lee to Francis Lightfoot Lee, July 14, 1787, ibid., 619.

29. Monroe to Jefferson, May 11, 1786, in Burnett, ed., *LMCC*, 8:359–60.

30. Edward Carrington to Jefferson, Oct. 23, 1787, in Boyd et al., eds., *Jefferson Papers*, 12:252–57.

31. "A correspondent says . . . ," *New-York Gazetteer*, Feb. 11, 1785.

32. Item d. Richmond, *Virginia Journal*, March 31, 1785. See also Pickering to Elbridge Gerry, March 1, 1785, in Pickering, ed., *Life of Timothy Pickering*, 1:504–507: "If but a single State be sold"; and Samuel Dick to William Hall, May 27, 1785, in Burnett, ed., *LMCC*, 8:126–27: the land ordinance provided for "Disposal of our new Western State."

33. Jay to Jefferson, April 24, 1787, in Boyd et al., eds., *Jefferson Papers*, 11:312–14.

34. The grid laid down in the land ordinance was altered by Congress May 12, 1786, by omitting the requirement that lines be run according to the "true meridian." Ford, ed., *JCC*, 30:262. At the same time the territorial government committee was abandoning Jefferson's proposed boundaries. See Pattison, *American Rectangular Land Survey System*, 19–36, 53–55, 90–92.

35. Madison to Lafayette, March 20, 1785, in Rutland et al., eds., *Madison Papers*, 8:250–55.

36. "Address from the Abbe Raynal to the Independent Citizens of America," *Freeman's Journal*, April 12, 1786.

37. Item in ibid., June 15, 1785.

38. Item d. Philadelphia, Jan. 26, 1786, *Maryland Gazette* (Baltimore), Feb. 3, 1786. For further discussion of the state size question, see Onuf, *Origins of the Federal Republic*, 34–36.

39. Jefferson to Madison, June 20, 1787, in Boyd et al., eds., *Jefferson Papers*, 11:480.

40. Monroe to Jefferson, Aug. 25, 1785, in Burnett, ed., *LMCC*, 8:202–203. Similar thoughts are expressed in Monroe to Jefferson, Jan. 19, 1786, in Boyd et al., eds., *Jefferson Papers*, 9:186–91.

41. King to Gerry, June 4, 1786, in Burnett, ed., *LMCC*, 8:380.

42. Madison to Jefferson, Aug. 20, 1784, in Rutland et al., eds., *Madison Papers*, 8:108.

43. Madison to Lafayette, March 20, 1785, ibid., 252.

44. "Lycurgus," no. 2, *New Haven Gazette and Connecticut Magazine*, Feb. 23, 1786.

45. "Extract of a letter from London," Oct. 14, 1784, *New-York Gazetteer*, Jan. 11, 1785. See also Richard Champion, *Considerations on the Present Situation of Great Britain and the United States of America* (London, 1784), 238–39, for a prediction that the union would break up into "three great Republicks."

46. From a Correspondent, d. New York, July 12, 1787, *Independent Chronicle*, July 19, 1787.

47. Washington to Hugh Williamson, March 15, 1785, in Fitzpatrick, ed., *Washington Writings*, 28:107–108.

48. Washington to Knox, Dec. 5, 1784, ibid., 3. Opening of the Potomac "will be one of the grandest Chains for preserving the federal Union." Item d. Alexandria, Nov. 15, 1784, *Virginia Journal*, Nov. 25, 1784.

49. Committee appointed Sept. 18, 1786, report of Sept. 19, 1786, in Ford, ed., *JCC*, 31:667n, 669–73; first and second reading of this committee's proposed ordinance, third reading postponed, April 26, May 9–10, 1787, ibid., 32:242, 274–75, 281–83 (text), 283; new committee appointed, first through third readings of adopted ordinance, July 9, 11–13, ibid., 310n, 313–20, 333, 334–43 (text, printed below), 343 (vote). Nathan Dane to King, July 16, 1787, in Burnett, ed., *LMCC*, 8:621–22. The complete text of the Ordinance was published in *New York Independent Journal*, July 18, 1787; *Massachusetts Gazette* (Boston) and *Maryland Gazette* (Baltimore), both July 27, 1787; and *Independent Chronicle*, Aug. 2, 1787.

50. Manasseh Cutler Journal, July 21, 1787, in William Parker Cutler and Julia Perkins Cutler, *Life, Journals and Correspondence of Rev. Manasseh Cutler, LL.D.*, 2 vols. (Cincinnati, 1888), 1:296. On Cutler's role, see ibid., 343–44; and William Frederick Poole, *The Ordinance of 1787, and Dr. Manasseh Cutler as an Agent in its Formation* (Cambridge, 1876).

51. Robert F. Berkhofer, Jr., "The Northwest Ordinance and the Principle of Territorial Evolution," in John Porter Bloom, ed., *The American Territorial System* (Athens, Ohio, 1973), 45–55; Peter S. Onuf, "Territories and Statehood," in Jack P.

Greene, ed., *Encyclopedia of American Political History*, 3 vols. (New York, 1984), 3:1283–1304.

52. Cutler, *An Explanation of the Map which Delineates that Part of the Federal Lands . . . Confirmed to the United States by Sundry Tribes of Indians* (Salem, 1787), reprinted in Cutler and Cutler, *Life of Cutler*, 2:393–406, quotation at p. 400.

53. Item d. New York, Nov. 4, 1785, *Virginia Journal*, Nov. 17, 1785.

54. [Madison], "Consolidation," d. Dec. 3, 1791, *National Gazette* (Philadelphia), Dec. 5, 1791.

4. From Territory to State

1. On the territorial system, see Peter S. Onuf, "Territories and Statehood," in Jack P. Greene, ed., *Encyclopedia of American Political History*, 3 vols. (New York, 1984), 3:1283–1304; Earl Pomeroy, "The Territory as a Frontier Institution," *Historian*, 7 (1944), 29–41; and the essays collected in John Porter Bloom, ed., *The American Territorial System* (Athens, Ohio, 1973). See also George M. Dennison, "An Empire of Liberty: Congressional Attitudes toward Popular Sovereignty in the Territories, 1787–1867," *Maryland Historian*, 6 (1975), 19–40. On constitutional and legal problems, see Don E. Fehrenbacher's excellent *The Dred Scott Case: Its Significance in American Law and Politics* (New York, 1978). The admission process is discussed in Jack Ericson Eblen, *The First and Second United States Empires: Governors and Territorial Government, 1784–1912* (Pittsburgh, 1968), 213–36. Jacob Burnet, *Notes on the Early Settlement of the North-Western Territory* (New York and Cincinnati, 1847), 335–69, is an extensive commentary on admission requirements. William A. Dunning raised the state equality question in his "Are the States Equal under the Constitution?" *Political Science Quarterly*, 3 (1888), 425–53. See also Peter S. Onuf, "New State Equality: The Amibiguous History of a Constitutional Principle," *Publius*, 17 (1987). For a convenient guide to key cases concerning the status of the territories and new state equality, see Edward S. Corwin, *The Constitution and What it Means Today*, revised by Harold W. Chase and Craig R. Ducat, 14th ed. (Princeton, 1978).

2. On the Ohio statehood movement, see John D. Barnhart, *Valley of Democracy: The Frontier versus the Plantation in the Ohio Valley, 1775–1818* (Bloomington, 1953), 138–60; Randolph Chandler Downes, *Frontier Ohio, 1788–1803* (Columbus, 1935); Beverley W. Bond, Jr., *The Civilization of the Old Northwest: A Study of Political, Social, and Economic Development, 1788–1812* (New York, 1934); and Alfred Byron Sears, *Thomas Worthington: Father of Ohio Statehood* (Columbus, 1958). The best account of factional alignments in early Ohio is in Donald J. Ratcliffe, "The Experience of Revolution and the Beginnings of Party Politics in Ohio, 1776–1816," *Ohio History*, 85 (1976), 186–230. See also Jeffrey P. Brown, "Frontier Politics: The Evolution of a Political Society in Ohio, 1788–1804" (Ph.D. diss., University of Illinois, 1979), 125–284. Andrew Cayton's comments on a draft of this chapter gave me a sharper understanding of early Ohio politics.

3. The enabling act, approved April 30, 1802, may be found in Francis Newton Thorpe, ed., *The Federal and State Constitutions*, 7 vols. (Washington, 1909), 5:2897–99.

4. Arthur St. Clair's Address, July 15, 1788, in William Henry Smith, ed., *The St. Clair Papers: The Life and Public Services of Arthur St. Clair*, 2 vols. (Cincinnati, 1882), 2:53–56, at 54.

5. St. Clair to James Ross, Dec. 1799, ibid., 480–84.

6. Acting Gov. Winthrop Sargent to Sec. of State [Timothy Pickering], Aug. 14, 1797, in Clarence E. Carter and John Porter Bloom, eds., *The Territorial Papers of the United States*, 28 vols. to date (Washington, 1934–), 2:622–24.

7. "The first Epistle of Paul," *Ohio Gazette* (Marietta), Sept. 28, 1802.

8. Meeting at Marietta, Jan. 12, 1801, *Western Spy* (Cincinnati), Feb. 11, 1801. For a discussion of this address, see Return J. Meigs to Thomas Worthington, Jan. 15, 1801, in D. M. Massie, *Nathaniel Massie, a Pioneer of Ohio. Sketch of his Life and Selections from his Correspondence* (Cincinnati, 1896), 166–68.

9. St. Clair to Oliver Wolcott [July 1795?], in Smith, ed., *St. Clair Papers*, 2:378–83. See also St. Clair to Wolcott, July 24, 1795, ibid., 383–85.

10. "Meeting at Columbia," Feb. 1, 1796, *Centinel of the North Western Territory* (Cincinnati), Feb. 20, 1796.

11. Ibid.

12. "A Citizen of the North-Western Territory," *Scioto Gazette* (Chillicothe), Nov. 27, 1800.

13. Thomas Worthington to Abraham Baldwin, Nov. 30, 1801, in Sears, *Thomas Worthington*, 64.

14. "A Friend to the People" [Edward Tiffin], "To the Inhabitants of the North-Western Territory," *Scioto Gazette*, Sept. 24, 1801; William Ludlow to Tiffin, Dec. 22, 1801, excerpted in Downes, *Frontier Ohio*, 211.

15. "Countryman," "To the Citizens of the North Western Territory," *Scioto Gazette*, Feb. 12, 1801.

16. William Goforth to Thomas Jefferson, Jan. 5, 1802, in Carter and Bloom, eds., *Territorial Papers*, 3:198–201.

17. St. Clair to Ross, Jan. 15, 1802, in Smith, ed., *St. Clair Papers*, 2:555–57. Goforth was not included in this list. On St. Clair, see Beverley W. Bond, "An American Experiment in Colonial Government," *Mississippi Valley Historical Review*, 15 (1928), 221–35; and Alfred B. Sears, "The Political Philosophy of Arthur St. Clair," *Ohio Historical Quarterly*, 69 (1940), 41–57. The best account of St. Clair's administration is in Eblen, *First and Second United States Empires*, 72–75 and passim.

18. On the developmental premises of American territorial policy, see Robert Berkhofer, Jr., "The Northwest Ordinance and the Principle of Territorial Evolution," in Bloom, ed., *American Territorial System*, 45–55.

19. James H. Kettner, *The Development of American Citizenship, 1607–1870* (Chapel Hill, 1978) is the best authority on this question.

20. Address, d. Cincinnati, Dec. 30, 1797, excerpted in Downes, *Frontier Ohio*, 184; see also circular letter, Dec. 30, 1797, in Julia Perkins Cutler, ed., *Life and Times of Ephraim Cutler* (Cincinnati, 1890), 319–20. A toast at the July 4, 1802, celebration at Columbia, Hamilton Co., suggested a solution to this impasse; celebrants drank to "The citizens of the North-Western Territory—may they soon pass into the ranks of freemen." *Western Spy*, July 10, 1802.

21. Goforth Speech, July 4, 1796, John Armstrong Papers, Indiana Historical Society, Indianapolis, Box 4, Folder 7.

22. Samuel Holden Parsons and James Varnum to St. Clair, July 31, 1788, Rice Collection, Ohio Historical Society, Columbus, Box 2, no. 3.

23. St. Clair to Wolcott [July 1795?], in Smith, ed., *St. Clair Papers*, 2:378–83, at 382.

24. Goforth Speech, July 4, 1796, Armstrong Papers.

25. "Peter Squib," "To his Grace, Lord Lingo," *Western Spy* (Cincinnati), May 22, 1802.

26. "Address to the Citizens," Dec. 6, 1797, excerpted in Downes, *Frontier Ohio*, 184.

27. "Friend to the People" [Tiffin], "To the Inhabitants," *Scioto Gazette*, Sept. 24, 1801.

28. Item d. Chillicothe, ibid., Feb. 13, 1802.

29. St. Clair to William Henry Harrison, Feb. 17, 1800, in Smith, ed., *St. Clair Papers*, 2:489–91.

30. See the digest of congressional legislation concerning the territories in Max Farrand, *The Legislation of Congress for the Government of the Organized Territories of the United States, 1789–1895* (Newark, 1896), Appendix B, 57–58.

31. Meeting at Columbia, *Centinel of the Territory*, Feb. 20, 1796.

32. Goforth to Jefferson, Jan. 5, 1802, in Carter and Bloom, eds., *Territorial Papers*, 3:198–201.

33. "Farmer," "To the People of Hamilton Co.," July 21, 1802, *Western Spy*, July 24, 1802.

34. "At a meeting of a number of the Inhabitants of . . . Columbia," *Centinel of the Territory*, Feb. 20, 1796: Congress would "cheerfully restore us to the rights of freemen" once the population reached thirty thousand, the number entitled to representation in Congress. William McMillan later asserted that the twenty thousand threshold for statehood specified in the 1784 Territorial Government Ordinance still remained effective: "the sales [of public lands] being made prior to any alteration in that ordinance precluded congress from making any without the consent of the people inhabiting the state in which such lands were situated." "Frank Stubblefield," no. 3, *Western Spy*, Aug. 14, 1802.

35. "An Act declaring the assent of the Territory . . . to an alteration of the ordinance," Dec. 3, 1801, in Salmon P. Chase, ed., *Statutes of Ohio and the Northwestern Territory*, 3 vols. (Cincinnati, 1833), 1:341; St. Clair to Ross [Dec. 1799], in Smith, ed., *St. Clair Papers*, 2:480–84. For St. Clair's public justification for the division—emphasizing "natural" boundaries—see his speech to the legislature, Dec. 19, 1799, *Western Spy*, Dec. 24, 1799; and *A Letter from Arthur St. Clair, Governor of the North-Western Territory, On the Subject of a Division of the said Territory* (Philadelphia, 1800). The best account of sectional politics and St. Clair's attempted "gerrymander" is in Downes, *Frontier Ohio*, 199–200.

36. Worthington, Memorandum to the President [Feb. 20, 1802], in Carter and Bloom, eds., *Territorial Papers*, 3:212–14.

37. See "The Memorial of the . . . inhabitants of Jefferson County," n.d., reprinted in *Scioto Gazette*, March 13, 1802. See also Worthington's account of congressional proceedings in his letter to Nathaniel Massie, Feb. 8, 1802, in Massie, *Nathaniel Massie*, 191–92; and the house debates of March 30, 31, and April 7, 8, 1802, recorded in *Annals of the Congress of the United States, 1789–1824*, 42 vols. (Washington, 1834–56), 7 Cong., 1 sess., 11:1103–26, 1155–62.

38. "Protest of the Minority Against the Division Act" [Dec. 1801], *Ohio Gazette*, Jan. 15, 1802.

39. "Jefferson County Memorial," *Scioto Gazette*, March 13, 1802. See also James Caldwell to Worthington, March 8, 1802, Rice Collection, Box 1, no. 12; and Sears, *Thomas Worthington*, 72–73.

40. *Annals of Congress*, 11:258, 259, 268, 275, 294–95, 296–97 (Senate); ibid., 11:427, 465–66, 470–71, 814, 985, 1017, 1097–1118, 1123–26, 1128, 1155–56, 1158–62, 1252, 1349–51 (House); extracts of proceedings, Jan. 26, 27, 1802, *Scioto Gazette*, Feb. 13, 27, 1802; Sears, *Thomas Worthington*, 81–85.

41. Robert Williams speech, March 30, 1802, *Annals of Congress*, 11:1107–11.

42. Joseph Nicholson speech, March 30, 1802, ibid., 1105–1107.

43. "A Countryman," "To the Citizens of the North-Western Territory," no. 1, *Scioto Gazette*, Feb. 12, 1801.

44. "An Address of New Market Township to their fellow citizens," *Western Spy*, Aug. 21, 1802.

45. "At a numerous meeting of the Republican Corresponding Society of Cincinnati," ibid., May 1, 1802.

46. Roger Griswold speeches, March 30, 1802, *Annals of Congress*, 11:1104–1105, 1112–14.

47. Nicholson speech, March 30, 1802, ibid., 1105–1107.

48. Goforth to Jefferson, Jan. 5, 1802, in Carter and Bloom, eds., *Territorial Papers*, 3:198–201.

49. James Finley to Worthington, Feb. 12, 1802, printed in *Report of the committee to whom was referred the census . . . of the territory* (Washington, 1802), 17–18.

50. Worthington to Massie, March 5, 1802, in Massie, *Nathaniel Massie*, 200–203.

51. "Friend to the People" [Tiffin], "To the Inhabitants," *Scioto Gazette*, Sept. 24, 1801. See also report of July 4 celebration at Cincinnati, where "The patriots in congress" were toasted for upholding the "rights and privileges of the citizens of the North Western Territory in opposition to our own representative." "At a meeting of the Republican citizens," *Western Spy*, July 10, 1802.

52. "A Farmer's Creed," *Western Spy*, June 5, 1802.

53. "Mentor's Reply," *Ohio Gazette*, Oct. 19, 1802.

54. "Dayton Association," *Western Spy*, June 26, 1802.

55. "Epistle of Paul," *Ohio Gazette*, Oct. 4, 1802.

56. E[lias] Langham, "To the Citizens of Ross County," *Scioto Gazette*, Sept. 4, 1802. Downes characterizes Langham as an "erratic Republican." Downes, *Frontier Ohio*, 197.

57. St. Clair speech [Nov. 3, 1802], in Smith, ed., *St. Clair Papers*, 2:592–97, at 596.

58. Nicholson speech, March 30, 1802, *Annals of Congress*, 11:1114–15.

59. Calvin Goddard speech, March 30, 1802, ibid., 1115–16.

60. "Frank Stubblefield" [McMillan], no. 4, *Western Spy*, Aug. 21, 1802. McMillan and the Cincinnatians aligned with St. Clair in order to gain more favorable new state boundaries for their city. A former territorial delegate, McMillan supported the Jeffersonians in national politics. Downes, *Frontier Ohio*, passim.

61. "Extract of a Letter from a member of the Senate," *Western Spy*, June 12, 1802. St. Clair objected to the tax exemption in similar terms in a letter to Samuel Huntington, July 15, 1802. "Letters from the Samuel Huntington Correspondence, 1800–1812." Western Reserve Historical Society, *Tracts*, 95 (1915), 55–151, at 80–81.

62. "Epistle of Paul," *Ohio Gazette*, Oct. 4, 1802.

63. "A Friend to Instruction," "To the Inhabitants of Waterford, Adams, and Salem," ibid.

64. "Peter Squib," "To his Grace, Lord Lingo," *Western Spy*, May 22, 1802.

65. St. Clair speech [Nov. 3, 1802], in Smith, ed., *St. Clair Papers*, 2:592–97, at 597, 594.

66. *Scioto Gazette*, July 10, 1802.

67. Tiffin to George Tod, July 25, 1802, Rice Collection, Box 1, no. 48. See also Francis Dunlavy to Worthington, Aug. 12, 1802, ibid., no. 35.

68. Albert Gallatin to William Giles, Feb. 13, 1802, in *Annals of Congress*, 11:1100–1103.

69. Item from *Ohio Gazette*, n.d., reprinted in *Scioto Gazette*, July 31, 1802. The comparison with the division bill is further developed in *Ohio Gazette*, Oct. 11, 1802.

70. Thomas T. Davis and Joseph Nicholson speeches, March 30, 1802, *Annals of Congress*, 11:1103–1104, 1105–1107, 1114–15. The Cincinnati Corresponding Society confidently asserted that "we may decide as we please" on Congress's terms, "and go into a state government notwithstanding." *Western Spy*, May 1, 1802.

71. Manasseh Cutler to Ephraim Cutler, Dec. 26, 1802, in Cutler, ed., *Life of Ephraim Cutler*, 82.

72. John Bacon (Mass.) speech, citing "necessary and proper" clause, March 30,

1802, and James Bayard (Del.) and Giles speeches, March 31, *Annals of Congress*, 11:1111, 1123, 1124–25.

73. Item from *Ohio Gazette*, n.d., reprinted in *Scioto Gazette*, July 31, 1802.

74. Sen. William Hendricks of Indiana was one of the leading proponents of this view: see the discussion and documents in Frederick D. Hill, "William Hendricks' Political Circulars to His Constituents: First Senatorial Term, 1826–1831," *Indiana Magazine of History*, 71 (1975), 124–80, esp. 127, 133. See also Raynor G. Wellington, *The Political and Sectional Influence of the Public Lands* (New York, 1914).

75. For a good introduction to these statehood movements, see R. Carlyle Buley, *The Old Northwest: Pioneer Period, 1815–1840*, 2 vols. (Indianapolis, 1950), 1:58–93; and Barnhart, *Valley of Democracy*, 161–215.

76. The Wisconsin Act, April 20, 1836, is in Carter and Bloom, eds., *Territorial Papers*, 27:41–52. "Democratization" can be traced through the digest of legislation included in Farrand, *Legislation of Congress*. It is also discussed in Eblen, *First and Second United States Empires*, 138–40, passim; and Onuf, "Territories and Statehood," 1296–99.

77. For Michigan, see Alec R. Gilpin, *The Territory of Michigan (1805–1837)* (East Lansing, 1970); and for Wisconsin, see Alice E. Smith, *From Exploration to Statehood*, vol. 1 of *The History of Wisconsin* (Madison, 1973).

78. Memorial to Congress [January 1816], in Carter and Bloom, eds., *Territorial Papers*, 17:285–87.

79. *Memorial of Sundry Inhabitants of the Counties of Randolph and St. Clair* (Washington, 1806), 6, complained about being "unwarrantably precipitated into the second grade of territorial government." See also "An Anonymous Protest Against Transition to the Second Grade" [1812], in Carter and Bloom, eds., *Territorial Papers*, 16:209–10. Michigan's belated arrival at second-stage, representative government in 1823 is discussed in Gilpin, *Territory of Michigan*.

80. "Address to the Freeholders of Indiana," Aug. 24, 1804, *Indiana Gazette* (Vincennes), Aug. 28, 1804.

81. Opposition to statehood in Wisconsin is discussed in Smith, *From Exploration to Statehood*, 648–51; and Alice E. Smith, *James Duane Doty: Frontier Promoter* (Madison, 1954), 290–93. Wisconsin voters rejected statehood on four different occasions between 1840 and 1845.

82. "State Government," no. 1, *Mineral Point Democrat*, Oct. 8, 1845, reprinted in Milo M. Quaife, ed., *The Movement for Statehood, 1845–1846* (Madison, 1918), 356–58.

5. Boundary Controversies

1. Peter S. Onuf, *The Origins of the Federal Republic: Jurisdictional Controversies in the United States, 1775–1787* (Philadelphia, 1983).

2. Arthur Bestor, "Constitutionalism and the Settlement of the West: The Attainment of Consensus, 1754–1784," in John Porter Bloom, ed., *The American Territorial System* (Athens, Ohio, 1973), 13–44; Chad Wozniak, "The New Western Colony Schemes: A Preview of the United States Territorial System," *Indiana Magazine of History*, 68 (1972), 283–306.

3. The relevant portions of the "postscript" to Cartwright's pamphlet are reprinted in Harold M. Baer, "An Early Plan for the Development of the West," *American Historical Review*, 30 (1925), 537–43.

4. Report adopted April 29, 1784, in Worthington C. Ford, ed., *Journals of the Continental Congress* (hereafter *JCC*), 34 vols. (Washington, 1904–37), 26:316.

5. Onuf, *Origins of the Federal Republic*, 153–54.

6. Robert Berkhofer, Jr., "Jefferson, the Ordinance of 1784, and the Origins of the American Territorial System," *William and Mary Quarterly*, 29 (1972), 231–62, at 260.

7. Onuf, *Origins of the Federal Republic*, 194–96. For an influential discussion of the need for balance of power, see Emerich de Vattel, *The Law of Nations, or the Principles of Natural Law Applied to the Conduct . . . of Nations* (Washington, 1916, trans. of 1758 ed.), 251.

8. Monroe to Jefferson, July 16, 1786, in Edmund Cody Burnett, ed., *Letters of the Members of the Continental Congress* (hereafter *LMCC*), 8 vols. (Washington, 1921–36), 8:404; and Onuf, *Origins of the Federal Republic*, 154–55, for a brief discussion and further citations. On sectionalism, see Staughton Lynd, "The Compromise of 1787," reprinted in *Class Conflict, Slavery, and the United States Constitution* (Indianapolis, 1967), 185–213; and Joseph L. Davis, *Sectionalism in American Politics, 1774–1787* (Madison, 1977).

9. Monroe to Jefferson, Jan. 19, 1786, in Burnett, ed., *LMCC*, 8:286.

10. See the discussion in Peter S. Onuf, "Territories and Statehood," in Jack P. Greene, ed., *Encyclopedia of American Political History*, 3 vols. (New York, 1984), 3:1283–1304.

11. "An Act declaring the assent of the Territory . . . to an alteration of the ordinance," Dec. 3, 1801, in Salmon P. Chase, ed., *Statutes of Ohio and the Northwestern Territory*, 3 vols. (Cincinnati, 1833), 1:341–42.

12. Arthur St. Clair to James Ross [Dec. 1799], in William Henry Smith, ed., *The St. Clair Papers: The Life and Public Services of Arthur St. Clair*, 2 vols. (Cincinnati, 1882), 2:480–84.

13. St. Clair to Ross, Jan. 15, 1802, ibid., 555–57.

14. See the discussion in Randolph Chandler Downes, *Frontier Ohio, 1788–1803* (Columbus, 1935), 199–200; and Alfred Byron Sears, *Thomas Worthington: Father of Ohio Statehood* (Columbus, 1958), 64–66.

15. "Dayton Association," *Western Spy* (Cincinnati), June 26, 1802.

16. Thomas Worthington, memorandum to Jefferson, Feb. 20, 1802, in Clarence E. Carter and John P. Bloom, eds., *The Territorial Papers of the United States*, 28 vols. to date (Washington, 1934–), 3:212–14. See also "Protest of the Minority Against the Division Act," *Ohio Gazette* (Marietta), Jan. 15, 1802.

17. The enabling act, approved April 30, 1802, may be found in Francis Newton Thorpe, ed., *The Federal and State Constitutions*, 7 vols. (Washington, 1909), 5:2897–99. For the convention, see "First Constitutional Convention, Convened November 1, 1802. Journal of the Convention," *Ohio State Archaeological and Historical Quarterly*, 5 (1897), 80–153; and Sears, *Thomas Worthington*, 94–114.

18. "Mentor," no. 6, *Ohio Gazette*, Aug. 17, 1802.

19. Sibley to Burnet, Aug. 2, 1802, reprinted in Jacob Burnet, *Notes on the Early Settlement of the North-Western Territory* (New York and Cincinnati, 1847), 494–96.

20. "Dayton Association," *Western Spy*, June 26, 1802; "Extract of a Letter from a Senator," ibid., June 12, 1802.

21. "Mentor," no. 6, *Ohio Gazette*, Aug. 17, 1802.

22. "Frank Stubblefield" [William McMillan], *Western Spy*, Aug. 28, 1802.

23. "A report is in circulation," ibid., Nov. 3, 1802. A house committee, reporting on a bill to create a new territory in the north country, Dec. 30, 1803, endorsed the Federalists' reading of the Ordinance: settlers in that region "have a right to be a part" of Ohio "until Congress shall think proper" to create another state. Carter and Bloom, eds., *Territorial Papers*, 7:163–64.

24. Jack Ericson Eblen, *The First and Second United States Empires: Governors and Territorial Government, 1784–1912* (Pittsburgh, 1968), 63.

25. Thorpe, ed., *Federal and State Constitutions*, 5:2897–99 (enabling act), 2901–

13 (constitution). On the Ohio-Michigan controversy, see Todd B. Galloway, "The Ohio-Michigan Boundary Line Dispute," *Ohio Historical Quarterly*, 4 (1895), 199–230; and Carl Wittke, "The Ohio-Michigan Boundary Dispute Re-Examined," ibid., 45 (1936), 299–319.

26. Edward Tiffin to Gov. Lewis Cass, Nov. 21, 1817, 24 Cong., 1 sess., H. Doc. 7 (Serial 286), 236–37.

27. Act of Jan. 11, 1805, in Thorpe, ed., *Federal and State Constitutions*, 4:1925–26.

28. For a discussion of these lines and reproductions of contemporary maps, see Thomas H. Smith, *The Mapping of Ohio* (Kent, 1977), 178–80. Anthony Finley's 1832 "Map of Ohio," reprinted in ibid., 179, shows the disputed area as part of Michigan. Maps showing the "Harris" and "Fulton" lines may be found in 24 Cong., 1 sess., H. Doc. 54 (Serial 287).

29. "J," "Michigan Nullification," *Toledo Gazette*, March 12, 1835; published separately as broadside titled "The Replication."

30. "A Citizen of the Contested Ground," "Toledo," *Ohio State Journal* (Columbus), Feb. 21, 1835. The editor of *Miami of the Lake* in Perrysburg (whose trade was threatened by Toledo) castigated those "who are determined to reap a golden harvest out of the NEW CITY SPECULATION, at the sacrifice of the interest of the state." *Miami of the Lake*, Aug. 19, 1834; also ibid., Sept. 18, 1834. See also editorial, *Scioto Gazette* (Chillicothe), May 20, 1835, predicting that Toledo would "eventually outstrip Detroit" if "Ohio retain[ed] possession." Michigan's claims were supposedly designed to prevent the new city's growth.

31. See Gov. Robert Lucas, Message to the Assembly, Feb. 6, 1835, the Preamble and Resolutions of Feb. 23, 1835, and the act of the same date defining the northern boundaries of certain counties, 24 Cong., 1 sess., S. Doc. 6 (Serial 279), 131–37. The legislative history of these measures may be followed in *Journal of the House of Representatives of the State of Ohio* and *Journal of the Senate*, 33rd and 34th General Assemblies, vols. 32 and 33 (Columbus, 1834–35), 32:8–18, 41, 576–643, 733, 768, 796, 799 (house action on boundary); 33:127, 136–49, 155–56, 158–59, 161–62, 167–73, 175–77 (house on Lucas Co., etc.); 33:67, 91, 634, 674, 678–80, 685, 692, 697 (senate on boundary); 33:6–122 (senate documents on controversy); 33:130–54, 161–63, 165, 170–74, 177–78 (senate on Lucas Co., etc.).

32. Act. of Feb. 12, 1835, 24 Cong., 1 sess., H. Doc. 7 (Serial 286), 82.

33. Item in *Detroit Free Press*, n.d., reprinted in *Michigan Whig* and *Michigan Argus*, both May 7, 1835. See also "A Friend to the Union," *Cleveland Herald*, April 24, 1835, reprinted in *Miami of the Lake*, May 13, 1835, criticizing the "authors of our *enlarged* edition of nullification principles."

34. The quotation is from a letter in *Cincinnati Gazette*, n.d., reprinted in *Michigan Sentinel* (Monroe), April 4, 1835. See also "Amaziah Downing" on Michigan's "pop-gun gentry," *Michigan Whig*, May 28, 1835. For a brief history of the "Toledo War," see Alec R. Gilpin, *The Territory of Michigan (1805–1837)* (East Lansing, 1970), 173–82.

35. According to "Old Miles Standish," writing in *Pennsylvania Enquirer*, Feb. 3, 1836, reprinted in *Michigan Sentinel*, Feb. 20, 1836: "The Ohio delegation has absolutely disgusted every one at Washington" by "its violence toward Michigan, who stands alone in her unprotected condition" and "is entitled by all that is sacred, and just, and legal, to the boundaries she claims." The *Sentinel* reprinted similar testimonials from papers throughout the country during the next few months. The editor of the *New Yorker*, 1 (July 23, 1836), 281, concluded (in "Michigan and Arkansas") that "Michigan may fairly seem to have had the older and therefore the stronger claim."

36. For comparisons between Michigan and Poland, see Public Meeting at

Tecumseh, July 21, 1835, *Michigan Sentinel*, Aug. 1, 1835; James Duane Doty, Report to the Legislative Council, Aug. 19, 1835, 24 Cong., 1 sess., H. Doc. 7 (Serial 286), 78–82; and editorial in *Adrian Watch-Tower*, n.d., reprinted in *Michigan Sentinel*, March 12, 1836.

37. Gov. Stevens T. Mason to Brig. Gen. Joseph W. Brown, Michigan Militia, Feb. 19, 1835, *Michigan Whig*, March 12, 1835. Mason's letter was reprinted in *Ohio Observer* (Hudson), March 26, 1835.

38. See, for instance, "Michigan's Appeal," in Report of the Committee on the Disputed Boundary, June 1, 1835, in Harold M. Dorr, ed., *The Michigan Constitutional Conventions of 1835–36. Debates and Proceedings* (Ann Arbor, 1940), 494–504: "We believe the question to be a judicial and not a legislative one." Ibid., 500. The quotations in the text are from Legislative Council Memorial to the House of Representatives, Feb. 12, 1835, in Carter and Bloom, eds., *Territorial Papers*, 12:857–60; and "The Case of Michigan," *National Intelligencer* (Washington, D.C.), Dec. 5, 1835.

39. John Quincy Adams's speech of Feb. 9, 1835, *Register of Debates in Congress*, 13 vols. (Washington, 1824–37), 23 Cong., 2 sess., 11:1254–57, at 1255.

40. The argument is developed in Doty, Report to the Legislative Council, March 5, 1834, 23 Cong., 1 sess., S. Doc. 235 (Serial 240).

41. Mason, Message to the Legislative Council, Jan. 12, 1835, in George N. Fuller, ed., *Messages of the Governors of Michigan*, 3 vols. (Lansing, 1925–27), 1:129–39, at 130. For another interpretation of the 1805 act, arguing that its "boundaries were made temporary, and as liable to be changed as the government which was created with them," see Memorial of Members of the Michigan Legislative Council, Jan. 27, 1834, in Carter and Bloom, eds., *Territorial Papers*, 12:711–15.

42. Resolution of Whig Convention, Ann Arbor, March 4–5, 1835, *Michigan Whig*, March 12, 1835.

43. Memorial to Congress by Inhabitants of Whiteford Township, March 18, 1836, in Carter and Bloom, eds., *Territorial Papers*, 12:1144–48, at 1145.

44. Gov. Mason to Sec. of State John Forsyth, Feb. 20, 1835, 24 Cong., 1 sess., H. Doc. 7 (Serial 286), 16–18.

45. *Michigan Statesman*, n.d., reprinted in *Michigan Sentinel*, Feb. 15, 1834. The argument that the constitutional force of the Ordinance derived from Virginia cession conditions was earlier elaborated with respect to the Indiana-Michigan boundary in a presentment of the Grand Jurors of St. Joseph's Co., Mich., n.d., *Detroit Courier*, March 15, 1832: "can full effect legally be given" to the Indiana enabling act, setting that state's boundary ten miles north of the Ordinance line, "without the consent" of the northern "state or states, and the people thereof, although both Congress and Indiana, may so have consented? *Can* it be *so* varied, without the consent also, duly evidenced of the State of Virginia?"

46. *Ontario Freeman*, n.d., reprinted in *Michigan Sentinel*, May 7, 1836.

47. "Ohio & Michigan," *Wooster Journal*, n.d., reprinted in *Miami of the Lake*, June 3, 1835. The editor believed the unidentified author "to have been for a long time, a prominent member upon the floor of Congress."

48. "A Friend to the Union," *Cleveland Herald*, n.d., reprinted in *Miami of the Lake*, May 20, 1835.

49. Editorial comments on Gov. Mason's speech of Sept. 1, 1834, calling upon Michigan "to act for herself," *Michigan Emigrant* (Ann Arbor), Sept. 11, 1834.

50. "State Government," *Michigan Argus* (Ann Arbor), March 12, 1835.

51. For the 1835 constitution and convention proceedings, see Thorpe, ed., *Federal and State Constitutions*, 4:1930–44; and Dorr, ed., *Michigan Constitutional Conventions*. Whigs concurred in opposing any "dismemberment of our Territory"

but counseled patience while Congress considered enabling legislation. Great Whig Meeting at Washtenaw Co., Jan. 17, 1835, *Michigan Whig* (Ann Arbor), Jan. 29, 1835.

52. Mason, Message to the State Senate and House, Feb. 1, 1836, in Fuller, ed., *Messages of the Governors*, 1:158–76, at 161.

53. Memorial to Congress from the Citizens of the Territory, March 18, 1836, in Carter and Bloom, eds., *Territorial Papers*, 12:1152–67, at 1152.

54. Mason, Message to the Legislative Council, Jan. 12, 1835, in Fuller, ed., *Messages of the Governors*, 1:129–39. See also the Legislative Council's Act to Enable the People of Michigan to Form a Constitution, Jan. 26, 1835, in Dorr, ed., *Michigan Constitutional Conventions*, 583–86, at 585, for a description of the state's boundaries based on the 1805 act.

55. Public Meeting at Shelby, March 14, 1835, *Michigan Sentinel*, April 4, 1835.

56. "Michigan's Appeal," June 1, 1835, in Dorr, ed., *Michigan Constitutional Conventions*, 494–504, at 496.

57. "Nunc Pro Tunc," *Michigan Argus*, April 30, 1835; on "nullification," see also "Pioneer of Michigan," *Michigan Sentinel*, Aug. 1, 1835.

58. Address to the Electors of Michigan by Democratic State Convention, *Michigan Argus*, Sept. 24, 1835.

59. Governor Mason, Message to State Senate and House, Nov. 3, 1835, *Michigan Argus*, Nov. 12, 1835, reprinted in Fuller, ed., *Messages of the Governors*, 1:153–56.

60. Lucius Lyon, John Norvell, and Isaac Crary to Hon. John M. Clayton, Chairman, Senate Judiciary Committee, Jan. 6, 1836, reprinted in *Michigan Argus*, Jan. 28, Feb. 4, 11, 1836; quotations, Feb. 4, 11.

61. Gov. Lewis Cass, Message to the Legislative Council, Jan. 5, 1831, in Fuller, ed., *Messages of the Governors*, 1:58–65, at 59.

62. Editorial, *Michigan Sentinel*, Nov. 8, 1834; "Disputed District," ibid., May 28, 1836.

63. Samuel F. Vinton to John F. Clayton, Chairman of Senate Judiciary Committee, May 10, 1834, *Ohio State Journal*, June 6, 1835.

64. Select Joint Committee, "Report on the subject of the Northern Boundary," June 15, 1835, ibid., June 20, 1835.

65. Lucas to Sec. of State Forsyth, June 1, 1835, 24 Cong., 1 sess., II. Doc. 7 (Serial 286), 149. The same point was made by residents of the Upper Peninsula who resented being included in Michigan Territory: "If what was supposed to be the temporary limits of a territory *must* be the limits when it becomes a *state*, empires have accidentally been established when nothing more was designed, than a compliance with the reasonable wishes of a people sparsely settled in almost unbounded wilderness" for temporary government. Petition to Congress by Inhabitants of Michilamackinac and Chippewa Cos. [July 24, 1829], in Carter and Bloom, eds., *Territorial Papers*, 12:55–58.

66. "Michigan," *Toledo Gazette*, March 25, 1835.

67. "Northern Boundary," *Cleveland Herald*, n.d., reprinted in *Miami of the Lake*, March 17, 1835.

68. "A Citizen," "Gov. Cass., Secretary of War, and the Boundary Question," *Scioto Gazette*, June 10, 1835.

69. Vinton to Clayton, May 10, 1834, *Ohio State Journal*, June 6, 1835.

70. Lucas to Sec. of State Forsyth, May 11, 1835, 24 Cong., 1 sess., H. Doc. 7 (Serial 286), 145–57. A copy of this letter and other relevant correspondence may be found in Robert Lucas Letterbook, Ohio Historical Society (hereafter OHS), Columbus.

71. Select Joint Committee, "Report," June 15, 1835, *Ohio State Journal*, June 20, 1835.

72. Ethan Allen Brown to Morris Jessup, May 15, 1835, Ethan Allen Brown Papers, OHS, Box 4. See also Memorial to Congress by Ohio Legislature, March 12, 1831, in Carter and Bloom, eds., *Territorial Papers*, 12:266–73, quotation at 267; Vinton to John Tipton, Chairman of Select Committee on Michigan, March 5, 1834, 23 Cong., 1 sess., S. Doc. 149 (Serial 240), 5; and Vinton to Clayton, May 10, 1834, *Ohio State Journal*, June 6, 1835.

73. Lucas to U.S. Rep. Taylor Webster, Feb. 5, 1835, Lucas Letterbook.

74. *Ohio Senate Journal*, June 18, 1835, 33:170. The resolution was adopted by a 20-13 vote. See also Lucas's letter to Forsyth, cited in note 70 above; and "Ohio," *Ohio State Journal & Sentinel*, June 17, 1835, reporting that "the flag of Ohio has been insulted." Michigan writers suggested that Ohio's determination to uphold its claims smacked of "nullification." *Michigan Sentinel*, April 15, 1835; *Michigan Whig* (Detroit), n.d., reprinted in *Michigan Sentinel*, April 25, 1835.

75. *Toledo Gazette*, March 25, 1835, reprinted in *Ohio State Journal*, April 4, 1835. For the United States to countenance Michigan's "forcible possession" of the disputed territory "places the United States in a state of *war* with Ohio." "Public Meeting in Geauga County," May 7, 1835, *Scioto Gazette* (Chillicothe), May 27, 1835.

76. "Buckeye" to Lucas, May [2], 1835, Robert Lucas Papers, OHS, Box 3.

77. *New York Commercial Advertiser*, n.d., reprinted in *Michigan Sentinel*, April 4, 1835.

78. See speech of Sen. Thomas Ewing of Ohio, Dec., 21, 1835, *Register of Debates*, 24 Cong., 1 sess.: "Next to the constitution itself (of which, indeed, this ordinance is by adoption a part) I hold it the most sacred among the muniments of our national liberty."

79. *Cleveland Whig*, n.d., reprinted in *Ohio State Journal*, June 6, 1835.

80. Thorpe, ed., *Federal and State Constitutions*, 3:1053–73 (Indiana); ibid., 3:967–1012 (Illinois).

81. "Common convenience has assigned . . . local police" over the Erie lakefront to Ohio, according to the Memorial to Congress from Citizens of the Territory [of Michigan], March 18, 1836, in Carter and Bloom, eds., *Territorial Papers*, 12:1152–67, at 1155.

82. "Ohio and Michigan," *Indiana Journal*, n.d., reprinted in *Niles Weekly Register* (Baltimore), 48 (July 25, 1835), 370–71.

83. "Michigan's Appeal," June 1, 1835, in Dorr, ed., *Michigan Constitutional Conventions*, 494–504, at 495.

84. *Michigan Sentinel*, Nov. 8, 1834. This argument is most fully elaborated in Lyon et al. to Clayton, Jan. 6, 1836, reprinted in *Michigan Argus*, Jan. 28, 1836.

85. "Michigan's Appeal," June 1, 1835, p. 495.

86. Editorial, *Michigan Argus*, Sept. 24, 1835.

87. Lyon et al. to Clayton, Jan. 6, 1836, reprinted in *Michigan Argus*, Jan. 28, Feb. 4, 11, 1836.

88. Vinton to Tipton, March 5, 1834, 23 Cong., 1 sess., S. Doc. 149 (Serial 240), 22.

89. Enabling Act, June 15, 1836, and Supplementary Act, June 23, 1836, in Thorpe, ed., *Federal and State Constitutions*, 4:1926–29.

90. Editorial, *Michigan Sentinel*, Feb. 13, 1836.

91. *Pontiac Courier*, n.d., reprinted in *Michigan Sentinel*, May 14, 1836.

92. *Adrian Watch-Tower*, n.d., reprinted in *Michigan Sentinel*, March 12, 1836.

93. For typical complaints from the Upper Peninsula, see the Memorial to Congress by the Inhabitants of Chippewa Co., August 1831, in Carter and Bloom, eds., *Territorial Papers*, 12:344–48; and Petition to Congress from Chippewa, July 1833, ibid., 604–606.

94. "Monroe County Convention," April 11, 1836, *Michigan Sentinel*, April 16, 1836.

95. "Address of the State Convention to the People of Michigan," Oct. 15, 1836, in Dorr, ed., *Michigan Constitutional Conventions*, 553–67, at 561; "The Crisis," *Michigan Sentinel*, April 16, 1836.

96. *Scott et al. v. Jones*, 5 Howard 343 (1847)

97. Address to the President of the United States [Sept. 30, 1836], in Dorr, ed., *Michigan Constitutional Conventions*, 548–53, at 552; and Resolutions Adopted by the Convention of Dissent, Sept. 30, 1836, ibid., 542–45, at 543.

98. "Address to the People," Oct. 15, 1836, ibid., 553–67, at 554.

99. Robert Clark to John Anderson, Pres. of the County Convention, Aug. 16, 1836, *Monroe Times*, Aug. 18, 1836.

100. Gilpin, *Territory of Michigan*, 183–92. It had become clear that "Michigan can effect nothing for herself," and only risked being thrown back into territorial dependency. "Extract of a letter from Washington, D. C." *Michigan Argus*, April 23, 1836. See also editorial in *Peninsular* (Centreville), n.d., reprinted in *Michigan Argus*, May 19, 1836, urging capitulation to Congress as "the least of two inevitable evils." The disputed territory "has become a part of the State of Ohio," broadside extra, ibid., Oct. 29, 1836.

101. State Sen. Barry's speech, Feb. 19, 1836, *Michigan Argus*, March 3, 1836. For a defense of the state government, see *Detroit Free Press*, Feb. 26, 1836.

102. "Peace and Union," *Loginsport Telegraph*, n.d., reprinted in *Michigan Sentinel*, April 25, 1835.

103. Dorr, ed., *Michigan Constitutional Conventions*; Thorpe, ed., *Federal and State Constitutions*, 4:1929–30.

104. Mason, Message to the State Senate and House, Feb. 1, 1836, in Fuller, ed., *Messages of the Governors*, 1:158–76, at 161.

105. Memorial of the Legislative Council to Pres. Andrew Jackson, March 23, 1835, 24 Cong., 1 sess., H. Doc. 7 (Serial 286), 33–34.

106. Petition to Congress by Inhabitants of the Disputed District, referred Jan. 10, 1835, in Carter and Bloom, eds., *Territorial Papers*, 12:844–49, at 846.

6. Slavery and Freedom

1. For the best treatment of congressional intentions with respect to slavery, see Paul Finkelman, "Slavery and the Northwest Ordinance: A Study in Ambiguity," *Journal of the Early Republic* (forthcoming).

2. Nathan Dane to Rufus King, July 16, 1787, in Edmund Cody Burnett, ed., *Letters of the Members of the Continental Congress* (hereafter, *LMCC*), 8 vols. (Washington, 1921–36), 8:621–22.

3. Timothy Pickering's proposal for a new state [April 1783], in Octavius Pickering, ed., *The Life of Timothy Pickering*, 4 vols. (Boston, 1867–73), 1:546–49; David McLean, *Timothy Pickering and the Age of the American Revolution*, (New York, 1982), 184–92.

4. See committee reports of March 1 and March 15, with revisions of March 22, 1784, in Julian P. Boyd et al., eds., *The Papers of Thomas Jefferson*, 22 vols. to date (Princeton, 1950–), 6:599–605. The April 19, 1784, vote to strike out the slavery clause is in Worthington C. Ford, ed., *Journals of the Continental Congress* (hereafter, *JCC*), 34 vols. (Washington, 1904–37), 26:246–47; and the adopted ordinance of April 23 is in ibid., 274–79. See Thomas Jefferson's comments in a letter to James Madison, April 25, 1784, and in his Observations on Demeunier's Manuscript [1786], in Boyd et al., eds., *Jefferson Papers*, 7:118–21, 10:58.

5. Rufus King's motion, committed March 16, 1785; committee report recom-

mending amendment to delay ban until 1800, April 6, 1785, in Ford, ed., *JCC*, 28:164, 239. King acknowledged the influence of Pickering's "Ideas on this unjustifiable practice." King to Pickering, April 15, 1785, in Burnett, ed., *LMCC*, 8:94. William Grayson of Virginia wrote Madison that a congressional majority would soon be found "liberal enough to adopt" King's motion. William Grayson to Madison, May 1, 1785, in Robert Rutland et al., eds., *The Papers of James Madison*, 15 vols. to date (Chicago and Charlottesville, 1962–), 8:274–77. See the brief discussions in Donald Robinson, *Slavery in the Structure of American Politics* (New York, 1971), 378–86; and David Brion Davis, *The Problem of Slavery in the Age of Revolution, 1770–1823* (Ithaca, 1975), 153–55.

6. Finkelman, "Slavery and the Northwest Ordinance."

7. See the excellent discussion in Drew R. McCoy, "James Madison and Visions of American Nationality in the Confederation Period: A Regional Perspective," in Richard Beeman et al., eds., *Beyond Confederation: Origins of the Constitution and American National Identity* (Chapel Hill, 1987), 226–58. See also Staughton Lynd, "The Compromise of 1787," in his *Class Conflict, Slavery, and the United States Constitution* (Indianapolis, 1967), 185–213; and Richard Henry Lee to George Washington, July 15, 1787, in Burnett, ed., *LMCC*, 8:620–21. On Manasseh Cutler's role, see Finkelman, "Slavery and the Northwest Ordinance."

8. Grayson to James Monroe, August 8, 1787, in Burnett, ed., *LMCC*, 8:631–32. For suggestive comments on the cultural significance of shifting from tobacco to wheat, see T. H. Breen, *Tobacco Culture: The Mentality of the Great Planters on the Eve of Revolution* (Princeton, 1985), 204–10.

9. Finkelman, "Slavery and the Northwest Ordinance."

10. For misgivings about the growth potential of the region, see Monroe to Jefferson, Jan. 19, 1786, in Burnett, ed., *LMCC*, 8:285–86. But see Madison's argument in the Constitutional Convention, July 11, 1787, that "population . . . would constantly tend to equalize." Max Farrand, ed., *The Records of the Federal Convention of 1787*, 4 vols. (New Haven, 1911–37), 1:585–86. Rufus Putnam made the same point to Fisher Ames in a lengthy letter justifying western development, Jan. 9, 1790, Rufus Putnam Papers, American Antiquarian Society, Worcester, Mass.: The western population would "greatly increase, while there are vacant lands in any quarter to be had." The best short discussion of contemporary population predictions is in McCoy, "Visions of American Nationality."

11. On the sectional origins of state makers, see John D. Barnhart, "The Southern Influence in the Formation of Indiana," *Indiana Magazine of History*, 33 (1937), 261–76; and Barnhart, "The Southern Influence in the Formation of Illinois," *Journal of the Illinois State Historical Society*, 32 (1939), 358–78. On emigration generally, see R. Carlyle Buley, *The Old Northwest: Pioneer Period, 1815–1840*, 2 vols. (Indianapolis, 1950), 1:1–57. The best general account of Northwestern attitudes toward race and slavery is Eugene H. Berwanger, *The Frontier against Slavery* (Urbana, 1967).

12. Arthur St. Clair's Address at Marietta, July 15, 1788, in William Henry Smith, ed., *The St. Clair Papers: The Life and Public Services of Arthur St. Clair*, 2 vols. (Cincinnati, 1882), 2:53–56. For similar rhetoric, see James M. Varnum, *An Oration Delivered at Marietta, July 4, 1788* (Newport, 1788).

13. [?] to Greenleaf [1789], Thomas Walcutt Papers, Massachusetts Historical Society, Boston, Vol. I, p. 123. See also Walcutt to Paul Fearing, August 1790, ibid., 137.

14. On the Federalists' attitude toward the national govenment, see Andrew R. L. Cayton, " 'A Quiet Independence': The Western Vision of the Ohio Company," *Ohio History*, 90 (1981), 5–32; and Cayton, "The Contours of Power in a Frontier Town: Marietta, 1788–1803," *Journal of the Early Republic*, 6 (1986), 103–26. Reginald

Horsman, *The Frontier in the Formative Years, 1783–1815* (New York, 1970), 39–49, provides a good introduction to the history of settlement during the period of hostilities with the northwestern Indians climaxing with the Battle of Fallen Timbers in 1794. On military operations, see Francis Paul Prucha, *The Sword of the Republic: The United States Army on the Frontier, 1783–1846* (1969; Bloomington, Ind., 1977), 17–42.

15. *Philadelphia Aurora*, April 12, 1802. For Duane's connections with Ohio Republicans, see Alfred Byron Sears, *Thomas Worthington: Father of Ohio Statehood* (Columbus, 1958), 74–75.

16. [Tiffin], "To the Inhabitants," *Scioto Gazette* (Chillicothe), Sept. 24, 1801.

17. "Hamilton Farmer," *Western Spy* (Cincinnati), Nov. 21, 1801.

18. Jehial Gregory to Return Jonathan Meigs, Jr., Aug. 8, 1802, in Julia Perkins Cutler, ed., *Life and Times of Ephraim Cutler* (Cincinnati, 1890), 66n.

19. "Republicanus," d. Marietta, July 6, 1802, *Ohio Gazette*, reprinted in *Western Spy*, Aug. 7, 1802.

20. Beverley W. Bond, ed., "Memoirs of Benjamin Van Cleve," *Quarterly Publication of the Historical and Philosophical Society of Ohio*, 17 (1922), 3–71, quotation at 70. These recollections about events in 1802 were composed in 1820 from contemporary journal entries. See also Cutler, ed., *Life of Ephraim Cutler*, 67. See also Richard Frederick O'Dell, "The Early Antislavery Movement in Ohio" (Ph.D. diss., University of Michigan, 1948), 97–104 and passim.

21. "Epistle of Paul," *Ohio Gazette*, Oct. 4, 1802. See also "Mentor," no. 6, ibid., Aug. 17, 1802.

22. Statement of John G. Macan, d. Chillicothe, Sept. 9, 1802, *Scioto Gazette*, Sept. 11, 1802. See also statement of John S. Wills, another unsuccessful candidate, Sept. 10, 1802, ibid.

23. Ohio Constitution, in Francis Newton Thorpe, ed., *The Federal and State Constitutions*, 7 vols. (Washington, 1909), 5:2901–13. See also "First Constitutional Convention, Convened November 1, 1802. Journal of the Convention," *Ohio State Archaeological and Historical Quarterly*, 5 (1897), 80–153. For discussion, see O'Dell, "Early Antislavery Movement," 108–10.

24. *Liberty Hall* (Cincinnati), July 7, 1806.

25. Petition to Congress by John Edgar, William Morrison, William St. Clair, and John Dumoulin, Jan. 12, 1796, in Jacob Piatt Dunn, ed., "Slavery Petitions and Papers," *Indiana State Historical Society Publications*, 2 (1894), 443–529, at 447–52. See the discussion in J. P. Dunn, Jr., *Indiana: A Redemption from Slavery* (Boston, 1890), 219–60. For earlier requests by French settlers for recognition of their slave property, see Memorials of Barthelmei Tardiveau, July 18, Sept. 17, 1788, in Clarence Alvord, ed., *Kaskaskia Records, 1778–1790* (Springfield, 1909), 475–88, 491–93.

26. Petition to Congress with 267 signatures, Oct. 1, 1800, in Dunn, ed., "Slavery Petitions," 455–61; Petition of the Vincennes Convention, Dec. 28, 1802, ibid., 461–70.

27. Resolution of Vincennes Convention, ibid., 469.

28. Memorial of St. Clair and Randolph Counties, Dec. 18, 1805, ibid., 483–92, at 484.

29. Finkelman, "Slavery and the Northwest Ordinance."

30. Letter to editor, *Indiana Gazette* (Vincennes), April 10, 1805.

31. "An Act concerning the introduction of Negroes and Mulattoes into this Territory," Aug. 26, 1805, in Francis S. Philbrick, ed., *Laws of the Indiana Territory* (Springfield, 1930), 136–39. See the editor's discussion at cxl–cxliii; and Emma Lou Thornbrough, *The Negro in Indiana: A Study of a Minority* (Indianapolis, 1957), 8–12 and passim.

32. "Chrisley Crum," *Western Sun* (Vincennes), May 13, 1809.

33. Thomas Randolph, "To the Citizens of Indiana," ibid., Feb. 25, 1809.

34. "A Citizen of Vincennes" [Elías McNamee], "To the Citizens of Indiana," ibid., Feb. 18, 1809. The resulting exchange is discussed in John D. Barnhart, *Valley of Democracy: The Frontier versus the Plantation in the Ohio Valley, 1775–1818* (Bloomington, 1953), 172–74.

35. Report of General W. Johnston, for committee on slavery petitions, Oct. 19, 1808, in Gayle Thornbrough and Dorothy L. Riker, eds., *Journals of the General Assembly of Indiana Territory, 1805–1815* (Indianapolis, 1950), 232–38; *Western Sun*, Dec. 17, 1808.

36. "Eumenes," d. Indiana Territory, May 21, 1806, *Liberty Hall*, June 2, 1806.

37. On territorial politics in this period, see Dorothy Burne Goebel, *William Henry Harrison: A Political Biography* (Indianapolis, 1926), 53–88; and Barnhart, *Valley of Democracy*, 168–77.

38. "A Citizen of Vincennes" [McNamee], *Western Sun*, April 22, 1809.

39. Legislative Petition, Sept. 19, 1807, in Dunn, ed., "Slavery Petitions," 515–17.

40. House to Gov. William Henry Harrison, Aug. 1, 1805, in Thornbrough and Riker, eds., *Assembly Journals*, 50–51.

41. Harrison's Address to the General Assembly, July 30, 1805, ibid., 38–47, at 44.

42. Memorial to Congress by Members of the General Assembly, Aug. 19, 1805, ibid., 101–108, at 103.

43. Resolutions Passed by the General Assembly [Dec. 20, 1806], ibid., 123–24. The date of the resolution is given in *Liberty Hall*, Feb. 17, 1807.

44. "Slim Simon," *Western Sun*, Feb. 11, 1809. This was a reply to General W. Johnston's "Answer to 'Citizen,'" ibid., Feb. 4, 1809. See also "Slim Simon," "To Citizen" [McNamee], ibid., Feb. 4, 1809.

45. "Slim Simon," "To Citizen" [McNamee], ibid., Feb. 11, 1809.

46. "Eumenes," *Liberty Hall*, June 2, 1806.

47. Legislative Petition to Congress, Aug. 19, 1805, in Dunn, ed., "Slavery Petitions," 476–83, at 478.

48. "Slim Simon," "To G. W. Johnston, Esq.," *Western Sun*, Feb. 11, 1809.

49. "Slim Simon," "To a Citizen of Vincennes," ibid., Feb. 11, 1809.

50. "Corpus Collosom," d. Clermont Co., Ohio, July 4, 1806, *Liberty Hall*, July 14, 1806.

51. "A Citizen of Vincennes" [McNamee], "To the Citizens of Indiana," *Western Sun*, Feb. 11, 1809.

52. "Benevolensus," d. Hamilton Co., Ohio, July 1, 1806, *Liberty Hall*, July 14, 1806.

53. "A Farmer," *Western Sun*, March 4, 1809.

54. "Farmer," ibid., March 18, 1809; General Johnston to "Slim Simon," ibid., Feb. 18, 1809.

55. James Beggs, "An Address to the Citizens of Clark Co.," unpublished manuscript [1809], William W. Borden Papers, Indiana State Library (hereafter ISL), Indianapolis.

56. "A Citizen" [McNamee] argued that as long as the Harrisonians challenged the slavery ban, Indiana "cannot reasonably expect emigrants from any part of the union." *Western Sun*, April 22, 1809. See also "A Friend to Truth," ibid., Aug. 16, 1809.

57. Elias McNamee ("A Citizen of Vincennes") called on assembly candidates to "declare unequivocally, whether they will oppose, or promote the introduction of slavery." Ibid., Jan. 28, 1809. See responses of Knox County candidates, ibid.: by General W. Johnston (against introduction), Feb. 4; D. Sullivan (for), Feb. 18; Thomas Randolph (for), Feb. 25; John Hadden (for), March 25. John Johnson, the only candidate who declined to take a position, and General Johnston were elected. Ibid., April 15, 1809.

58. "An Act to repeal the act entitled 'An Act for the introduction of negroes and mulattoes,'" 1810, in Philbrick, ed., *Laws of the Indiana Territory*, 138–39. See, for instance, Walter Taylor, "To the People of Indiana Territory," *Western Sun*, June 23, 1812; and Thomas Posey to John Gibson, Secretary of the Territory, March 13, 1812, English Collection, ISL.

59. Solon Justus Buck, *Illinois in 1818* (Springfield, 1917); Norman Dwight Harris, *The History of Negro Servitude in Illinois and of the Slavery Agitation in that State, 1719–1864* (Chicago, 1904).

60. "Caution," d. Silver Creek, St. Clair Co., March 29, 1818, *Western Intelligencer* (Kaskaskia), April 15, 1818. For the claim that the new state was free to institute slavery regardless of Article VI, see "Candor," d. St. Clair Co., April 25, 1818, ibid., May 6, 1818.

61. Governor Coles's speech to Senate and House, Dec. 5, 1822, *Illinois Intelligencer* (Vandalia), Dec. 7, 1822; replies of Senate, Dec. 12, and House, Dec. 20, ibid., Dec. 14, 21, 1822. On the convention question, see William H. Brown, *An Historical Sketch of the Early Movement in Illinois for the Legalization of Slavery* (Chicago, 1865); George Flower, *History of the English Settlement in Edwards County, Illinois* (Chicago, 1882); Merton L. Dillon, "Sources of Early Antislavery Thought in Illinois," *Journal of the Illinois State Historical Society*, 50 (1957), 36–50; Merton L. Dillon, "The Antislavery Movement in Illinois, 1809–1844" (Ph.D. diss., University of Michigan, 1950), 73–122; Helen Louise Jennings, "John Mason Peck and the Impact of New England on the Old Northwest" (Ph.D. diss., University of Southern California, 1961), 86–95; and Janet Cornelius, *Constitution-Making in Illinois, 1818–1970* (Urbana, 1972), 20–24. For background on Illinois newspapers in this period, see Leonard John Hooper, Jr., "Decade of Debate: The Polemical, Political Press in Illinois, 1814–1824" (Ph.D. diss., Southern Illinois University, 1964).

62. Horatio Newhall to his family, April 14, 1824, Horatio Newhall Papers, Illinois State Historical Library (hereafter ISHL), Springfield.

63. For a review of state court decisions bearing on the Ordinance, see Walter C. Haight, "The Binding Effect of the Ordinance of 1787," *Publications of the Michigan Political Science Association*, 2 (1896–97), 343–402.

64. Public Meeting at Vandalia, Feb. 15, 1823, *Edwardsville Spectator*, March 1, 1823.

65. "Truth," *Illinois Intelligencer*, May 24, 1823.

66. "Young Freeman," d. Dec. 31, 1823, *Illinois Gazette* (Shawneetown), April 3, 1824.

67. William Berry, editorial, *Illinois Intelligencer*, Feb. 22, 1823.

68. "Federal Logic and the Missouri Question without Disguise," *Richmond Enquirer*, July 25, 1823; editorial, *National Intelligencer* (Washington), Aug. 1, 1823.

69. George Churchill, "To the People of Madison County," March 4, 1823, *Edwardsville Spectator*, March 15, 1823. Churchill was justifying his vote in the Illinois house of representatives against calling a convention.

70. Edward Coles to Nicholas Biddle, Sept. 18, 1823, in E. B. Washburne, *Sketch of Edward Coles, Second Governor of Illinois, and of the Slavery Struggle of 1823–4* (Chicago, 1882), 159–62.

71. See particularly "Marcus," "The Illinois Convention," *New York American*, July 16, 1823; and "Senex," ibid., Sept. 24, 1823.

72. See, for instance, the Constitution of the Morganian Society [1823?], ISHL.

73. "Brissot," d. Jackson Co., March 17, 1824, *Kaskaskia Republican*, March 30, 1824; "A Plain Man," "On the Convention," no. 1, *Illinois Gazette*, June 12, 1824.

74. "Copy of a Letter from a Gentleman in Mercer Co., Ky., to his friend in Kaskaskia," *Kaskaskia Republican*, May 4, 1824. See also "Vindex," ibid., June 15, 1824, attesting to the authenticity of these letters. For an unpublished letter to the

same effect, see Henry Berry to ? Fitzhugh, June 15, 1824, Berry Family Papers, ISHL.

75. Editorial, *Kaskaskia Republican*, July 20, 1824.

76. "A Man that owes Government for his land," ibid., June 15, 1824.

77. "The Convention," *Illinois Gazette*, June 14, 1823, reprinted in *National Gazette* (Washington), July 3, 1823; "A Plain Man," "On the Convention," no. 3, *Illinois Gazette*, July 10, 1824; "The American Bottom," *Kaskaskia Republican*, July 13, 1824.

78. "A Yankee," d. Bond Co., March 19, 1823, *Illinois Intelligencer*, March 29, 1823.

79. Thomas F. Burgess toast, Convention Dinner at Lebanon, April 4, 1823, *Edwardsville Spectator*, April 17, 1823. This item was reprinted in *National Intelligencer*, May 27, 1823. See also "X," *Illinois Gazette*, Jan. 10, 1824.

80. "Convention," *Illinois Intelligencer*, April 26, 1823. For good statements of the diffusion argument, see "Extract of a Letter from a Gentleman in Illinois," *Scioto Gazette* (Chillicothe), June 7, 1823; and "Impartial," *Western Sun* (Vincennes), May 10, 1823. "No Methodist" argued that legalization would be the means of making slaves "acquainted with the religion of Jesus." *Illinois Gazette*, Oct. 11, 1823.

81. "To the People of Illinois," *Illinois Gazette*, July 5, 1823. See also "A Friend to Liberty," *Edwardsville Spectator*, April 12, 1823: "We require the extension of slavery in this state to give zest and enterprize to its inhabitants and to introduce others that are wealthy and able to give a stir to business amongst us."

82. Alton meeting, April 19, 1823, *Edwardsville Spectator*, May 10, 1823; "Extract of a letter from a gentleman in Fredericksburgh, Va., to his correspondent in this state," ibid., June 7, 1823; "Laocoon," "Convention," no. 2, ibid., May 3, 1823.

83. "Jonathan Freeman" [Morris Birkbeck], *Illinois Gazette*, June 28, 1823. See also "Martus," *Republican Advocate*, June 26, 1823.

84. "Address of the Monroe Society," *Edwardsville Spectator*, May 31, 1823.

85. "Jonathan Freeman" [Morris Birkbeck], *Illinois Gazette*, June 21, 1823. The best sustained attack on diffusion is Birkbeck, "An Appeal to the People of Illinois on the Question of a Convention," ibid., Oct. 11, 18, 25, 1823.

86. "Democracy," *Republican Advocate* (Kaskaskia), June 26, 1823.

87. "Address of the Board Managers of the St. Clair Society to prevent the further introduction of slavery in the state of Illinois," *Edwardsville Spectator*, April 12, 1823. Jennings, "John Mason Peck," 90, says Peck was the author.

88. "Laocoon," "Convention," no. 1, ibid., April 26, 1823. See also Daniel Stookey to Citizens of Illinois, Sept. 1, 1823, ibid., Sept. 6, 1823.

89. For typical statements of this view, see "A Farmer," ibid., March 29, 1823; "A Farmer of St. Clair Co.," ibid., May 10, 1823.

90. "Aristides," "To the People of Illinois," no. 2, ibid., May 17, 1823. See also "Spartacus," *Illinois Gazette*, July 23, 1824: "The independence of slaveholders would render them but little benefit to the neighborhood in which they lived, because they would have but few wants which the people could supply."

91. "A Friend to Freedom," "Another Convention Toast," *Edwardsville Spectator*, April 19, 1823.

92. "Address of the Board Managers of the St. Clair Society," ibid., April 12, 1823.

93. "A Friend to Illinois," ibid., Oct. 4, 1823.

94. "Martus," "Crisis," no. 3, *Republican Advocate*, June 19, 1823.

95. "One of Many" [Edward Coles], no. 9, *Illinois Intelligencer*, July 16, 1824; "Looker-On," *Edwardsville Spectator*, May 10, 1823; "A Mechanic," ibid., July 13, 1824.

96. "Aristides," "To the People of Illinois," no. 2, *Edwardsville Spectator*, May 17, 1823; *Remarks Addressed to the Citizens of Illinois, on the Proposed Introduction of Slavery* (n.p., n.d.), 9. Copy in Boston Public Library.

97. Daniel Stookey to the Citizens of Illinois, Sept. 1, 1823, *Edwardsville Spectator*, Sept. 6, 1823.

98. "Jonathan Freeman" [Birkbeck], *Illinois Gazette*, July 10, 1824.

99. "A Farmer," *Edwardsville Spectator*, April 6, 1824.

100. Editorial, ibid., June 28, 1823; Coles to Biddle, Sept. 18, 1823, and to Roberts Vaux, Dec. 11, 1823, in Washburne, *Sketch of Edward Coles*, 159–62, 162–64. Horatio Newhall predicted that the convention would be defeated by a margin of two thousand. Newhall to his family, May 21, 1823, Horatio Newhall Papers, ISHL.

101. "Honestus," *Illinois Republican* (Edwardsville), June 28, 1823; "Americanus," *Illinois Gazette* (Shawneetown), reprinted in *Illinois Intelligencer*, Jan. 16, 1824; "The Convention," *Illinois Republican*, June 16, 1824.

102. Item reprinted from *Republican Advocate*, n.d., *Illinois Intelligencer*, Jan. 30, 1824; "Yankee," ibid., May 24, 1823; "Yankee," ibid., May 3, 1823.

103. "The Legitimate Power of the People," *Republican Advocate*, Jan. 22, 1824. See also, "Mercutio," ibid., March 9, 1824, on the Ordinance's "cabalistic character."

104. Toast by Seth Converse, Esq., Monroe Co., July 4, 1823, *Illinois Intelligencer*, Aug. 9, 1823.

105. David J. Baker to *Republican Advocate*, d. Kaskaskia, Jan. 28, 1824, *Edwardsville Spectator*, Feb. 17, 1824. See also "Whiteman," *Illinois Intelligencer*, June 7, 1823; "Another Citizen of Illinois," *Edwardsville Spectator*, Jan. 20, 1824; and "Farmer," no. 3, ibid., May 4, 1824.

106. Alfred W. Cavarly speech, Carrollton, July 4, 1823, *Edwardsville Spectator*, Aug. 9, 1823.

107. "A Citizen of Illinois," "To the People of the State of Illinois," ibid., Jan. 6, 1824.

108. "Common Sense," ibid., June 29, 1824.

109. "Address of the Minority," ibid., March 1, 1823.

110. Coles emphasized the state's responsibility to uphold the "principles which gave birth to the American Revolution" in his "One of Many" series in *Illinois Intelligencer*, particularly nos. 2 and 4, May 21 and June 4, 1824. If the legalization effort succeeded in Illinois, proslavery forces would pursue the same "monstrous . . . object in Indiana, and perhaps Ohio." *National Gazette*, May 1, 1823.

111. Sangamo Celebration, July 4, 1823, *Edwardsville Spectator*, July 12, 1823.

112. Converse toast, July 4, 1823, *Illinois Intelligencer*, Aug. 9, 1823.

113. "An Old Resident of Illinois," "To Ninian Edwards esq." (calling on the former governor to take a stand on the convention issue), *Edwardsville Spectator*, April 12, 1823.

114. "Reasons for Opposing a Convention," *Illinois Intelligencer*, June 4, 1824.

115. "The Climate," ibid., June 11, 1824; and James Lemen, Jr., in *Edwardsville Spectator*, March 9, 1824.

116. Theodore Cone, Esq., Oration at Albion, Ill., July 4, 1823, *Illinois Gazette*, Aug. 2, 1823.

117. Theodore Calvin Pease, *Illinois Election Returns, 1818–1848* (Springfield, 1923), 27–29. "The state will hereafter support the interests of the other free states," Horatio Newhall promised his family. Letter of Aug. 1, 1824, Newhall Papers, ISHL.

118. Birkbeck to Coles, March 1, 1823, in Washburne, *Sketch of Edward Coles*, 173–76; "A visitor from Illinois," "To the Editors of the American," *New York American*, July 2, 1823; *National Gazette*, July 3, 1823.

119. Item from *Trenton True Republican*, n.d., reprinted in *Edwardsville Spectator*, May 17, 1823.

120. "A Farmer," "Hemp and Flax," ibid., March 29, 1823.

121. "A Friend to Inquiry" published data showing that "more than three times as much land was sold in the free states and the territory in the first six months of the year 1823, than in the slave states and territory!" Ibid., March 9, 1824.

7. From Constitution to Higher Law

1. Hoar's speech is excerpted in Wager Swayne, *The Ordinance of '87 and the War of '61* (New York, 1892), 63–64.

2. Ibid., 79.

3. Clinton Rossiter, ed., *The Federalist Papers* (New York, 1961), 238.

4. Philip Barbour speech, Feb. 15, 1819, in *Annals of the Congress of the United States, 1789–1824*, 42 vols. (Washington, 1834–56), 15 Cong., 2 sess., 33:1187.

5. *Strader et al. v. Graham*, 10 Howard 82 (1850), 96. See also *Pollard's Lessee v. Hagan*, 3 Howard 212 (1845), 223; and the discussion in Francis Philbrick, ed., *The Laws of the Illinois Territory, 1809–1818* (Springfield, 1950), ccxvi–ccxxii.

6. "Yankee," d. Bond Co., *Illinois Intelligencer* (Kaskaskia), May 3, 1823.

7. Rudolphus Dickinson speech, May 10, 1848, *Congressional Globe*, vol. 18 (Washington, 1848), 30 Cong., 1 sess., 747.

8. Don E. Fehrenbacher, "The Federal Government and Slavery," paper delivered at Bicentennial Conference, Claremont, Calif., February 1984. For an excellent analysis of constitutional issues in antebellum territorial history, see Don E. Fehrenbacher, *The Dred Scott Case: Its Significance in American Law and Politics* (New York, 1978). See also the stimulating discussion in Arthur Bestor, "State Sovereignty and Slavery: A Reinterpretation of Proslavery Constitutional Doctrine," *Illinois State Historical Society Journal*, 54 (1961), 117–80.

9. Thomas Ewing speech, Dec. 21, 1835, *Register of Debates in Congress*, 13 vols. (Washington, 1824–37), 24 Cong., 1 sess., 12:17.

10. Caleb Atwater, *A History of the State of Ohio, Natural and Civil*, 2d ed. (Cincinnati, 1838), 353.

11. Arius Nye, "A Fragment of the Early History of the State of Ohio, Being the Substance of an Address Delivered at Marietta, on the Forty-Eighth Anniversary of the First Settlement of the State," April 9, 1836, *Transactions of the Historical and Philosophical Society of Ohio*, I, part 2 (Cincinnati, 1839), 304–34, quotation at 312.

12. Timothy Walker, *Annual Discourse, Delivered before the Ohio Historical and Philosophical Society, at Columbus, on the 23d of December, 1837* (Cincinnati, 1838), 9, 5.

13. Salmon P. Chase, ed., *The Statutes of Ohio and of the Northwestern Territory Adopted or Enacted from 1788 to 1833 Inclusive* (Cincinnati, 1833), 16–17.

14. Edward D. Mansfield, *The Political Grammar of the United States* (New York, 1834), 145n, 145.

15. William M. Corry, "Native Citizens," in *Celebration of the Forty-Seventh Anniversary of the First Settlement of the State of Ohio* (Cincinnati, 1835), 5; Atwater, *History of the State of Ohio*, 352.

16. James H. Perkins, " A Discourse Delivered before the Ohio Historical Society," n.d., *Transactions of the Historical and Philosophical Society of Ohio*, I, 268–85, at 282.

17. Chase, ed., *Statutes of Ohio*, 18.

18. Timothy Walker, *Introduction to American Law* (1837; New York, 1972), 44; Manasseh Cutler, *An Explanation of the Map which Delineates . . . the Federal Lands* (Salem, Mass., 1787), reprinted in William Parker Cutler and Julia Perkins Cutler, *Life, Journals and Correspondence of Rev. Manasseh Cutler, LL.D.*, 2 vols. (Cincinnati, 1888), 2:393–406, at 404.

19. *Hogg v. Zanesville Canal and Mfr. Co.*, 5 Ohio 410 (1832), 416–17; Walker, *Introduction to American Law*, 45. For an earlier opinion supporting this view, see Huntington, C. J., in *Rutherford v. McFadden* [1807], reprinted in *Liberty Hall* (Cincinnati), Nov. 3, 1807. For a good review of the cases, see Walter C. Haight, "The Binding Effect of the Ordinance of 1787," *Publications of the Michigan Political Science Association*, 2 (1896–97), 343–402.

20. *Strader v. Graham*, 10 Howard 82 (1850), 95–96; James G. Birney, *Examination of the Decision of the Supreme Court of the United States, in the Case of Strader, Gorman and Armstrong vs. Christopher Graham* (Cincinnati, 1852), 22, 26n (citing Sen. Salmon P. Chase). See also *Permoli v. First Municipality of New Orleans*, 3 Howard 589 (1845), for an earlier ruling (written by Catron, J.) that the Ordinance, which had been extended to Orleans Territory, was "superseded by the state constitution" (quotation at 610); and William M. Wiecek, *The Sources of Antislavery Constitutionalism in America, 1760–1848* (Ithaca, 1977), esp. 191–93, on Birney and Chase's earlier use of the Ordinance.

21. Mansfield, *Political Grammar*, 145.

22. N. C. Read, *The Anniversary Oration of the Buckeye Celebration, 7th April, A.D., 1841* (Cincinnati, 1841), 8 (my emphasis).

23. Atwater, *History of the State of Ohio*, 352; William D. Gallagher, *Facts and Conditions of Progress in the North-West. Being the Annual Discourse for 1850, before the Historical and Philosophical Society of Ohio* (Cincinnati, 1850), 18.

24. Review of Salmon P. Chase's edition of *The Statutes of Ohio*, *North American Review*, 47 (1838), 1–56, at 2.

25. Jordon Pugh Oration in *Celebration of the Fifty-seventh Anniversary of the Settlement of Ohio, April 8th, 1844* (Cincinnati, 1844), 21, 13.

26. The historiography is discussed in Ray Allen Billington, "The Historians of the Northwest Ordinance," *Illinois State Historical Society Journal*, 40 (1947), 397–413; Philip R. Shriver, "America's Other Bicentennial," *Old Northwest*, 9 (1983), 219–35; and James David Griffin, "Historians and the Sixth Article of the Ordinance of 1787," *Ohio History*, 78 (1969), 252–60.

27. Daniel Webster speech, Jan. 20, 1830, *Register of Debates*, 21 Cong., 1 sess., 6:39.

28. Nathan Dane, *A General Abridgement and Digest of American Law*, 9 vols. (Boston, 1823–29), Note A, Appendix to vol. 9, 75–76. For Dane's analysis of the Ordinance text, see Dane to Webster, March 26, 1830, Massachusetts Historical Society, *Proceedings*, 10 (1869), 475–80. Dane noted that the adopted draft was in his hand in a letter to John H. Farnham, May 12, 1831, Indiana Historical Society, *Publications*, 1 (1897), 69–71.

29. Minutes of the Indiana Historical Society, Nov. 8, 1831, Indiana Historical Society, *Publications*, 1 (1897), 27, "Natives of Ohio," *Celebration of the Forty-Fifth Anniversary of the First Settlement of Cincinnati and the Miami County, on the 26th Day of September, 1833* (Cincinnati, 1834), 14.

30. William Corry speech, in *Celebration of the Forty-Seventh Anniversary*, 12; toasts to the Ordinance and to Dane (by Samuel Findlay), ibid., 23, 62. See also "Biography: *Nathan Dane*," *Boston Daily Advertiser and Patriot*, n.d., reprinted in *Miami of the Lake* (Perrysburg), March 24, 1835.

31. Walker, *Annual Discourse*, 9; Walker, *Introduction to American Law*, 44.

32. An article in the *Cincinnati Chronicle*, n.d. ("The Ordinance of 1787, Its History—Thos. Jefferson, Rufus King, and Nathan Dane"), reprinted in *National Intelligencer* (Washington), Aug. 6, 1847, had argued that Rufus King's March 16, 1785, motion to exclude slavery from the national territory was the real source of "the anti-slavery clause, as it now exists in the Ordinance." Peter Force responded with an accurate reconstruction of events, properly crediting Dane. *National Intelligencer*, Aug. 26, 1847. (See chapter 6 above.)

33. Dane, *General Abridgement*, 9:75; article in *Cincinnati Chronicle* cited in note 32.

34. See, particularly, *Remarks Addressed to the Citizens of Illinois, on the Proposed Introduction of Slavery* (n.p., n.d.). Copy in Boston Public Library. Jefferson's discussion of slavery in his *Notes on Virginia* was reprinted in *Illinois Intelligencer*, July 2, 1824. See also "Democracy," *Republican Advocate* (Kaskaskia), Oct. 9, 1823.

35. Pugh Oration, in *Celebration of the Fifty-seventh Anniversary*, 21. Pugh tried to apportion credit for the Ordinance fairly, "acknowledg[ing] our indebtedness to the sage of Monticello," while still insisting that "the great merit of framing this Ordinance belongs to Mr. Dane." Ibid., 17. But the arguments of Salmon P. Chase and other antislavery leaders about the founders' true devotion to freedom tipped the balance decisively away from Dane. I have found no subsequent northwestern reference to his authorship. On Chase and the founders, see the discussion in Eric Foner, *Free Soil, Free Labor, Free Men: The Ideology of the Republican Party before the Civil War* (New York, 1970), 73–102.

36. Thomas Corwin, Speech on Compromise Bill, July 24, 1848, in Isaac Strohm, ed., *Speeches of Thomas Corwin, with a Sketch of His Life* (Dayton, 1859), 404–61, at 406–407, 451. For more on the founders' intent and a refutation of "popular sovereignty," see Corwin, Speech on Current Political Issues, ibid., 477–510, at 495–99.

37. Edward Coles, "History of the Ordinance of 1787," read before Historical Society of Pennsylvania, June 9, 1856, reprinted in Clarence E. Alvord, ed., *Governor Edward Coles* (Springfield, 1920), 376–98, quotations at 377, 385–86, 397–98. New Englander Charles Francis Adams agreed that "the celebrated ordinance" of 1787 "reinstated the Jefferson proviso respecting slavery." Adams to Edwin Legg, Sept. 26, 1859, Adams Family Papers, American Antiquarian Society, Worcester, Mass.

38. Sangamo Grand Jury (April term), *Edwardsville Spectator*, May 4, 1824.

39. Isaac Naylor, "Pioneer Life in Clark County," unpublished manuscript, Isaac Naylor Papers, Indiana Historical Society, Indianapolis.

40. "The Ordinance of 1787," in Neville Craig, ed., *The Olden Time*, 2 vols. (1848; Cincinnati, 1876), 2:277; Nye, "Fragment of the Early History," 308. For an excellent discussion of the importance of free land in Republican ideology, see Foner, *Free Soil, Free Labor, Free Men*, esp. 1–39 and, on the intentions of the founders, 73–102.

41. Nye, "Fragment of the Early History," 309–10.

42. Naylor, "Pioneer Life." Foner notes that many of his Republicans made similar distinctions between areas in the Northwest settled by enterprising Yankees and those settled by southerners. Foner, *Free Soil, Free Labor, Free Men*, 48–50.

43. James Hall, *Letters from the West* (1828; Gainesville, Fla., 1967), Letter XV, "National Character," 246.

44. Elias Pym Fordham, *Personal Narrative of Travels in Virginia, Maryland, Pennsylvania, Ohio, Indiana, Kentucky; and of a Residence in the Illinois Territory, 1817–1818*, ed. Frederic Austin Ogg (Cleveland, 1906), 93, 229. For a useful analysis of travelers' accounts, see John Jakle, *Images of the Ohio Valley: A Historical Geography of Travel, 1740 to 1860* (New York, 1977).

45. Adlard Welby, *A Visit to North America and the English Settlements in Illinois* (London, 1821), reprinted in Reuben Gold Thwaites, ed., *Early Western Travels, 1748–1846*, 32 vols. (Cleveland, 1904–1907), 12:139–341, at 228.

46. Stephen C. Smith, *An Oration . . . at the New Meeting House in Marietta* (Marietta, 1808), 14. See also Benjamin Ruggles, *An Oration, Delivered at the New Meeting House, in Marietta* (Marietta, 1809).

47. George W. Ogden, *Letters from the West* (New Bedford, 1823), reprinted in Thwaites, ed., *Early Western Travels*, 19:19–112, at 96, 95.

48. Atwater, *History of the State of Ohio*, 330–31.

49. Walker, *Annual Discourse*, 21.

50. Atwater, *History of the State of Ohio*, 351. For a similar prediction, see John A. Bryan, *The Ohio Annual Register . . . for the Year 1835* (Columbus, 1835), 9.

51. Toast by Judge Goodenow, "Natives of Ohio," *Celebration of the Forty-Fifth Anniversary*, 43.

52. Caleb Atwater, *The Writings of Caleb Atwater* (Columbus, 1833), 204–205.

53. Nye, "Fragment of the Early History," 312; Perkins, "Discourse Delivered before the Ohio Historical Society," 268–85, at 282.

54. Caleb Atwater, *The General Character, Present and Future Prospects of the People of Ohio* (Columbus, 1827), 20–21.

55. "Michigan," *Detroit Courier*, March 15, 1832.

56. [Lewis C. Beck], "Union of Lake Michigan with the Illinois River," *St. Louis Register*, n.d., reprinted in *Illinois Gazette* (Shawneetown), April 6, 1822. This piece was included in Lewis C. Beck, *A Gazetteer of the States of Illinois and Missouri* (Albany, 1823), 27.

57. [Beck], "Union of Lake Michigan," citing Robert Fulton, *A Treatise on the improvement of canal navigation* (London, 1796).

58. John Pendleton Kennedy to organizers of 47th anniversary of first settlement at Cincinnati, March 27, 1835, *National Intelligencer* (Washington), n.d., reprinted in *Scioto Gazette* (Chillicothe), June 10, 1835.

59. "Our Name," *Toledo Blade*, Dec. 19, 1835.

60. [Beck], "Union of Lake Michigan."

61. Frederick Jackson Turner, "The Significance of the Section in American History," in *The Significance of Sections in American History* (New York, 1932), 22–51, at 45. For a useful discussion of the Old Northwest as a distinctive region, see Harry N. Scheiber, "Preface: On the Concepts of 'Regionalism' and 'Frontier,'" in Harry N. Scheiber, ed., *The Old Northwest: Studies in Regional History, 1787–1910* (Lincoln, 1969).

62. Toast at "Natives of Ohio," in *Celebration of the Forty-Seventh Anniversary*, 23.

63. Walker, *Annual Discourse*, 9.

64. "Kentucky and Indiana," *Buffalo Bulletin*, n.d., reprinted in *Miami of the Lake* (Perrysburg), Jan. 27, 1835.

65. Harry V. Jaffa, *Crisis of the House Divided: An Interpretation of the Issues in the Lincoln-Douglas Debates* (1959; Chicago, 1982), 296.

INDEX

☆☆☆☆☆☆☆☆☆☆☆☆☆☆☆☆☆☆☆☆☆☆☆☆☆☆☆☆☆☆☆☆☆☆☆☆☆

PETER S. ONUF, Professor of History, Southern Methodist University, is author of *The Origins of the Federal Republic: Jurisdictional Controversies in the United States, 1775–1787.*